Ted Langelar 7/ 24 / 24

Six Remarkable Ministers

Six Remarkable Ministers

Edited by B. A. Ramsbottom

"Behold, God exalteth by His power: who teacheth like Him?"
(Job 36. 22)

1994

Gospel Standard Trust Publications,
12(b) Roundwood Lane,
Harpenden, Hertfordshire, AL5 3DD,
England

ISBN   1 897837 04 6

Published by:
Gospel Standard Trust Publications,
12(b) Roundwood Lane,
Harpenden,
Hertfordshire,
AL5 3DD

Cover Picture: Nant Ffrancon Pass, North Wales
(Andy Williams)

Printed and bound in Great Britain by
Biddles Ltd.
Walnut Tree House,
Woodbridge Park,
Guildford, GU1 1DA

CONTENTS

INTRODUCTION

This book tells the story of six interesting men whom God raised up to preach the gospel. They were all completely different. Thomas Godwin was a poor, illiterate cobbler in Wiltshire, who taught himself to read and write, on his knees. A. B. Taylor was brought up in formal Presbyterianism in Scotland, where singing and shooting were his chief delights. Francis Covell was a Croydon tradesman who stammered so badly that often his customers could not understand him. Nisan (later, Edward) Samuel was a strict Jew in Poland. George Mockford was a Sussex shepherd boy who knew grinding poverty. Robert Moxon lived in Yorkshire and as a young man only narrowly escaped committing murder. Though so different, God raised up each of them to be preachers of the gospel. All these men were remarkable in several ways:

1. Not one of them was brought up under clear preaching of the truth, neither did any of them ever hear a true gospel sermon till after they had been savingly converted to God. Some had no religion at all, some had just a formal religion, and one was a strict Jew.

2. Not one of them was brought up a Baptist, yet all became clearly convinced that baptism by immersion is the baptism of the Word of God.

3. All of them became convinced Calvinists through the teaching of the Holy Spirit. One or two of them were told that they were "Calvinists" before they knew what the word meant. In fact, one of them, Robert Moxon, was convinced of the truth of sovereign election whilst in the pulpit of a Methodist chapel where he had gone as a "free will" preacher.

All became staunch, unflinching preachers of the doctrines of God's free and sovereign grace, denying offers of salvation to all. In varying degrees each of them became eminent preachers, and all were wonderfully used by God.

So it is right to describe them as "six remarkable ministers."

*   *   *

Each of the "six remarkable ministers" became Strict Baptist ministers connected with the *Gospel Standard* magazine. Not all

David's mighty men "attained to the first three," (1 Samuel chapter 23) but they were all valiant men, and the Holy Ghost has left them on record. The six ministers whose lives appear in this book are not so well known as Gadsby, Warburton and Kershaw, but they are certainly among the "valiant of Israel" and their lives deserve to be better known. They all knew the depths and heights of sin and salvation.

But apart from the spiritual quality of their lives, they are all extremely interesting. What light we have on life in the last century in the household of a strict Jew, or among the poor in Wiltshire and Sussex, or in the highlands of Scotland! And what interesting adventures and escapes some of them had!

*   *   *

The accounts are written with varying ability and style – for instance, what a difference in the style of writing of the first two accounts. In the case of Francis Covell's life, this was not written by himself but compiled after his death. All the other accounts have the serious shortcoming of having been written a considerable time before the author's death (one 50 years!) or if written in later life, the account ends some years previously and usually abruptly. In these cases we have given a few details of what took place afterward – but the earlier part is the cream.

In these days when life is more easy, and when many want religion to be more easy, may the faithful witness of the six ministers bear fruit to the honour and glory of God.

B. A. Ramsbottom
1994

Mrs. Hazel Parish, Mrs. Joy Wiltshire and Mr. John Kingham are specially thanked for all their work in preparing *Six Remarkable Ministers* for publication.

yours affectionately
Thos S Godwin

THOMAS GODWIN: 1803-1877

*The remarkable account of a poor, illiterate cobbler raised up by
God to be a minister of the gospel.*

*Brought to a knowledge of salvation without ever hearing a
gospel sermon, Thomas Godwin learned to read and write on his
knees, crying to God to help him. After two short pastorates, he was
minister at Godmanchester, Huntingdonshire, for the last sixteen years
of his life. He preached occasionally for John Warburton at Trowbridge and J. C. Philpot at Stamford, and after William Gadsby's
death was invited to succeed him at Manchester (which he declined).
Mr. Godwin was perhaps J. C. Philpot's closest friend.*

CHAPTER 1

BIRTH AND EARLY DAYS

The Lord God of Abraham, of Isaac and of Jacob help me to
do the thing which I have had on my mind for many years, and
help me to be honest before God and men and with my own
conscience. I have for many years past been much exercised about
giving an outline of my poor unprofitable life, and of the gracious
dealings of my covenant God and Father in the Lord Jesus Christ.

My first birthplace was at Purton, in Wilts. I was born at
Purton, in the county of Wilts, a village about five and a half miles
from Swindon, in the year of our Lord 1803. My father's name
was Ralph Godwin, and my mother's Susan. My parents were
poor, and my father's calling or trade was that of a shoemaker.
There were eight of us in the family – five boys and three girls –
and I am the youngest son of my mother.

As I grew in years, and everything was so dear, I was obliged
to go out to work just after I was turned six years of age. My first
employment was to ride about with an old farmer, to open the
gates for him, as he was a cripple; and my wages were two pence
per day – one shilling (5p) per week. As I grew older, my wages
were advanced; and when I was about ten years of age I became a
milk boy, and cut my own loaf. But I was then a steady and a

hard-working boy, and had to rise in the morning about four o'clock.

And so I was moved on, by God's good providence, from one step to another until I became about fifteen years of age; and then I began to think myself something. The pride of my heart and the lust of my flesh began to show themselves in a most rapid way and manner. I was then living with a widow woman, at the vicarage house in a village called Rodbourn Cheney, near Swindon, in the county of Wilts. She feared God, and would often correct me. I lived with her three years, and then went home to my father and learned shoemaking, as I had done a little at it before.

Then I ran further into sin than ever. I was then just nineteen years of age, and I commenced in business as a shoemaker at a village called Shaw, about three miles and a half from Swindon, in the county of Wilts. There I ran further into sin and wickedness than ever, until I was just over twenty-three years of age.

At this time I was married; and as we were much addicted to card-playing, and visiting from place to place, and people getting into my debt [sic]; although my wife and I worked very hard for the bread that perisheth, and tried hard to pay our way, yet we were never satisfied unless we were card-playing or visiting. And we were both as proud as the devil and the pride of our hearts could make us.

Conviction of Sin

But now troubles and afflictions of one kind and another began to fall upon us, and I began to be very unhappy and very miserable, so that I did not know what to do with myself. One day, I had been into a neighbour's house, where I often used to resort, as I was so fond of foolish talking and making sport of one and another, and an awful blasphemer when in a passion, and that was often. But, as I was passing from this person's house to my own, just as I got into the centre of the road, these words dropped into my heart and soul with such power: "Every idle word that men shall speak, they shall give account thereof in the day of judgment."

And now the Lord put a damper upon all my wicked practices, and spoiled all my sport in this world. At that time I was very fond of singing, but the arrow was shot into my conscience, and stuck fast there. I tried with all my might and power to get it out and shake it off; but all was in vain. The Lord began to show me that I was a sinner in His sight, and I began to make vows and promises that I would mend my life and go to church; and I then thought that I should soon grow better.

At that time I could not read at all, no, not the alphabet, and what to do I could not tell; for, I thought, if I could read, the Lord may be pleased with me, as I wanted to do something to try and please the Lord. I knew that we had got one old book in the house, and I thought it was a Bible, because I knew some of the letters, but not all. So I got this old book and went up into my cutting-room, and kneeled down and opened the old Bible, and began to try to pray over it, to ask the Lord to teach me to read.

On a Lord's day morning I used to be up before the sun all through the spring and summer, as my soul's trouble commenced in the spring of the year 1826. I had been very diligent in business, but yet not so earnest in it nor at it as the Lord had made me about my never-dying soul. Here I used to spend all my Sabbaths, from daylight in the morning until dark at night, with the exception of going to the parish church twice on a Lord's day.

When I could read the little words without spelling, this encouraged me to press on and redeem all the time I could; but as convictions grew within my conscience, and one sin and another was opened up in my soul, I felt that all my seeking and trying to read and pray did not make me any better, but I rather grew worse and worse. But still, as the Holy Ghost showed me what was wrong, He gave me power to leave it off. And here I went on until the Lord made me leave off all the business that I had practised on the Lord's day from the commencement of my marriage. All my old companions looked with a scornful eye upon me; before they could do nothing without me, neither could they go anywhere with pleasure without me; but now they hated me, and began to persecute me, and say all manner of evil against me.

But still, my soul was on the full stretch after something; but I was as ignorant of salvation as a beast.

After a time I got a New Testament, which was better print than this old Bible, and down I fell upon my knees to thank the Lord for it, and tried to ask the Lord to teach me to read it, and often with weeping eyes. After a long time I could read a little, and then I began, as I thought, to be thankful to the Lord for teaching me this little. As I had left off all my former practices, and was very diligent in the use of the means, and tried to do all the good I could to my neighbours, and never lost a moment in idleness, therefore pride and self-righteousness sprang up in my heart to that degree that I began to think that I really had become a better man. The church minister that I sat under began to praise me, and set me up very high among the congregation, until I thought that I must be a Christian in deed and in truth; and I used to go from house to house to talk about, as I thought, *religion*. But, alas! alas! I neither knew my own heart, nor anything of the fall of man, nor anything of the bitterness and evil of sin.

As I had then two small children, I took my little girl to a weekly boarding school. And as I had a brother who lived close to this school, I looked in to see him and found another brother with him. As I was in my own eyes too holy to talk about anything but religion, I began to tell them what state and condition we were all in by nature and practice. My eldest brother said to me, "Tom, thee dost think that thou art righteous." I answered him by these words: "There is none righteous, no, not one." And the Holy Ghost brought the same words back into my own heart and conscience like a sharp two-edged sword, and cut me down at a stroke. I trembled from head to foot, within and without, and the tears ran down my cheeks.

Out of the house I came. All my supposed religion was swept away in a moment; and down my soul fell, like a bird shot, into a state of despondency. But before I had got three stones' cast, these words came with such killing power: "For it is impossible for those who were once enlightened, and have tasted of the heavenly gift, and were made partakers of the Holy Ghost, and have tasted the good Word of God, and the powers of the world to come, if they shall fall away, to renew them again unto repentance; seeing they crucify to themselves the Son of God afresh, and put Him to an open shame."

Now the enemy told me that I had committed the unpardonable sin, that there was no ground whatever for me to hope for mercy, and that I was a reprobate, and must be cast for ever into hell. All my profession was turned into sin and transgression; the curse of the law was brought into my heart and conscience; and the devil let loose upon me, so that my soul sank into the lowest hell. Sin and transgression became so bitter and hateful in my soul, I seemed to suffer the torments of hell within; and I could neither eat nor drink, sleep nor work. My flesh and strength failed me, and I very soon became like a walking ghost. Here I saw a just God, and His strict justice; and the wrath of a broken law was let out into my conscience like a burning fire. Truly my soul did experimentally know the right meaning of these words: "Moreover, the law entered, that the offence might abound. But where sin abounded, grace did much more abound."

CHAPTER 2

The Lord kept me shut up here in this prison of sin, guilt and condemnation, tortured and tormented in my very heart, soul and conscience; and I envied the dog, horse, cow and fowl, and wished that I had never been born. With such a heavy load of sin and guilt, law and wrath, working within, I felt afraid to close my eyes in sleep, for fear I should wake up in hell. I was tempted day and night to destroy myself, sometimes with poison, sometimes with a knife, and sometimes with a razor, sometimes in the water, and sometimes with a rope, until my life became a burden to me, and the torment seemed as bad as hell itself, and the solemn weight of eternity. With the fear and dread of eternal torments, fearing that the earth would open her mouth and swallow me up, or else that the judgment of God would come down upon me and strike me dead on the spot, I went backward and forward to the parish church, and heard the law read over every Sabbath day. I used to look at the minister and the dead congregation; they all seemed dead together; and not one word about my case could I hear.

Here I was, with my mouth stopped, my soul lost; and no one seemed to know my case nor care for my soul. My flesh had gone off my bones, and my strength was dried up like a potsherd. Here my soul could feelingly and experimentally join with David, and say, "There is no soundness in my flesh because of Thine anger; neither is there any rest in my bones because of my sin. For mine iniquities are gone over my head; as a heavy burden they are too heavy for me." And I could feelingly say with Jeremiah, "I am the man that hath seen affliction by the rod of His wrath." And here my soul was kept at Mount Sinai; and as the trumpet sounded long and louder in my poor burdened and condemned conscience, and expecting to be cut off and sent to hell, my flesh trembled for fear of Him. I was indeed afraid of His judgments.

In this awful state I cried to God for mercy day and night; but I wanted repentance before God. I felt that I could not repent of myself, and my soul cried to God day and night for it. And yet godly fear and godly sorrow were at that time working within my soul; because sin was so hateful and bitter, and the tears of sorrow were running down my cheeks day and night. Satan was tempting me on every hand and on every side, until my soul was in such an agony that I felt as though hell could be no worse, and the devil set in upon me like a flood.

A HOPE IN GOD'S MERCY

Being at home by myself on a Monday morning, Satan and I had agreed together to go up into my cutting-room and hang myself. Upstairs I went to put an end to my miserable life, trembling from head to foot, and under these feelings: that my poor dear wife and children would come home and find my dead body, and my soul would be in hell. But Satan got defeated. Before I could get up into my room, these words dropped into my heart and soul: "Who can tell but what God may have mercy on such a hell-deserving sinner as I have felt myself to be before a heart-searching God?" I cast my eyes up to the beam where the execution was to take place. All of a sudden the Lord brought before my mind all the vile characters that He had saved, as they are set forth in the Bible; such as the harlot Rahab, Manasseh, Mary Magdalene, Saul of Tarsus, and others. Down I fell upon my knees once more, and the publican's prayer was put into my heart and soul. My heart was broken all to pieces. The tears ran down my cheeks in streams, and a hope was raised up in my soul in the free mercy of God.

How long I was kept here I could not say; but this I can say, that while on my knees, pouring out my soul before God, I felt He was *able* to save me; but my soul said, "Art Thou *willing* to save such a black sinner as I am?" I felt willing to be saved in any way; but all this time my soul had no knowledge of the Saviour. Although I felt nothing but the strict justice of God against me, yet I could see that He was a God of mercy to His people. But when the Lord raised up this hope in my soul in His free mercy, I had such a sight and felt sense of His long-suffering mercy and forbearance towards me that I came down out of my cutting-room, trying to thank the Lord for making a way for my escape once more.

After this my soul sank lower and deeper than before. I was now tempted to kill my wife and two dear children, and then destroy myself. I must leave my reader to judge what my feelings must be. Here my soul was tormented day and night. I had no one to speak to, and there was no truth to hear on the Lord's day. I went to the parish church twice a day, and sometimes used to go out between the services into fields, creep into the ditch, and try to cry for mercy. I always walked with my guilty head down, looking on the earth, with my mouth shut. When any one came to my house on business, I could only receive their orders; I could not talk to them. If any one asked me what was the matter, I used to say, "I am lost and going to hell." The byword was, respecting me, "Godwin has gone out of his mind"; and I thought so too, and that I should be taken off to an asylum and die there, and that my wife and two children would die in a poor-house.

DELIVERANCE FROM THE LAW

Now the time drew near that the Lord had fixed for my deliverance. My soul was suffering a hell upon earth, between the guilt of sin, the weight of transgression, the strict justice of God, the wrath of the law, the power of temptations, the terrors of God, the fears of death, the pains of hell, a never-ending eternity, and everlasting separation from God and my poor wife and children. These things sank me into black despair.

But the memorable morning was come. I walked round my garden and my nice little cottage at Shaw, which the Lord had given me, for the last time, I thought; for I expected to be in hell in a few minutes. But, honours for ever crown the dear Lamb of God! I staggered into my shop. I passed my front door, and looked upon my wife and children for the last time, as I thought. But just as I stepped into my shop, the Lord Jesus came down into my heart and soul, and took off my burden of sin and guilt, and blotted out my transgression. He removed the curse and terrors of the law out of my conscience, and brought pardon and peace into my soul; and these words came with such power: "O that I had wings like a dove! for then would I fly away and be at rest." My soul mounted up on the wings of love and faith, and upon the

14

wings of the Holy Ghost, and entered into the dear bosom of the precious Jesus.

My soul was so happy, and as full of the love of God in Christ Jesus as it could hold. I sang, I danced, I shouted; and I loved, I blessed the dear name of the Father, Son and Holy Ghost. My soul saw by faith the Three Divine Persons, yet but One Eternal God. The Word of truth came with weight, power and sweetness into my heart night and day; the Holy Ghost opened it up unto my soul, and then I could read the letter of the Word. I opened the Bible, fell upon my knees, and asked the Lord to teach me and guide me into all truth. The glorious revelation and manifestations, and the applications, with the operation of the Holy Ghost, filled my heart and soul with joy and peace in believing; and under the Spirit of adoption my soul cried, "Abba, Father!"

For over twelve months my soul walked in the life, liberty, and love of the gospel of the Three-One God, eating and drinking the truths of the everlasting Son of the Father, full of grace and truth. Although my mourning days were many under the burden of sin and the hard bondage and curse of the law, yet my glorious days of life, love and liberty weighed down all my sorrow, mourning, grief and torment. And the continual operations and applications of the Holy Ghost, the dear Comforter, made my soul dance like the poor prodigal son when he entered into his father's house and had his filthy garments taken off and the best robe put on. And although it is nearly forty years since this took place in my soul, yet it is as fresh and clear as though it was but as yesterday. Under this enjoyment I fell to work with my hands to try to get out of debt, and pay every man twenty shillings in the pound. I worked eighteen and twenty hours out of the twenty-four for years together.

———————

CHAPTER 3

PROVIDENTIAL TRIALS AND DELIVERANCES

Here I must go back a little. I might enlarge, and write much on the difficulties by the way in providence, and how I tried hard to make money. My wife was anxious we should go into Wales, for she had heard such good tidings of that part. Nothing would satisfy her but I must go over and see about settling there. I left home soon after Christmas, and walked to Bristol the first day, and over into Wales the next. But when I came there I did not try to get a house, for I hated the place, and I could not understand the people's language. The day I went over it was a very calm sea, but when I returned it was very rough. The sea wrought, and was tempestuous. When we got into the Bristol Channel, I thought my life was at stake, and I ran upon deck to cast myself into the sea, to swim to shore; but the captain soon cried, "No danger!" But, before we could land at Bristol, a poor woman fell overboard, but the poor ungodly wretch, Godwin, got safe to land. I walked home to my wife the next day, and told her I would never go into Wales to live, for I did not like it well enough. My wife was much disappointed. "There are many devices in a man's heart; nevertheless the counsel of the Lord, that shall stand."

I had taken an apprentice boy, and received twenty pounds with him. He was a very good boy, and would have got on very well, but when he had been with me about half his time, the Lord struck the poor boy with a stroke, and took the use of his right side away. Now here was a great trial, for I had engaged to keep him in food and raiment until the seven years had expired, and also to find a doctor, if needed. So I had to send for the doctor, and soon I had a bill of £5. But the doctor could do him no good. Then I got him to Bath, but all was useless. He had served half his time and had been very handy, and I had set great store by him, as he was quiet and willing to work, and I could also trust him. But the Lord knew what was best for me, and also what I needed. Although at that time I had no religion, yet I was enabled to perform my covenant with him. But I had many temporal troubles and trials with a poor afflicted wife, who had the fever, and I had heavy doctors' bills to pay. But I had strength to work, and the Lord brought me out of all my temporal troubles, as regards my debts, and enabled me to forgive all my debtors.

SPIRITUAL DARKNESS AND TEMPTATIONS

But, again, after the blessed Lord had taught me to read His precious Word of truth, and my soul so enjoyed it, I thought that my soul was near entering heaven. I longed to die, to be with the blessed Jesus. But the Lord had another furnace for me to be plunged into. Although my conscience was kept tender, and the fear of the Lord flowed in my heart like a fountain of life, and my temper was mild and meek, yet the Lord began to hide His face, shut up His Word, and let a cloud down upon the mercy-seat. Thick darkness gathered over my soul, and my heart sank fathoms within me. The sins of my heart began to rise, and the devil was let loose upon me. The Bible became a sealed book, and all prayer seemed to have left me, so that I could not get my heart up to the Lord, for it lay within me like stone or lead. The old serpent, the devil, tempted me to curse God the Father, God the Son and God the Holy Ghost.

These temptations followed me day and night, and whenever my eyes or hands fastened on the Bible, the curses and blasphemous thoughts rose up within my heart like so many mountains. These things crippled, wounded and killed me; but as fast as the blasphemous thoughts passed within my heart, my soul kept saying, "Bless the Lord, bless the Lord," day and night, when my eyes were open. And to think that these awful thoughts should go out against my best Friend, and also that the curses should go out in thoughts against the people of God! My soul again reeled to and fro, and staggered like a drunken man, and I was brought to my wit's end. But my heart was so hard, I could not cry here as my soul did under the law; and this followed me wheresoever I went for about twelve months, until I felt sure I must have committed the sin against the Holy Ghost; for I had inwardly blasphemed His name, and Satan told me that I had committed the unpardonable sin. As I had nowhere to go to hear but to the parish church, and never had any spiritual companion to open my mind to, nor yet any minister of truth to hear, I thought I must be the man out of whom the unclean spirit went, and now he had come back again, and brought seven other spirits more wicked than himself.

Under these feelings and fightings I was compelled to live. I used to walk about, wringing my hands and stamping my feet like a madman. I could not think for one moment that I could be a child of God. I dared not read my Bible, because these awful curses went out so strong against the Bible and its Author. And when I dropped off to sleep for a time, Satan told me that the curses came out of my mouth in my sleep. This distressed me beyond measure, so that my flesh and strength gave way again, and I felt so weak in body and soul.

O! my dear friends, you that have a gospel minister to sit under, thank God for it; and you that have a few spiritual friends to meet with from Sabbath to Sabbath, set a value upon them. If you cannot get a preacher, remember the poor wretch that is now writing had no truth to hear, no friend to speak to, and could not cry to the Lord in this state.

One day, I could not sit in my shop, but walked into my house in bitter agony of soul. The New Testament lay on the table, and I took hold of it and threw it open. These words took hold of my soul: "Then was Jesus led up of the Spirit into the wilderness to be tempted of the devil." My poor devil-tempted, sin-tormented soul was delivered in a moment. My soul danced within me. O how my heart and soul thanked, blessed and praised my dear Lord and Saviour for coming down into my heart once more, to give me peace and rest! The Holy Ghost showed my soul that Jesus was led by the Spirit into the wilderness on purpose to be tempted of the devil. And He also showed me that going through all these temptations that my soul had been passing through was following Jesus through the wilderness; and I could clearly see that the Holy Ghost was leading my soul all through these cutting and killing temptations, and that divine grace enabled my soul to fight against them from the commencement of this hot war in my heart.

How sweet and precious was the Word of God to my soul in those days, and what pleasure I felt in reading it! The Holy Ghost led my soul into it, opened up the beauty and sweetness of it within my heart, and taught me to read the letter of it. I used to sit up nights, after my wife and children had gone to bed, and rise up hours before them in the morning, and eat and drink the Word of life; walk off miles on a week evening to try to pick up a crumb, but could find nothing but husks; return home on a dark night, and have a little persecution to go to bed with. But I could then bear it with patience, without returning a word.

LEARNING THE TRUTH

As the dear Lord led my soul on in divine things, revealed His precious Word of truth home into my soul, taught me to read the letter of His Word, for which I have blessed Him over and over again, and as it was opened up in my heart, I could not help speaking of it. An old man that had heard of me, who lived in the adjoining parish, came to see me. After he had talked with me some time, he said, "Why, you are a Calvinist." I could not think what he meant by saying that I was a *Calvinist*, so ignorant was I of the meaning of the word. Indeed, I had never heard the word before. I kept on turning this word "Calvinist" over and over in my mind, and I could not get rid of it.

CHAPTER 4

About this time, I heard that a poor woman who lived in the upper part of the village was brought to feel her state as a sinner before God. This set fire to my zeal. It came into my mind that the parish clerk, who at that time was a friend of mine, had a book that would suit her case; but it being late at night when I heard of it, I did not know how to manage to get the book for her to have it that night, as she lived about half a mile from my house one way, and he about a mile the other. But my soul being so full of love to Jesus and zeal for the welfare of poor sinners' souls that there was scarcely a house in the place but what I had been into to tell them of their state, and that they would go to hell if they died in their sins, I started for this book, and felt she must have it before I slept.

I set off running, for fear the man would be gone to bed; but I had not gone far before these words dropped into my heart: "It is not of him that willeth, nor of him that runneth, but of God that sheweth mercy." I stopped my pace all of a sudden, and could not think what it meant, for I did not know that these words were in the Bible. But I began to run on, when the words returned again: "It is not of him that willeth, nor of him that runneth, but of God that sheweth mercy." I reached the house before the man had gone to bed, told him my business, and said there was nothing like driving the nail while it was hot; and I wanted to give it a good clench.

Off I went with the book; but no sooner was I got out of the house when the words came again: "It is not of him that willeth, nor of him that runneth, but of God that sheweth mercy." This followed me all the way to where the woman lived, and back to my house, and also when I awoke in the morning; so that, instead of my driving the nail into the poor woman's mind and clenching it, the Eternal Spirit drove a nail in a sure place into my conscience, and clenched it; for it has never been drawn out unto this day, and I believe it never will be, because "the Word of the Lord endureth for ever."

Now the Lord began to inform my judgment, and open up the doctrines of grace in my heart and conscience. My soul was very earnest at the throne of grace, and over my Bible. I was led to beg the Lord to lead my soul by His blessed Spirit into the truth as it is in Jesus, and that He would never suffer me to go astray. And, bless His dear name, He opened up His blessed Word of truth in my soul day after day; so that when the church clergyman, whom I still sat under, came to see me, which he mostly did once a week when he came round to visit what he called his "flock," I began to talk to him about election and predestination, and also what I saw in them, and what my soul felt from them. He looked at me, smiled, and said that he loved the doctrines of election and predestination; and that none would ever go to heaven unless they were elected. My soul kept on crying to the Lord for Him to teach me and lead me into His truth, and was still led to search the Bible with more earnestness than ever; and His Word and Spirit searched my heart and conscience in such a powerful way.

Now I could read some of the easy chapters in the Gospel of John through; and every time the parson came to see me I had some fresh testimonies to speak about. He still said that he loved those things, and what precious doctrines they were. He had said to the people in the parish, those he called Christians, and some out of the parish that used to hear him, "Be sure and go to see Godwin when you want to talk about religion; for he is such a bright Christian." And as my soul was so full, I could not help speaking about it.

One day, when I called on a person in the next village who made a profession, and I hoped the wife knew something about soul-trouble, the conversation turned upon religion. I could not help telling them a little of what the Lord had revealed to my soul; and having known them for some years, I felt a freedom to open my mind. But when the clergyman called on her, she told him that I had called there to see her (indeed, I had done their work for years), and had talked about election, saying that there was a people that God had chosen in Christ before the world began, and that those people must go to heaven. This frightened the poor woman so much that she could not sleep. She began to look at her children, and wondered what would become of them if that was a truth.

When he came to see me again, he did not forget to tell me about it, and also told me to mind what I said to people about such doctrines. But, as the Lord led my soul on, and revealed these precious doctrines of truth to my soul, I began to look into the New Testament he had got for me, with Bucket's Commentary [does he mean *Burkitt?*]; and I was led to see that Mr. Bucket was a rotten-hearted man, who did not know the life and power of truth in his soul. The more the Lord opened my understanding in the mysteries of godliness, the more my eyes were opened to see into error. "Then opened He their understanding, that they might understand the Scriptures."

Once on a time I went to hear an Independent minister, who preached in a house on a week evening in a village near Wootton Bassett. People told me that he preached the doctrine that some were to go to heaven and some to hell; and let them do what they would, they must go to hell. I said that if ever I heard him or any other man say such things, I would never believe him, but would attack him as soon as he had done speaking. But he never mentioned such a thing, neither did he come any nearer the truth than the church parson. But, before the Lord brought my soul out, the enmity of my heart boiled up against the doctrine called election; and I said I would never believe such a doctrine, for I would not believe that God was such a God as that, to save one and leave another, without giving all a chance. But God made my soul believe it, for "it is not of him that willeth, nor of him that runneth, but of God that sheweth mercy." This truth settled the matter in my soul's experience, and this one passage came upon the back of it: "Therefore hath He mercy on whom He will have mercy, and whom He will He hardeneth."

Again, as the dear Lord led my soul on experimentally into the truth, and applied His precious Word to my heart with divine power and life, the Bible was increasingly dear to me, and Mr. Bucket was laid aside. Then the doctrines of divine grace were opened up more clearly within my heart and soul, and my stammering tongue was more and more loosed to speak of them.

The people looked shy upon me. About this time a man called at my house with a roll of papers in his hand. When asked what he had, he said, "I will leave you one if you will promise to stick it up in your house after you have read it." I replied I would not promise that. He left it, and walked away. When I looked at it, down I threw it; for I saw what it was on the first page. It said that the doctrines of election and predestination were not the doctrines of the Bible, and that they came from hell. My feelings rose up so strong against the doctrines of free will, and so strong on the side of free grace, that I felt indignation against the man and his party for ever publishing such blasphemies against God and His precious truth.

I then heard that a man had come to Swindon who preached those precious doctrines, and that the enemies of truth had these bills printed against him. As they had heard of me, they sent me one, or rather brought me one. Then I said I would go and hear this man. My wife and I fixed to go one Thursday evening. When we had found out the chapel, I stood and looked up and down the street to see if anyone whom I knew would see us go in, as I had been a strict Churchman so many years.

We got into the chapel, and the people's eyes were upon us, as we were strangers. The old gentleman read and prayed, and began to preach. He spoke of the blackness of the heart, and the preciousness of the Lord Jesus Christ, and also of the everlasting love of God towards His elect people, and many other things. It was just what my soul wanted to hear; yet he did not say how the poor sinner was exercised and tried in his soul, nor yet how he was plagued with sin and the devil. Yet he said a good deal about the devil, and that the Lord Jesus had made an end of sin and trans- gression, and brought in an everlasting righteousness to justify the election of grace. I had never heard any man preach the doctrines of God's free grace and mercy before, though the Lord had been leading my soul experimentally into it for some months before this, therefore I was much taken by the man's preaching, and it spoiled me for hearing the church minister, although I continued to hear him for some time after this, and went to hear at the chapel on week evenings. The Word of God was so sweet to my heart and conscience that my soul was diligent in searching it, with earnest prayer in my heart for the Lord to lead me into all truth.

About this time I heard that a minister by the name of Tiptaft [William Tiptaft of Abingdon (1803-1864)], was going to preach in the same chapel at Swindon. I was told that Mr. Tiptaft had not long left the Church of England. I felt such a desire in my soul to go and hear him, particularly as he had been in the Church of England; so I went to hear him. When he began to read, every word came with power and weight. I had never heard any one read so before. Then he began to pray, and I could not keep my eyes off him. Then he read this text: "And they shall call them, The holy people, The redeemed of the Lord; and thou shalt be called Sought out, A city not forsaken" (Isa. 62. 12). He went into it in such a feeling way and manner, and knocked everything down as he went that stood in his way, and rooted out, and pulled down, and destroyed; and then began to plant. As he went on, he beat down infant sprinkling, and set up believers' baptism; and this had a firm hold on my conscience, for I had seen it in the Word of God. And when Mr. Tiptaft entered into it, and opened it up as a Bible ordinance for believers only, then my soul was led more and more to the Word, to see whether the things that he spoke of were true. "They searched the Scriptures daily," to see "whether those things were so."

The next time the clergyman called I entered into the subject of infant sprinkling and believers' baptism, and also spoke of the sermon that I had heard that dear man of God preach. I told all the people that I would walk twenty miles any time to hear another such sermon as Mr. Tiptaft preached. Then commenced a union with that dear man, and we walked in love and peace until his death, which took place at Abingdon, August 17th, 1864.

But now my troubles began with the clergyman. He was filled with rage and jealousy against me, and began to chide me that I was going astray, that the doctrines I held were erroneous, and that they were doctrines of devils. Then I turned and fought him with his own words; how he had confessed and owned to me before that he loved the doctrines of election and predestination; and that he had testified to me that there would never be a soul saved if it was not chosen to salvation. But the more he persecuted me, the more the Word of truth multiplied within me, according to that word: "The more they afflicted them, the more they multiplied and grew."

As he was for ever taunting and plaguing me, both at my own house and elsewhere, after trying to drive the truth out of my heart, and finding that he could not move me, for it was burned into my heart and conscience by the living power of a living God, he looked angrily at me, and said, "Godwin, you are led by the devil." I answered him, under a meek and quiet spirit, "If I am led by the devil, Christ is precious to me; and if that is being led by the devil, may God give my soul more of it." He now began to warn all his friends not to come near me, for I had become a dangerous man. Now I saw that this poor man had never had the enmity of his heart slain; therefore he hated God's truth, which was so precious to me.

One Sabbath day he said, "Godwin, you say that I am in error." I replied, "You *are* in error." "Then," he said, "we had better have a meeting. You get a man, and I will get one." He fixed the day for the following Thursday, at my house. He came, with the clerk and more of his friends; I had only one friend for whose soul I thought the Lord had done something; and he came with the minister. When he came, he wanted to know whether my man was come or not. I said, "No; I have not asked one, neither do I intend to do so. I have the Word of truth, and the eyes of the Lord upon me; and my soul has called upon God to be a witness." Then he began to pray in his way. Then I said, "Before you begin, I will tell you my creed. In the first place, God the Father loved my soul in Christ before the world began, and He gave me to Christ. In the fulness of time the Lord Jesus fulfilled the law, and made it honourable for me, and died, and redeemed my soul from all my sins and transgressions. In God's own time, the Holy Ghost quickened my dead soul into life, and brought me, as a perishing sinner, to Jesus, and revealed Christ within my soul as my Saviour." I also said that Christ only died for His people, and that the invitations of the gospel were only held out to the quickened sinners. Then I said, "Now, you contradict it by the Word of truth if you can." He shook and trembled, with my old Bible on his knees; and himself, his clerk and his friends were all confounded. At length he said, "You want to get wiser than your teacher." And the man he had chosen, who had been a close professing friend of mine, spoke up, and said, "Some people do want to get wiser than their teachers." But my soul testified that God the Spirit alone had taught my soul, and that he had never put one finger to it; and how was it likely, when he, with his friends, hated the very things that God had taught me, and that my soul loved better than life itself. So "none of those things moved me."

After the Lord had so blessed my soul, I was greatly exercised about my dear wife; and many prayers and petitions I put up on her account. I used to watch her in the church, to see whether she was paying attention or not. I knew that I could do nothing for her. It must be the power of God to bring her to know anything aright. Still I was kept begging the Lord to quicken her dead soul into life, and always checked everything I saw her do or say wrong. After a time, the Lord was pleased to lay her on a bed of affliction, and brought her down very low. My mouth was opened to talk very closely about the state of her soul, and also to tell her what I had passed through under the curse of God's righteous law, and under the guilt and burden of sin in my conscience; also the blessed deliverance the Lord had given me, and the sweet enjoyment that my soul had rejoiced in for a long time. She heard me with all the quietness imaginable. She knew that she had never passed through those things. The Lord heard my prayer, and restored her to health again.

Still, my soul was led to beg for her on my knees before the Lord, out in the shop, and in my cutting-room; for I then knew the worth and value of a soul, and also the preciousness of a Saviour. My eyes and ears were opened to all her words and ways. I could see she was more quiet and not so much after the world. Once in particular the Lord brought me down on my knees, and let down such a spirit of prayer into my soul on her behalf to bring her out, that my soul will never forget that night, nor the power I felt in my soul. From that time she was brought into great distress, and after a time was sweetly brought into the liberty of the gospel, and we sang and praised the Lord together. I can never describe my feelings of thankfulness to the Lord for bringing my dear wife unto Himself with me. I had indeed travailed in birth for her; and as she had lived with me in all manner of sin, and had been a persecutor to me, and was now brought to fear and love and serve the Lord, how my soul wept for joy! I said, "Now my soul will have a heaven on the earth, and shall never have trouble; for the Lord has answered my prayers on the behalf of my dear wife. 'As for me and my house, we will serve the Lord.'"

I now opened my house for prayer and reading. The Lord greatly honoured it; for the Lord called five or six by His grace, so that we had some blessed times together, my dear wife being one among the number. So the persecuting wife was turned into a good companion in tribulation. The sweet meetings we had together in my house at Shaw I cannot forget. They were golden days indeed.

———————

CHAPTER 5

MY BAPTISM AND CALL TO THE MINISTRY

Now begins another long and heavy trial. All at once, the thought of preaching fell upon me, and sprang up in me. I tried to shake it off because I had no human learning and never was taught a word by man or woman. I said, "Lord, I am in debt, and I cannot stand up before Thy people in the world, and not be out of debt."

While I was a hearer in the Church of England, the Lord laid believers' baptism upon my conscience, and He opened it up in my soul. I felt that I must go through it. As there was going to be a baptizing at Uffington, in Berkshire, off I walked on a cold winter's morning, and a friend went with me. I had never seen a baptizing. I took a change of raiment with me. When I arrived at Uffington, I was sent to Mr. W——'s to see the minister, and give in my experience. I went with a willing heart, for my soul was full of the love of Jesus; therefore I longed to walk in His ordinances. I was asked into the parlour to see the minister. I began where the Lord began with my soul, and entered into a law-work on my conscience, and told when my soul was quickened into divine life, and how my soul sank under the curse and bondage of the law, the power and guilt of sin and transgression; and then in what way the Lord Jesus came and delivered my soul, and brought pardon and peace into my heart. He said, "That will do." When I went down into the water, my soul was so happy. There for the first time I saw Mr. Shorter [at this time pastor at Blunsdon Hill]. He gave out the hymns at the water side; Mr. Husband [founder of South Moreton Chapel] addressed the people; and Mr. Hitchcock [a seceding clergyman who also baptized William Tiptaft] baptized.

And then came on persecution from the Church people.

About this time Mr. Gadsby, of Manchester, came to Swindon to preach in an Independent chapel. I heard of it, and went to hear the dear man of God. This was his text: "Who is this that cometh from Edom, with dyed garments from Bozrah? this that is glorious in His apparel, travelling in the greatness of His strength? I that speak in righteousness, mighty to save" (Isa. 63. 1). And O, how I loved that dear man! for he entered into all the ins and outs of my pathway. I had about half an hour's talk with him after the service, and our hearts were closely knit together in love and affection.

But to return to the deep exercise of soul about the ministry. Day and night, at home and abroad, I told the Lord over and over again, that I was such a fool, and again He told me that He had chosen the foolish things of the world to confound the wise. And then again the Lord poured into my heart His precious love, and then my soul wanted to give vent to my feelings, and felt willing to go. Then darkness and temptation came upon me; and then I said, "No, I will not go; I cannot"; for I had been led to count the cost over and over again. I saw what a host of enemies I should have. But still it came upon me again with such an overwhelming weight.

This went on for about twelve months, so that I had no rest. Then my soul said, "Lord, if Thou wilt make it plain to me, I will go"; but feeling jealous of my own heart, my soul cried unto the Lord for Him to apply a word to my soul in my sleep, and awake me up out of my sleep, and then I should be sure that it came from Him and that I did not steal His Word; for, Gideon-like, I wanted the fleece wet and dry. I followed this on for some time.

One Wednesday night, a little past one o'clock, these words came with such power: "Set thy house in order; for thou shalt die, and not live." This awoke me up in a moment, and set me up in the bed. A horror of great darkness fell on my soul, and all my faith, hope and confidence seemed to leave me. I thought I must die, and my poor dear wife thought so too. She tried hard to get a light, which was not so easy in those days as at the present; and I sat trembling, fearing every breath would be the last, under this awful horror of darkness and distress, and the perspiration running down my face. But before she could get a light, the Lord Jesus Christ revealed Himself to my poor distressed soul in such a powerful way and manner that I fell down in my bed, and said to my wife, "I do not want a candle. The Lord is come, and has brought life and immortality to light." And the Holy Ghost led my soul into heaven, to hold communion with the Lord Jesus Christ for about one hour in such a sweet way and manner that I felt saved in the Lord with an everlasting salvation. The Holy Ghost showed me that my name was written in the Lamb's book of life. My soul well understood the meaning of "setting my house in order," for He had done it Himself, and I felt willing to die. O how my soul longed to be with Him! But He told me that I should not die, but live, and declare the works of the Lord. I could not let my wife speak a word to me. I could join holy John and say, "Behold, what manner of love the Father hath bestowed upon us," or upon *me,* that I should be manifested a son of God!

The glorious truths of the gospel were opened up in my soul at that time as my soul had never seen them before. The precious blood of the everlasting covenant, and my soul's interest in it, were opened to me in such a way that I never saw before nor since. Nor do I expect to have it opened up to my soul's view again in the same way in this world, for my soul saw all my sins washed away in and through this precious atoning love and blood. As I had an invitation to go out to speak some time before this took place, at once I said, "Lord, I will go and tell the people what Thou hast done, since Thou hast done so much for my soul." I said to my soul that I would not consult with flesh and blood any longer. This took place in the month of August 1834.

I had told my wife to get my clean things ready on the Saturday night, for I should rise early in the morning. But I got but little sleep through the night, thinking about standing up before a people and carrying a message to them from the Lord. As I sat up in the bed, thinking this solemn matter over, I began to fear and tremble, fearing I should run and not be sent by the Lord; and such a cloud of gloom and darkness came over my soul that I sat and trembled in my bed. Then I lay down again; and then my vows and promises came to my mind and memory which I had promised the Lord under that glorious revelation. Then I got up in the bed, and I followed this up and down until it was too late. Then, after this, I cannot tell what I went through in my mind until the following December, but I kept it all to myself. I said, If the Lord wants me to speak in His name, He knows where I am and what

I am. And my prayer was this: "Lord, if it is Thy will that I should speak in Thy name, incline Thy people to press me."

Soon after, the preacher at Swindon was taken ill, and they published me to speak. I said, "Well, if the Lord inclines my mind to do so, and will give me a text, I will try to come and speak." On December 25th, 1834, I stood in a pulpit for the first time. After I came out of the pulpit I received invitations from two different quarters. So my labours commenced at once, and although I was such a poor ignorant fool, yet I do not remember ever having an idle Sabbath day from that time to this. The first year of my speaking, I have walked twenty-six miles and preached three times at three different places on one day.

After I had had an invitation to preach at Pewsey, in the county of Wiltshire, and had been there a few times, the people there wanted me to settle over them. But I had a good business; therefore I could not see my way to do so. Therefore, I engaged to go up on a Saturday and return on Monday. This commenced in December 1835. I often walked the twenty-two miles, spoke three times on the Lord's day, and went off on the Monday morning early, getting home after walking the same distance, all winds and weather, hail or snow, rain or frost; and then off with my coat, and went to work until the next Saturday. The Lord only knows what trying journeys I had when passing over the Wiltshire downs, the winds and weather meeting me, and my fleshly mind looking back. Sometimes, through the winter months, I have turned round and looked back, and thought, Well, I will not keep on. But then the fear of the Lord began to move in my soul, and that noble word was felt: "No man, having put his hand to the plough, and looking back, is fit for the kingdom of God." Then my soul would press on again.

SETTLEMENT AT PEWSEY

And now began another trying time. The people would have me go to live among them. So the church gave me a call to become their pastor. This put me into a trying box because I had a comfortable home of my own, and the Lord had enabled me to pay all my debts; for my soul had told the Lord over and over again that I could not stand up before a people until I owed no man anything. Bless His dear and precious name, He enabled me to do so! But to return. How can I leave my home and my good business? But the Word of the Lord followed me up day and night, that I must forsake all to follow the Lord Jesus Christ – house, land, wife, children, father, mother, sisters and brothers, for the Lord's sake and the gospel's. So, at the beginning of November 1836, I put a bill up in my window: "A House to be Let." In came a gentleman to say a lady wanted to buy it. But I did not want to sell it, though I was compelled to do so. The day was fixed for my removal from my pretty home at Shaw, where the Lord had so favoured my soul for the last ten years, to Pewsey.

On the Saturday morning before my removal on the following Wednesday, God only knows what I went through. I had sold my house, given up my business, and then the Lord hid His face, and my soul was left in such a state of rebellion. I left my house, and could not wish my wife goodbye. I walked on for about six miles, and felt ready to burst with grief, sorrow and rebellion. But before I got over two miles through Swindon, the Lord broke in upon my soul with these words: "Thy shoes shall be iron and brass, and as thy days, so shall thy strength be." This subdued the anger and rebellion, and the words returned again with double power, and brought my soul out into a wealthy place. My soul began to sing and rejoice in the Lord, and I took my little Bible out of my pocket and soon found the words, and they so enlarged within my heart and soul that I walked on to Marlborough as strong as a giant refreshed with the new wine of the everlasting kingdom of our Lord and Saviour Jesus Christ, and as happy as I could live. The house and business were nothing at all to me. I felt I could give up anything for His name's sake. This day, and the blessings my soul received, I cannot forget, for it was a hill Mizar. This was on November 19th, 1836. On the following Wednesday, the 23rd, we removed to Pewsey, and remained there until September 18th, 1846.

CHAPTER 6

But again. What did my soul undergo there during nearly ten years! I arrived at Pewsey with my wife and two children and my household furniture, and owed no one a penny, and had about £100 of my own money. I went into a house at about £10 per year. As I had gone backwards and forwards for about eleven months, I thought there never was such a loving people as those I was going to live amongst. And now, I thought, I have done with my long journeys twice a week, and am come to live amongst such a loving and religious people that I must be happy. I could not see how I could have any trouble.

So, when we had our house in order, I commenced my business, and took the pastoral charge of the church there. My salary amounted to about nine or ten shillings a week. I went on preaching and working at my trade. The church increased, and the congregation was large; and I thought things were going on well. But, after some time, I began to see that there were many that I had thought to be good people who were loose livers. And here begins my trouble at Pewsey; for truth and conscience compelled me to take the sharp two-edged sword, and use it Sabbath after Sabbath until the fire became very hot.

About this time I walked over to Allington to see Mr. Philpot, as I had heard a good report of him. He was then living with Mr. Parry, before his marriage. When I entered the house, he just looked at me, and then turned almost his back upon me, and spoke roughly; but as I spoke a few words to Mr. Parry about the grace of God, Mr. Philpot spoke up, and said, "What do you know about the grace of God?" I began to tell him what my soul knew about the grace of God that bringeth salvation; and he turned himself round with such a smile on his countenance, and with such heartfelt affection towards me. This was in the year 1837. Now I am writing in 1867, and our hearts have been knit together in the affection and spirit of the gospel from the first time of our meeting to this present time.

But to return to my troubles at Pewsey. Still they were not all troubles. No; blessed be the name of the Lord, He often blessed my soul with His precious smiles, and gave me much life and power in the pulpit, and much pain and persecution out of it. But, as I said, I found many loose livers amongst the congregation. Still, we went on for some time. The Lord led me more and more into myself, and also into others; and the Holy Ghost led my soul more and more into the experimental part of the gospel, and also what the gospel, received in the heart and conscience with life and power, produced in the life, conversation and actions of the elect vessels of mercy. As the Lord continually led me and kept me to those three great points in preaching, viz., doctrinal, experimental and practical religion, and much favoured me in my own soul in the pulpit and also out of it, and after I had been kept on in those things, closely insisting upon a feeling religion, and that it made a man honest and upright in his movements in life; then I began to find that there were many ungodly characters standing in a profession, and my soul was much tried to see them still attend the chapel. I feared I was not honest; and continually kept begging the Lord to make me honest and upright before Him and the people, and also with my own conscience, as I was such an ignorant fool that I could not read a chapter through without making some blunder, or pronouncing some word wrong.

So I was continually under correction in every sense of the word. Now the Lord kept my soul begging by night and by day. Therefore the Lord fulfilled in me this word: "Behold I will make thee a new sharp threshing instrument, having teeth; thou shalt thresh the mountains, and beat them small, and shalt make the hills as chaff. Thou shalt fan them, and the wind shall carry them away" (Isa. 41. 15, 16). The people began to give up their sittings by whole pews together; the congregation grew less and less; the deacons began to fear that the cause would never be carried on; and things began to take such a turn that many of the poor sheep feared that they should never stand their ground, but that they should follow the goats.

Before this, the friends had talked of enlarging the chapel by building a side gallery; but I told them there would be plenty of room for the congregation in a very short time, without enlarging. But they thought there was going to be a wonderful church and congregation there; but I did not think so. After I had been among them for some time, I found the foundation was rotten; therefore I knew the building must decay, and the rubbish come down. Then I began to find out that one whom I had baptized before I went to live there was a loose liver and an unprincipled man; and then my troubles began in such a way that my soul had not witnessed before, and sometimes I really thought it would be the death of me.

This went on until Christmas Day 1837, when I was led to preach from this text: "But when the fulness of the time was come, God sent forth His Son, made of a woman, made under the law, to redeem them that were under the law, that we might receive the adoption of sons. And because ye are sons, God hath sent forth the Spirit of His Son into your hearts, crying, Abba, Father" (Gal. 4. 4-6). I spoke twice on the Christmas Day, and also the Lord's day morning following, and God favoured my soul with much life and power. The Lord fastened the truth of it home on my dear wife's conscience, as she had been in a backsliding state for some time. I had charged it home upon her; but still she kept it from me, as she knew I was then very severe against any one that made a profession of religion yet lived in any known sin. God had made and kept my conscience very tender in His fear, so that I had no mercy whatever on backsliders, nor did I then think any poor soul could backslide which had had pardon and peace brought into the heart and conscience by the blood of sprinkling. I had so suffered for my sins under the curse and killing power of the law that I thought I should never sin again; but I little knew what was before me. In the afternoon of the same Lord's day, I was led to speak from these words: "Be not afraid; but speak, and hold not thy peace; for I am with thee, and no man shall set on thee to hurt thee" (Acts 18. 9, 10).

I saw for some few days that my poor wife was in a dreadful state of mind; but at last she had to speak out and confess her departures from the Lord, and beg me to pray for her. After a short time, God made manifest His pardoning love and blood to her conscience, and washed all her guilt away; and it was the means of bringing us nearer together in soul union and communion from that time.

CHAPTER 7

But the enemies of the cross continued to rage against the truths the Lord enabled me to bring forth; and as I was still using the sharp two-edged sword from Sabbath to Sabbath, and cutting up and cutting off all who did not come up to the Bible standard, and kept threshing away upon empty professors and rotten hypocrites, the chapel began to get emptier than ever, and the friends fearing that the cause could not be kept on. Still, our collections kept up every year whether there were many or few people at the chapel. The devil roared, the enemies gnashed, and professors persecuted; so that, between one thing and another, my path got more and more trying.

There were a few that used to meet at an inn on week nights and Sabbath days to make up all the lies they could against me, and send it to the newspaper. One of the party used to come to the chapel to hear what he could pick up to make sport of me at the inn; but little did he know what lay before him, for after he had followed this on for some time, he was left to commit suicide. He would have destroyed my character, but the Lord took care of me and left him. There were four other men who would have destroyed me and the dear tried few, and the Bible also; but the Lord took care of us, and cut them down one after another in a solemn way and manner. They fell into the pit they would have dug for us.

The dear Lord wonderfully supported my soul under all my persecutions and made His truth very dear to me. I had a few dear friends who were knit very closely to me for the truth's sake, but still it was trying to them to hear such lies reported about my preaching. They could not find anything else, because the Lord had kept me upright in my movements. Sometimes it seemed more than I could endure, to stand against the scandals and persecutions I had to pass through; but still it was no more than what the Lord promised me; for, "In the world ye shall have tribulation"; and, "They that will live godly in Christ Jesus shall suffer persecution."

About this time, too, I was much tried with Satan's temptations, and I used to sink very low when out of the pulpit. One

Thursday evening I had been preaching, and had had a sweet time. But soon after I came out of the pulpit, my soul sank so low and such a mist of darkness and gloominess came over my mind that I wandered away into the fields. I called upon a friend, but was so dumb that I could not talk. I went home, could not eat my supper, crept off into my bedroom, and fell down before the Lord, and begged Him to tell me why I was so low, entreating Him to show me whether there was any secret sin that I was practising, and yet ignorant of it.

After a time I got into bed. I had very little sleep all that night but kept on begging the Lord to bring it to light in my conscience if there was any one thing He had not stripped me of. I got up in the morning as low as I went to bed, and got out in the shop to work under deep examination of heart, lip and life. I came in to my breakfast as low as ever, and could not talk to my wife. While I sat at the table I took up a little book by William Hunting-ton that had been lent to her. I opened just at the very spot where he speaks of the bosom sin, and backs it up with the Word of God. I threw down his book, took up the Bible, turned to the chapter and verse, and looked at it, showed it to my wife; and from that day that snare was broken, and my soul escaped.

And now came another thing to try me and exercise me. My enemies were so bitter against me, both little and big; and as my little boy was ill in bed, one Saturday night, a crowd of men got together and broke my bedroom window. The stone went near my boy's head as he lay in bed. I was sitting in my house and heard the crash. I took to my heels and ran after the fellows in such a rage, and overtook them. I felt determined to give them the law. I found out which man it was, and returned back to my house very angry, and knew not how to contain myself.

But, all of a sudden, the Lord broke in upon my soul. I cried out before my wife that I did not care if every window in the house was broken. I thanked, blessed, praised and loved the Lord for ever making manifest His love, mercy and goodness to such a wretch, at such a time, when I seemed more like a devil than a man. So that it was not for works of righteousness which I had done, but according to His great mercy that He saved me through and out of that trial.

But some of my friends wished me to make him pay for the mending of the window; but no, I could not. The dear Lord had given me such a blessing in and through it, and He had freely forgiven me all my sins in my rage and anger, and therefore I freely forgave them for breaking the window.

But I was not long in this sweet spot. I had been speaking on a Lord's day of what grace did in the hearts of the children of God, what fruits it produced in their lives, conduct and conversation, both in the master and servant, mistress and maid, father and son, mother and daughter, wherever the life and power of God was received in the heart and conscience. And as there ever were and ever will be, as long as there is a sinner left upon the face of the earth, characters that are full of religion in the head, tongue and judgment, but have none in the heart, conscience and life, these are sure to kick and fight against that religion which makes a man honest and produces fruits to the honour and praise of the Lord.

So, on the following Saturday night, one of the enemies of the truth put a note under the door, the contents of which so wrought on me that I was determined not to preach that Lord's day. When near chapel time, off I started quite another way, to run from my work; for I felt I could never stand against nor bear up under these persecutions that I then had on every hand. But I had not run far before these words dropped into my heart: "The hireling fleeth, because he is an hireling, and careth not for the sheep." The power of these words stopped me, and I dropped my guilty head, and returned back like any thief.

After I entered my house, I took up the Bible and opened it at the thirty-second of Jeremiah, and these words laid hold of my heart: "And they shall be My people, and I will be their God. And I will give them one heart and one way, that they may fear Me for ever, for the good of them, and of their children after them. And I will make an everlasting covenant with them, that I will not turn away from them to do them good, but I will put My fear in their hearts, that they shall not depart from Me" (Jer. 32. 38-40). And as I preached then three times, so I spoke all day from those verses, and my soul never had a better day in the pulpit. So that my soul can testify that all things work together for good to them that love God, to them who are the called according to His purpose.

Again, soon after this trouble and deliverance there was something else to try my faith and patience; and that was on a Lord's day evening. I had had a good day in speaking of the Lord's dealings towards me and His tried children, and after calling on a friend, we went home. I was unlocking the door, when one of the children saw something the matter with the front door. On putting her hand to see, she found a hole right through. On looking, I found all the bottom part kicked in, so that there was a road into the house. What to do we did not know. After a little while I said, "Let us go to bed, and leave all in the Lord's hands," for the Lord had wrought faith and patience in my heart, and enabled me to bear it just then. But I often cried out with Jeremiah, "Woe is me, my mother, that thou hast borne me a man of strife, and a man of contention to the whole earth!"

My two dear children were a great anxiety to me to bring them up in the nurture and admonition of the Lord. How I watched their every movement! But here I would give God's people a caution. Beware of making your children professors, as it is easily done, if they are steady. My two children would deceive any in a strange place if they were left to talk about religion, as they had heard but little else from time to time at home all their growing up, so that they knew the truth in their judgment. The grace of God will not suffer you to let them go on in their own ways without checking and warning them; but I fear and believe that there are many brought up in a religion from their childhood, and some even get into churches, and yet die destitute of grace and spiritual life at last. This is a solemn fact. But grace will lead the parents to do all they can to bring their children under the sound of God's blessed truth, and they will use all lawful means to do so. "And ye fathers, provoke not your children to wrath, but bring them up in the nurture and admonition of the Lord."

Now began another trouble. Some of the people got in my debt. I felt compelled to pay for everything, both in my business and in the house; and my salary for preaching was small, so that my money began to get short, and troubles set in fast upon me. I feared we should be obliged to get in debt again. Then my cry to the Lord was: "Do open some way for me to keep from getting into debt again." Well, I thought, we will make little do, as we have but little. I went over to Allington to hear that dear man of God, Mr. Warburton, of Trowbridge [John Warburton (1776-1857), author of *Mercies of a Covenant God*]. As I had never seen him before, when he stood up in the pulpit I looked him through and through, and when he began to preach, he soon looked *me* through and through. I had never heard but one such a preacher before. In the following year, I heard for the first time that beloved man of God, Mr. Philpot, and a searching sermon he preached. But I never heard a man preach too close for me yet. Many times since then I have heard him with pleasure and profit.

CALLS FROM OTHER CHURCHES TO SUPPLY

But again. I very soon received an invitation from Mr. Warburton to go to Trowbridge to preach for him. I answered him in this way: "I am such a fool; therefore I cannot think about standing in your pulpit." He answered, and said, "Our people want fools to preach to them. They have too many wise men." So that he would make me engage to go; but God only knows what I went through before the time was up to fill this engagement. The devil set in upon my soul in such a way that I wished I had never made this engagement. This made my soul groan and sigh to the Lord day and night for help; and then the cursed pride of my heart sprang up and said, "Why, I shall become a great preacher now. I am invited to preach in the great John Warburton's pulpit."

But when the Saturday morning came for me to start off to Trowbridge, and I had about twelve miles to walk, my soul sank fathoms within me. I trembled and shook from head to foot. I walked out into the little back kitchen, and fell down upon my knees, ready to faint, and poured out my soul before the Lord. He spoke these words into my heart, with life and power: "The Lord shall preserve thy going out and thy coming in, from this time forth, and even for evermore." And, bless His precious name for ever and ever, He went before me, and gave me life and liberty in the pulpit, and comforted the dear people's souls together. Mr. Warburton had told the deacons before he left home that, if they heard the stranger well, they were to try and get him for the following Sabbath. So I returned home to Pewsey, a distance of about twenty-two miles. I travelled the first ten miles by coach to

Devizes, and walked the other twelve to Pewsey. They gave me a sovereign for my labour and travelling expenses. This did not make me very fat; because there was no business going on at home. I went on the following Saturday morning. The Lord was with me again; and the people's souls were all alive under the word, for there were some precious jewels at Zion Chapel, Trowbridge, at that time.

After these two visits to Trowbridge, the people wanted me when Mr. Warburton left home. Then I began to feel the pride of my heart rise very high, and I thought, Surely, now Mr. Warburton's people have heard me so well, I shall soon be sent for to go to London. But upon the back of this Satan was let loose upon me. His temptations and the pride and lust of my heart worked together; and enticements of one kind and another almost drove me mad. I used to walk about, and wring my hands, and stamp my feet in an agony of soul night and day, and was trembling and fearing lest I should fall into the temptations, and bring a reproach upon the cause of God and the truth. For about three years my poor tortured and tormented soul passed through floods and flames of temptations. Sometimes I thought, if I crossed the broad ocean, I should be out of the reach of these temptations; but then, I thought, I shall carry my wretched heart with me, and the devil will be there. Here my soul cried heartily unto the Lord for deliverance; for I felt I could not live under it.

I stood engaged to preach with Mr. Warburton and Mr. Philpot at Calne anniversary on May 23rd, 1843, and a most trying time it was to me to go into the pulpit. But the Lord helped me. I returned to Allington with Mr. Parry and Mr. Philpot, and stopped there that night. My dear and much esteemed friend wanted to send me part of the way home on the morning of the 24th; but I said, "No, I would rather walk." So off I went. It being such a hot day, I took off my coat. After I got about two miles on the road, a sweet spirit of meditation fell upon my soul, and I walked on through the village of Alton. As I was mounting the hill, under prayer and supplication for the Lord to appear and subdue the sins of my base heart, and rebuke the devil, and open His hand to me in providence, just as I had got up to the top of the hill, the Lord Jesus revealed Himself to my soul in such a blessed way and manner by these words: "Behold the Lamb of God, which taketh away the sin of the world." And truly my soul did behold Him as taking away all my sins and transgressions, and washing them away in His precious atoning blood.

I had still between three and four miles to walk, and the sun was shining hot upon my body; but the Sun of righteousness was shining so gloriously into my soul that I walked and sang by the way, with the sweet tears of love and joy running down my face, with all my inward sins slaughtered, and the devil driven into his den. My soul came forth with a shout of "Victory!" through love and blood. I have never felt the power of sin and temptation in such a trying way and manner since. The Lord raised my faith so high that day on the road to believe that deliverance was near at hand in temporal matters.

As my soul was delivered out of that awful state of captivity, I longed to get home to my house to give full vent to my feelings; for my soul was as full as it could hold of the love of God the Father, God the Son and God the Holy Ghost. My soul loved the Father for making choice of me, the Son for redeeming me, and the Holy Ghost for calling me by His grace. When I got into my house, I shut myself in my room, and fell down and gave the Lord thanks for all His goodness and mercy to me and mine; and, strange to say, when I got home, there was a letter from London for me to go and preach at Eden Street for the first time for two Lord's days in the month of July 1843. Here I saw the hand of the Lord towards me in opening doors for me and supplying my every need.

When I had filled those two Lord's days, they gave me an invitation for the month of December. The Lord was with me to bless His own Word. Then I received an invitation to go to Woburn, in Bedfordshire, to preach; and I engaged to go for two Lord's days in the month of April 1844. I was then called out a great deal from place to place, so that I was at home at Pewsey very little.

CHAPTER 8

LEARNING TO WRITE

But to return to Pewsey. I must recall here a thing which took place in the year 1840. For eleven or twelve years before this time, this scripture was applied with power to my mind: "Write"; and it followed me up. Sometimes I thought I would put myself to school, but I had to support my wife and family. I kept promising myself that I would try, but when I had a little time, then I had no will. My soul kept on praying for the Lord to open the way. So in the year 1840, in the month of May, I had nothing much to do; then what to do I could not tell. Sometimes I thought I would try; and then again something said it would be of no use for me to try to learn to write. I was too old. But something said, Try, try.

At last I got a strip of writing paper, and asked my son to put down the alphabet in large letters on one side, and small on the other. I went up into my bedroom, fell upon my knees, and asked the Lord to teach me to write, as He had taught me to read Himself; for if there were letters to write my wife had to do it. I took the pen, ink and paper, and began to make a trial. I tried all one day and the next, and kept on through the week until I was almost beside myself; down upon my knees, and pleading that word "Write," and up and trying again.

At last I gave it up, and walked into my garden, groaning and crying to the Lord, saying, "Lord, didst not Thou tell me to write?" I could not form a letter for the life of me. I went up into my room again, took up the pen, sat down, and thought that I would just have one more trial, and then give it up for good. The Lord guided my pen, showed me how to form a letter, and I went on writing without any copy being set for me, and wrote anything that sprang up within my heart of the Word of God. After I had been writing for some little time, down I fell on my knees to thank the Lord for teaching me to form a word or letter. After I had followed this on for a few days, I began to think, How shall I put this together?

Some time after this I received a letter from Exeter to go and supply at the late Mr. Tanner's[1] chapel, called the Tabernacle. I felt that I must write a few lines to my dear and much esteemed friend, Mr. Philpot. But, I thought, such a fool as I am, with no human learning, to write to an Oxford scholar and eloquent orator as he is! It seemed like presumption. Still, I could not get it off my mind; but I felt I could not spell or put words together. Then I went to a bookshop and bought a spelling book; but I could not learn to spell a word. So I got a little writing paper, pen and ink, and went up into my bedroom and tried to ask the Lord to teach me; and then I began to write to this great preacher. And the Lord broke in upon my soul, broke my heart all to pieces, and the tears ran down my face; so that my soul by precious faith had such a sight and felt sense of the great Saviour, and my interest in Him, that I lost sight of the great preacher. My tears ran down on the paper as I scribbled.

O! what a precious time my soul had! I sent it off to Stamford to him; and in a short time I received a letter from him. And then I had to cry to the Lord to ask Him to teach me to read it. And, bless His dear and precious name, He did. I could not tell any one what my soul enjoyed in reading it. He encouraged me to press on and lose no time. And on I went with fresh courage, and never spent an hour's idle time for years. As I was continually asking the Lord to teach me how to spell and put the words together, it seemed to me as though there was a voice within my heart telling me how to spell and put words together. And what my soul has enjoyed in writing to friends, and feeling thankfulness and gratitude to the Lord for teaching me how to read and write! And He Himself hath done it. No man nor woman ever taught me anything of the kind. Then "bless the Lord, O my soul, and all that is within me, bless His holy name."

FURTHER TRIALS AT PEWSEY
As persecutions continued, we were anxious to get out of the High Street; and as there was a house, garden and a little land to be

---

[1]Henry Tanner's autobiography appeared in the *Gospel Standard* in 1982.

let, and I had some money left to take it, one of the deacons and my wife and self went and took it. My mind was swallowed up in it. We began to reckon what stock we should want, and what money it would take to stock it; and off my wife went to call my money in. This was on a Saturday. I was left at home and got no sleep, I was so busy with this new place. All of a sudden the word came into my soul: "No man that warreth entangleth himself with the affairs of this life," and truly they cut me up root and branch.

After evening service, the sister of the widow woman that I took this place of was standing at the chapel door; and she said: "You are not to have this place now." I answered her, "But I *will* have it, in spite of any one." Then this scripture came with such killing power into my heart: "Vengeance is Mine; I will repay, saith the Lord." And O! what a night I had on my bed between these two scriptures cutting me all to pieces, like so many swords, when my mind was hard at work in it: "No man that warreth entangleth himself with the affairs of this life." As I did not like to give way to the son-in-law, who was a lawyer, therefore I said, "I will have it, in spite of any one." Then this scripture came again with double power; and it made me cry, "Lord, what shall I do?" And the Lord showed me what I must do; and that was to give it up, and let Himself inflict the vengeance on the man. And, solemn to say, the Lord soon struck him blind; and one Sabbath evening, as he was eating, a bone got into his throat and killed him.

The Lord laid a heavy affliction upon my poor wife. She was a great sufferer; and my engagements at this time lay so far from home – at Manchester, Liverpool, Wolverhampton, Stamford and Oakham; so that I have come out of the pulpit hot, gone off to the railway station, and have travelled all night to and from these places to go home and see the dear sufferer.

INVITATIONS TO MANCHESTER AND WOBURN

About this time, I had an invitation from the church at Manchester to supply for them for so many months on probation [this would be after the death of Gadsby]; but I could not see my way to do so. The first time of my preaching at Woburn, in Bedfordshire, was in April 1844; and the first time of my supplying at the late Mr. Gadsby's chapel, Manchester, was in September

1844. So that doors opened to me on every hand. This supplied me with everything needful to meet my heavy expenses through my wife's long illness. But, being from home so much, I was obliged to give up my little business, and had wholly to live on the ministry. As I only received £25 a year from the friends at Pewsey, and had about £15 to pay for house rent and taxes out of that, I could not live to stop at home; and as the greater part of the people were poor, and God's grace in my conscience would not suffer me to impose upon them (because the poor that oppresseth the poor is like a sweeping rain that leaves no food), so, when I went from home so much, my conscience was impressed to give up my yearly pay, and only receive pay for the Lord's days that I was at home. Then I received ten shillings (50p) for the Sabbath; and I trust the Lord gave me a conscience towards my brethren, as well as one towards myself.

After going to Woburn two or three times, the friends wished me to settle amongst them, which caused me much exercise of mind. But I could not then see my way, but continued to supply for them as often as possible, and felt the power of the truth the Lord enabled me to deliver from time to time.

At one time, when I went to supply at Eden Street, London, in 1845 for the first two Lord's days in July (I had been to Zoar before), and came to my lodgings at Southampton Street on the Saturday night, there was a note for me. I opened it, and saw that it contained but a few words, and no name on it. I read it. The first words were: "Be sure your sins will find you out," and the other words: "There is nothing covered that shall not be revealed, nor hid that shall not be known." I turned it over and over in my mind, and as my wife was with me, I read it to her and showed it to the friends in the house.

I went to bed, but had little sleep. I got up, looked at this note again: "Be sure your sins will find you out." Well, I felt that this was a truth, for I knew it by every day's experience, and had done so for many years past; and the other portion troubled my mind at times. I could not think what it could mean, for I greatly feared there was some secret sin in me, or practised by me, that had never been brought to light. I was much perplexed and cast down, and had no text. So, between one thing and another, I verily thought it was all over with my preaching for that day. But I thought I would take my Bible and look at the connection.

When I had found it and had read the whole verse, the words entered into my soul with such life and power that I had a text. The person who wrote it took care not to take the whole verse, which reads thus: "Fear them not, therefore; for there is nothing covered that shall not be revealed; and hid that shall not be known." And the whole secret was opened up within my soul, which had been hid in those words from my understanding. So Satan missed his mark and was confuted, and my soul drew sweetness out of the text whilst I was speaking from it; and the Word of the Lord ran and was glorified.

I have had anonymous letters since then; for many are the trials and afflictions of the righteous, but the Lord will deliver them out of them all. And "no weapon that is formed against thee shall prosper; and every tongue that shall rise against thee in judgment thou shalt condemn. This is the heritage of the servants of the Lord; and their righteousness is of Me, saith the Lord."

SETTLEMENT AT WOBURN

As the Woburn people would not let me rest unless I would accept their call to become their settled pastor, I was greatly tried and exercised between the Manchester and the Woburn people. But I gave the Manchester friends a denial, and the leading gentleman at Woburn was continually pressing me until I would go and settle among them. He said he never heard any preacher like he heard me, and showed me great kindness; not that I received so much of his money; for after I had paid my travelling expenses from Pewsey to London and from London to Woburn, and back home again, I had but a few shillings left, because I had a great many miles to travel by coach in these days. My salary at Woburn was to be thirty shillings a week. At last I consented to go to Woburn, and the time and day were fixed for our removal. But the Lord only knows what my soul went through until about one hour before we left Pewsey.

There were a few poor souls there that my heart was closely knit to, and I could not get a word from the Lord. My poor wife was ill in bed, and I had but little bed that night, and less rest and sleep. I went up to my wife in bed about four o'clock in the morning to get her up, when she said, "I cannot get up. I cannot stand that long journey." My soul sank fathoms. I walked downstairs and into the garden for the last time in such distress of mind; and the dear and blessed Lord spoke to my heart and soul: "Fear thou not; I will help thee, and go before thee." I walked into the house quite happy, and felt sure that my wife would be able to take the journey, though a long one; and she was much better when we arrived at Woburn on the morning of the 18th of December, 1846, than when we left Pewsey.

We went into an empty house; for one cab took me, my wife, son and servant, and all our luggage and furniture from Paddington to the North-Western Station. My daughter was just married, and we left them in the house with the furniture; and now we had to furnish this house. I thought, of course, they would pay our travelling expenses; but no, not one shilling. The gentleman often asked me whether I did not want some money; but I always said No. I never borrowed any money of him; and he never gave me but one £5 note all the years of my friendship with him, which was about seven; and then his wife told him that he had not given me enough to pay my travelling expenses, as I had got my wife in London, she being unwell. He sent it to me there in a letter. Neither did I want his money, for I wanted to keep a good conscience towards both God and man.

My wife got better, and the Lord was with me in the pulpit. The church increased under my ministry, and we had peace among ourselves. Invitations came from every quarter, and the Lord greatly favoured my soul with life and liberty, and kept my conscience tender in His blessed fear.

After I had been there some time I received an invitation to go to Leicester. The first time I went there, the Lord blessed the Word to the people's souls, and Mr. Harrison[2] spoke of the Word coming with power into his heart and soul; and therefore he showed great kindness to me. But I am sorry to say that my Woburn friend began to be a little jealous. But still, I took no

---

[2]There is an account of Isaac Harrison in *The Seceders, Volume 2.*

notice of that. We still walked together in a friendly way and manner for about five years and two months until, after a church meeting, on the following morning, we got a little crooked because I told him my own faults, and then told him his.

And now began my troubles and deep-felt grief because I could not endure to see the poor of the flock trodden upon. So then troubles came in upon me like a wide breaking in of waters; but the Lord stood by me and enabled me to come up into the pulpit Sabbath after Sabbath with a "Thus saith the Lord," and with sword in hand. I had much enmity manifested against me; but I had a good conscience before God and man, and therefore the Lord stood by me.

This went on for over twelve months. Before the year was ended, some of them wanted me to leave quietly; but I said the church brought me there, and the church should send me away, and that I came there in an honourable way and manner, and that I wished to leave in the same way. But no, they would not send me away, so I stood my ground. God only knows what my soul went through during the twelve months. As I called a church meeting, some few sent in their resignation because they would not meet me.

During this trying year, my son left his situation. My daughter, her husband and children came to us in the month of May, and remained with us to the end of September; and I had them all to keep. This was a trying time indeed; it was in the year 1851, and some of the people said they should starve me out. But my Lord and Master fed me and all my family. Soon the dear Lord opened a way for my son-in-law at Oakham, in Rutland, and my son went into business at Luton, in Bedfordshire. Then we were only three left – myself, wife and servant. But here I was, with only the poor of the flock; but the Lord greatly blessed our souls, and the other few that left us opened a place close by our chapel, in the very place where I used to resort in my trouble.

And there is another thing that took place with me at Woburn. The Lord laid affliction upon my body. I was preaching at Eden Street, London, and went into the country to preach, and lay in a damp bed. I cannot say that I *slept* in it, because I lay and shook all night. I was obliged to return home before my engagement was completed, and very ill I was, and I thought I must die. The Lord hid His face from my poor soul, and shut me up in darkness and confusion, and the devil set in upon me in such a way, and told me my religion was a cheat and delusion. I lay and groaned and sighed like a poor prisoner in deed and in truth. My poor wife would say to me, "Why, father, it is all well with you." "Ah!" said I, in answer to her, "it is very well for you to say so, because you are out of the furnace, but I am in it." She would try to comfort me, for she had witnessed so much of the Lord's goodness and mercy towards me, but all the past mercies and deliverances would not do for my soul in that trying affliction and hot furnace. This was the first bodily affliction that ever I had. I had flattered myself that, if ever I was ill, how I should lie and love and serve the Lord. But, alas! alas! I had no love, no faith, to love and serve the Lord with.

A few days before I was taken ill, as I was walking down the City Road in London, before I got to the city toll-gate, these words were applied to my heart and soul with such power: "Have faith in God," and they kept on speaking in my heart. I wondered what was coming upon me. But in this furnace and fire my soul was led to understand them, for I felt that my soul needed faith in God.

This affliction brought down both body and soul. On the Friday, my soul sank so low, when all of a sudden these words came with such power: "Be still, and know that I am God." My little faith laid hold of the Lord Jesus in a moment. My soul was delivered from all my doubts, fears, groans, sighs and cries, and I came forth with a shout of "Victory!" through the blood of the everlasting covenant. These words: "Be still," sounded in my soul so sweetly that I said to my wife, "It is indeed all well with me now." I also added, "I shall dress myself and go and preach on Lord's day." She could not believe me, but I felt I must crawl out and preach from this text, for it seemed to me that there was not another such an one in all the Bible, because it so enlarged within my soul.

All day on the Friday, and also on the Saturday, my heart and soul was all on fire under the burning love of God in Christ Jesus. On the Lord's day morning I dressed myself, put on a large travelling cloak, and into the chapel I went and preached twice that day from my text; and truly the pulpit medicine, with the words: "Be still," was the best remedy and physic my body and soul had through all my illness. And now, my dear fellow preachers, *beware of sleeping in damp beds.*

As the house we lived in belonged to the party who had risen up against me, during an engagement of mine from home my poor wife was driven out of it, and she took four top rooms in a house in the market place. It being such a hot summer, and living day and night close to the blue slates, her poor head was affected. Here we were for fifteen months, and could not get a house anywhere. But when I was called out to preach, and saw a house shut up, O how I did long for that place! Now, my dear readers, I will leave you to judge the state and condition of our poor minds. I did not care so much about myself as I did about my poor afflicted wife, because she had been brought up more tenderly and better than I had; and she would often say in those rooms, "I am afraid I shall lose my reason." What trouble this gave me! I saw nothing but poverty and distress before me.

But at about the end of fifteen months there was a house to be let a little way out of town on the Leighton Road. I went with my wife to see it, and took it at once, and went into it; but all to no use and purpose. The malady was set in upon my wife, and she grew worse and worse daily. What to do I could not tell. Our old servant married away; and here I was, left to do as I could. I was compelled to try and fill my engagements; so I got a young woman to come and stop with her during the time I was gone to Leicester. At the same time, my daughter and her husband lay down at Oakham with fever, one on one bed and one on another. And although the Lord gave me such good health and strength, yet the enemy told me that the hand of the Lord was gone out against me, and my enemies would have an opportunity to say, Aha, aha, so we would have it; and that into deep poverty I must come, and all my family. But the dear Lord opened the hearts of the dear friends at Oakham, Stamford and other places, so that the needs of my poor daughter, her husband and children were well supplied. My dear and much esteemed friend, Mr. Philpot, was a great friend to them.

My poor soul kept crying to the Lord to open a way for me, that I might be able to pay my way, as I had done for many years; and I felt that faith and confidence in the Lord that He would do it. But I could not see in what way He would do it. But He knew the way that I must go; and when He had tried me, He brought forth my soul as gold. "For He performeth the thing that is appointed for me."

As my wife still grew worse and worse, my little faith was sharply tried in every way. The enemy of my soul tormented me, and told me I should never be able to stand my ground in this town as an honest man, for the people were all so poor. Poor dear things, they did all they could; and when I was out, they paid their supplies very well. And the Lord enabled us to do more to the inside of the chapel when the rich were gone than ever was done in their time. For we had made a new baptistery in the chapel, and brought the gas in, which cost over £16.

CHAPTER 9

AN INTERPOSITION OF THE LORD'S PROVIDENCE

But to return. Now the time was up for a great door to be opened for me in providence. My dear and much esteemed friend Mr. Harrison, of Leicester, died on the 3rd of March, 1855, and left me a farm at Besthorpe, in Nottinghamshire. As Mr. Harrison died on the 3rd of March, the first rent was due to me on the 6th of April. I said to myself, "Now I will preach to the poor things at Woburn free." So I published from the pulpit that I should not take anything from them for preaching after Lady Day. But this caused me another great trial; for the people whispered among themselves that Mr. Harrison left it as much to them as to me. Poor things, they did not understand the meaning of "absolutely" – "I give and bequeath to my friend Thomas Godwin, minister of the gospel, the farm at Besthorpe *absolutely*." So I had to get a copy of the will to convince them. On the 7th of April, 1855, another friend died, and left me £20.

So you can see, my reader, that my covenant God and Father had appointed some good things for me, a vile wretch, so that I could feelingly say, "The Lord is my Shepherd; I shall not want"; and "Thou preparest a table before me in the presence of mine enemies; Thou anointest my head with oil; my cup runneth over."

Now it was all over with that class of people; their hope was lost respecting starving me out. And there was another thing nearer than all this: there was no room for my devilish heart to fear that they would have their ends, and distrust my God. What hath God wrought? Then, my poor tried brother and sister, trust in Him, and commit thy way to Him, and He shall direct thy ways.

DEATH OF MY FIRST WIFE

But the Lord gave me ballast; for my poor wife grew worse and worse, and became very violent and as strong as a lion. She took me by the throat and almost strangled me, but the Lord gave me just strength enough to escape out of her hand. Then I strapped her hands to show her that I could master her. Then the devil set in upon her to destroy herself; and as the Lord had now given me the means to send her away, and she wished me to do so, I had made up my mind to go to Bedford to the asylum, and make an appointment to take her there. But, before the time came for me to go, she became more calm and quiet, and said, "Father, do bear with me. It will not be long." This broke my heart all to pieces, and I said, "No, I will never put you into an asylum." When I went from home, I used to get someone to take care of her, and when at home I used to look after her myself. I often used to hear her say in the night, when that awful spirit was upon her, "I will kill him"; but I used to sleep by her side very comfortably, for the Lord had assured me that she would never destroy herself nor yet her husband.

One day, when my son and daughter drove over to see their poor mother, they took her back with them while I got the house painted and papered; but she never returned home again. I then engaged a person to look after her, and I lived by myself, and travelled backwards and forwards from Woburn to Luton. She lived about a year and six months after she got to Luton with her daughter.

Now, there is no one on earth that can enter into these trials and troubles but those that have been in them, because they are always set against their best friends; and this is killing work to the poor husband or wife that has great affection towards the afflicted one. If ever this little work should fall into the hands of those who may have the same affliction to do with and to bear, be sure and be kind to them, and pray for patience to bear with them.

But now comes the closing scene. I was in the country preaching, and was just going to remove on to Bedworth to my dear old friend's house, the late Mr. Congreve [G. T. Congreve, a book of whose letters was published], when a letter came to say that my wife was a great deal worse. This was on the Friday morning, December 26th, 1856. A friend at Winslow drove me to Leighton to take the train for Luton, but it was gone; then another friend drove me on to Luton, and I sat and watched her all night by myself, and attended to her until about five o'clock in the morning, when she fell asleep, as quiet as a lamb, with a beautiful smile on her countenance, December 27th, 1856. I lost one of the best wives any man could have before her deranged state of mind came upon her, which was about three years before her death. Many a sly blow she gave me; but the Lord ever preserves His people, because He keepeth the feet of His saints. When I used to ask her if I should go out to preach and leave her, she used to say, "Go, father; you must be about your Master's business." Her mortal remains lie in the Luton cemetery.

A HEAVY AFFLICTION

Now, this change of life set me thinking; and as I had lived by myself eighteen months, and had done everything in the house for myself, I felt I would not keep either servant or housekeeper, as my wife took her servant to Luton with her; and that I would do for myself. But as I was called out so much, I came after a long journey into a cold, damp house, and nothing to eat; but I had some good drink in the pump, as I had been a water drinker for many years, and I used to call at the butcher's and get a chop, and go home and light my fire, and cook it.

But before the month of January was out, I went to Alvescot to preach, and on my return I called to see the late Mrs. Day. She was a member at Abingdon with that dear and precious man of God, the late William Tiptaft. As she was ill in bed, she wished to see me, so I went up into her bedroom. As soon as I saw her, I said, "You have got the fever"; for I felt it go down my throat. As dear friend Tiptaft had engaged to change pulpits with me, he went to Woburn for the Lord's day, and I preached at Abingdon for him morning and afternoon. Then I went over to Oxford and preached in the evening, and left Oxford by the first train to Bletchley, and walked the six miles to Woburn to meet Mr. Tiptaft at my house, my daughter being there to provide for Mr. T. When I got home, Mr. Tiptaft told me he was going out to preach that evening, and he said, "Mr. Goodman is coming after me at such an hour." "Then," I said, "I shall hope to go with you." So we went, and returned home after the service.

We took our supper together, and went to bed about eleven o'clock; and at one I was taken very ill with the fever. My dear friend and brother Tiptaft left me in the morning, and my daughter left me the next morning, because her husband and children needed her at home. There I was, left ill in bed, and no one to do anything for me. I used to get a man to get me a little milk, and took a little at a time. Here I lay until the following Monday morning. And in connection with this heavy affliction, I received a letter from my much esteemed friend Mr. Philpot, which contained heavy tidings. Between the painful feelings this letter gave me in soul, and the affliction of my body, I thought I should soon be in the grave with my poor departed wife. But, on the Monday morning, a friend came in to see me. I said to him, "Will you go and order a fly [a one-horse carriage] for me? I must try and go to Luton to my son's." Although it was a bitterly cold morning, yet I dressed myself and got into the fly; but the snow being so deep, the poor horse could not make any speed at all. But before we had got four miles on the road, we met my dear son with a fly and two horses, coming for me; so they drove close up by the side of our fly, so that I managed to get out of the one into the other. But when we got to Dunstable, the poor horses were so done up that the driver was obliged to take them out and give them a feed of corn.

As I sat in the carriage, I thought the Lord was about to make a full end of me, I was so dark and dead in my soul. When I got to my son's, I went to bed, and still grew worse and worse; but the affliction of my body was nothing to that of my mind. God only knows what I went through on that bed. My flesh wasted away on my bones, my strength of body and soul was gone, and Satan set in upon me, and said, "Your wife has only been dead a month, and now the Lord is about to cut you off at a stroke." My soul said, "Lord, what? Am I to die in this awful state of death and darkness, after so many deliverances and blessed testimonies that my soul has had from time to time?" My poor children kept coming to look at me, and my poor dear daughter who knew the Lord, and also her husband, and my dear son's wife, who herself attended to me all through my affliction. They would not let the servant come near me, neither the children, because mine was a very bad fever.

One night my soul was led out in nearness to the Lord, and two lines of a hymn dropped into my mind. My soul kept on repeating them. The lines were these:

> "A sacrifice of nobler name
> And richer blood than they";

the only two lines of a hymn that ever were made useful to my soul. After some little time, the Lord Jesus, the great sacrifice for sin, was opened up in my soul and manifested to my heart, so that my soul was brought out into a "large place" again, because the Lord delighted in me. And He made my soul delight in Him, so that I could lie and love the Lord Jesus, His people and His ways. Now I felt sure I should be raised up again to declare the truth and faithfulness of the Lord; and from that time I began to get better. I longed to go forth again into my labours, as the love of the Lord Jesus Christ flowed into my heart like so many warm springs from the fountain of everlasting life. So, without saying a word to my good nurse, I dressed myself for the first time, walked down stairs, put on my hat and cloak, walked out the back way, and went to see my dear daughter, as she then lived in Luton.

On the Saturday morning I rode five miles in the omnibus to the Dunstable railway station. It being the month of February 1857, the roads were so very rough that I thought it would have shaken me to pieces. I was ready to faint; but I got into a first-class carriage, and travelled about seventy miles to Leicester, and on Lord's day morning walked up into the pulpit more like a dead man than a living one. I preached twice that day, and the Lord was with me to bless His Word to the people's souls.

I began to gather strength fast, and my soul was very happy. I had been at Leicester but a few days before a lawyer's letter came to me. When I read it, down my soul sank lower than before; and what to do I could not tell. But very soon these words came with great power: "I will overturn, overturn, overturn."

My highly-esteemed friend at Oakham said that he would stand in my shoes, and that all letters that came to me I was to forward to him. I did so. I stopped at Leicester for three Lord's days, then came to Godmanchester for one, went to Hitchin for a week evening, and from there to Luton to my son's. There I found another letter from another lawyer at Woburn, for my enemy lived at Woburn. He said, "Godwin has some money, and I will ruin him." But these words kept on running through my heart: "I will overturn, overturn, overturn." So my soul committed all my case into my Lord and Master's hands.

When I reached Woburn, I went to the lawyer at once, and told him that I had received his letter, but that I never raised the report about his man; it was a common byword in the town. In a few days the lawyer came to me and wanted to know why I did not attend to his letters myself. I told him I should have nothing to do with them. And I heard no more about it. So the dear Lord overturned all their craftiness, and made their wisdom foolishness. "For He taketh the wise in their own craftiness."

Now my soul loved my blessed Lord and Master for making His own Word good again to me; and I wanted to honour Him and glorify Him in body and spirit, which are His.

MY SECOND MARRIAGE

Now I travelled on a little more smoothly for a little time, but very lonely, having nobody to speak to, and having to do all the household work myself, for I had made up my mind not to have a woman in my house. But after a few months, I felt that I could not live such a lonely life, and come home so often into a damp house. Then my soul began to cry to the Lord to give me another good wife, one that He Himself had appointed for me, one that was in the possession of the life and fear of God. "O Lord," cried my soul, "do not let me be deceived. Do not let me set my mind on one of my own choice. Do lead me to the one that Thou hast appointed for me." And the dear Lord answered my cry, and gave me a good, kind-hearted wife, liberal to the Lord's poor people. And never was a better nurse or more diligent wife in the house, and she cannot do enough for me. She is indeed a helpmeet. No man ever had two better wives than myself.

THOMAS GODWIN

DEATH OF MY SON

As my house at Woburn was too small, and there was not another in the town to be let, I took a house at Linslade, near Leighton Buzzard station, because we were continually travelling the country over. But soon there was another trouble and deep trial for me in the death of my dear and only son, who I hoped would be a comfort to me in my old age. I was preaching at Allington, in Wiltshire, when the heavy tidings of his illness reached me. I said that he would die, because my soul had been led to pray for him day after day.

After we arrived at home, we took a cup of tea, and started by the last train to Luton. My dear son had been crying out all day, "Has father come? Has father come?" and then, I believe, when it got so late, he gave me up. But when we drove up to the door, his dear wife met us with her baby in her arms, and the first words she said were: "Dear grandpapa, you are just in time to see the last of your dear son." My heart seemed almost to come into my mouth. I ran upstairs, and saw him with his eyes closed and nearly gone. I could not speak to him. His wife said, "John, my dear, here is your dear father come." He opened his eyes, turned, and fixed them upon me, and said, "Father, I am saved! Saved with an everlasting salvation!" I said, "Are you sure that you are saved, my son?" He said, "Yes." Then my heart and mouth were opened, and I preached the Lord Jesus Christ to him in that powerful way and manner, so that he did not seem like my son. Then he made motions for me to pray, and the heavens were opened to my soul. I could not pray for his life, but for an easy dismissal to glory, after which he made some motions to me about his three little children. Then he said, "Free grace; free grace. It is all of grace," and was gone in a moment. We had been with him just half an hour.

This was a trying stroke for my soul to pass through; but the blessed evidence and testimony that the Lord had given his soul, and the dying testimony that I witnessed myself of his soul being saved with an everlasting salvation, buried and covered all my sorrows for some time. But I had to witness this truth: "Thou broughtest us into the net; Thou laidest affliction on our loins. We went through fire and through water; but Thou broughtest us out into a wealthy place." Little did we think, when his poor mother died, that he would so soon be laid in the same grave with her. He departed this life September 21st, 1859, aged 32. "The Lord gave, and the Lord hath taken away; blessed be the name of the Lord."

INVITATIONS TO LIVERPOOL, ALLINGTON AND GODMANCHESTER

About this time I received a call from the church at Shaw Street, Liverpool. This caused me great exercise of mind for a long time, and much prayer to the Lord to know His mind and will respecting the matter; because sometimes it is the voice of the church, and not the voice of the Lord. Therefore I have been obliged to look closely into this matter. As I could not feel any leadings of the Lord within my soul that way, therefore I gave them a denial. But they would not receive it as such; so, after a long while, I gave them a second.

After this, two other churches asked me, but I wanted to see my way out from Woburn. At last, the Lord led me to give up my charge over them as a pastor. I still drove over to Woburn from Leighton every Lord's day when I was at home, and preached to them. But in the year 1860, the friends at Godmanchester gave me a call to become their pastor, and my dear and much esteemed friends at Allington wanted me to go and be settled over them. Here again my poor mind was so tried, night and day, to know the mind and will of the Lord in this trying matter. I had known the dear friends at Allington for about twenty-five years, and had proved their kindness to me over and over again, and my heart and soul was closely knit to them in the bonds of the gospel. But Godmanchester kept following me so closely until it was quite a trouble, for I had said, over and over again, that I would never settle over any other church, for I had had so many church troubles for so many years, again and again, that when I gave up my charge at Woburn, I made up my mind not to take the charge of another church. And the Lord only knows what trouble and sleepless hours this caused me on my bed, until the month of January 1861.

I was preaching at Oakham, and in the bedroom, on the morning of the 13th of January, the dear Lord decided the matter for me; for I felt I could not live any longer under the painful exercise. My poor soul cried out in the distress of my mind, "O Lord, do tell me what I am to do. I am so troubled. Am I to go to Godmanchester, or am I not?" The word came with such power: "Go; and I will be with thee"; and my soul was delivered in a moment, and I was as happy as I could be.

SETTLEMENT AT GODMANCHESTER

As I stood engaged to supply at Godmanchester in the month of March 1861, I then engaged to take the pastoral charge over the church. My labours were to commence on the first Lord's day in July. When this was settled in my mind, I wrote to my much esteemed friend Mr. Parry and told him in what way the Lord had settled the matter, and that I must go to Godmanchester.

After we had settled to go to Godmanchester, we wanted a little improvement in the chapel house. So one thing was suggested, and another; at last it was agreed upon to build two more rooms, and I gave twenty pounds to start with. All the money was soon raised. It cost a hundred and thirty pounds, and it is now a good family house – five rooms above, and five below. The Lord greatly blessed my soul on the first Lord's day in a marked way and manner, for I felt such life, liberty and power through the day in the pulpit from this text: "Take heed, therefore, unto yourselves, and to all the flock, over the which the Holy Ghost hath made you overseers, to feed the church of God, which He hath purchased with His own blood." I felt the Lord Himself ordained me over this church and people, and He gave testimony to the Word of His grace.

CHAPTER 10

And now begins a new scene in my poor life. On the 10th of July, 1861, we arrived here at this house, Chapel House, Godmanchester, with our household furniture. A vast number of kind-hearted friends were waiting to help us unload our furniture at the Chapel House. There was no road then to the house, but there were two green fields in the front of it, therefore the friend that rented them gave us liberty to draw the waggons across his field, and we cut down the hedge, and the furniture was soon in the house. Mr. J. Gadsby and Mr. Harper sent their waggons to Leighton Buzzard, and brought the furniture all the way by road; and although the waggons did not arrive until six o'clock in the evening, yet the bedroom and parlour were ready by supper time. So that we could lie down to rest under a feeling sense of the Lord's goodness and the kindness of the people. The house is called "Chapel House," although some little distance from the chapel; but it is the sole property of the church, therefore it is called Chapel House.

The dear Lord was with me in the pulpit, and fed His church and people under me, so that our hearts and souls were united together in the bonds of the gospel, and we walked together in love and union. On the 6th of October, I baptized in the River Ouse, and in the afternoon received them into church fellowship; and among them my present wife, who had been a member for years at Stadhampton before I married her. The church increased under my ministry, and we walked together in love; peace and prosperity ruled and reigned among us, each one esteeming others better than themselves. And we all pulled together, as we were all of one heart and one soul.

We began to see that something must be done to the chapel. One side was all decayed; we therefore saw that there must be a new wall built. A few of us met together, and we mutually agreed to do so. We collected the money among ourselves, and we set the men to work, and pulled the wall down, and got the new wall up before the Sabbath; and it was finished and paid for at once, which cost £90.

Soon something else came to cause us a little exercise. That was a Sabbath school. At once a few of us met together, and talked the matter over, and we found that there was no room for the children to sit, although the chapel is large. Then one of the friends said, "Shall we build a new gallery?" After a few minutes' consultation, one friend said, "We will have one, if we pay for it ourselves" (the committee). We began to see how much money we could raise; and the builder was sent for, and the contract entered into. The school was opened in the new gallery on the 1st of May, 1864, commencing with eighty-one children. This cost £97 13s., and the builder came and took his money as soon as it was done.

Surely the Lord is on our side; therefore we need not fear what man can do unto us. The cause prospered, and the Lord was truly among us, so that we could say that the Lord had done great things for us as a church and people, whereof we were made glad.

[Mr. Godwin then gives an account of how a drive to his house was made and a new kitchen built. Later the chapel was extensively repaired, a new floor, new seats and a new pulpit being put in. For all these improvements the money was remarkably provided.]

Now, my dear readers, I will leave you to judge what our feelings must have been, for I cannot describe them. During the time this work was going on, we met in the British School, and when we re-opened the chapel, we had no public collection because the kind friends made up what was wanting, so that all the money was ready when the work was completed. And I do believe that the Lord re-opened our hearts to bless, praise and thank Him for all His great favours to such unworthy wretches. We were like Manoah and his wife, and had nothing to do but to look on and wonder at the great things the Lord had done for us; for now we had built a new side wall to the chapel, a new gallery and a new inside to the chapel, and all was paid for when it was done. O my Lord, surely Thou hast made Thy promise good, which came with such power into my soul in the bedroom at Oakham: "Go, and I will be with thee." And, bless His precious name, He *has* been with me. And although we have lost by death twenty-two precious saints since I have been here, yet we have added between thirty and forty members [this would be over a period of nine to ten years], so that "the Lord is good; and a stronghold in the day of trouble." Also we have lost by death many out of the congregation, so that the congregation is not so large; but the great blessing is that we are walking in peace and union.

[Mr. Godwin then tells how a stable and coach house and a horse and carriage were bought for him.]

But none of these things moved me. The Lord keeps the running sore opened in my heart, and the old serpent is for ever tempting and tormenting me; so that the pride of my heart is kept down, for there is nothing in this world but what is connected with trouble and sorrow.

Just upon the back of this great gift, the dear teachers of the Sabbath school gave me a new Bible for the pulpit; and this broke my heart, and the tears of love and joy sweetly ran down my cheeks. Then a few of the poor members gave me one of Mr. Gadsby's best hymnbooks. This I record to show their love and affection towards me as their minister. And I must record this – that the first seven years of my ministry here were the most peaceful and the happiest time of my life in the ministry; for we never had any unpleasantness in the church and congregation, and we have walked together in love, spiritual union and affection, and I believe have had each member's prosperity in view, and have wept with them that wept, and rejoiced with them that rejoiced. And the school prospered, and the teachers agreed together in the school; and although many teachers have been removed, yet others have come forward; so that the number has been kept up.

[Here follows an account of the building of a schoolroom, the enlarging of the burial ground, and the provision of a minister's vestry.]

But to return. Many years ago, I was much tried that, if I should be laid aside, and be a burden to the people, what should I do, as I never had been a burden to any people, and hoped I never should. In the year 1867, a member of this church in Cambridge Street died, and left me three hundred pounds, free of legacy duty.

My dear readers, I cannot tell you what my feelings have been, from time to time, under the great goodness and mercy of the Lord to me and mine. "O that men would praise the Lord for His goodness, and for His wonderful works to the children of men!" I cannot bury these things, but must bring them to light, and lay them open before the public, that they may encourage some of the poor ministers of the Lord Jesus Christ when my body shall be laid in the grave; for here is an old man, nearly sixty-eight years of age, whom the Lord hath brought through many troubles, trials and sorrows, and given his soul such sweet testimonies and deliverances out of all his troubles and temptations, and made His promises good to my heart and soul: "Seek ye first the kingdom of God and His righteousness, and all these things shall be added unto you." And again: "Consider the ravens, for they neither sow nor reap; which neither have storehouse nor barn; and God feedeth them. How much more are ye better than the fowls?"

These two portions of God's Word were applied to my soul, and the Lord gave me strength and courage to cast myself upon Him when I left the Church of England and all my former friends; and, notwithstanding all the bitterness and enmity of friends and foes, the Lord hath stood by me. And He has gone beyond His promise to me and mine, for He is not only a promise-making and a promise-keeping God, but He is a promise-fulfilling God, that keepeth covenant and mercy for ever toward them that fear Him, and hath said that He will never leave nor forsake His poor tried family that are scattered abroad all over the earth. So that His name is still "Jehovah-jireh" – "The Lord will provide."

I must just say, to the honour and praise of His great name, that I have received four small legacies from strangers in blood, besides the two large ones. So that you, my dear reader, can see that the Lord has made His goodness to pass before me in the way on every hand and on every side; and He hath made me willing to labour among His poor children. And He hath led me about in His vineyard, and given me health and strength to travel the country over. I have preached in nearly two hundred different pulpits, and have had a large circle of close friends scattered over the land. And my unprofitable life has been lengthened out to see the end of most of my old friends in the ministry. They are gone to the place appointed for all the living family of God. What changing scenes I have witnessed, both in myself and others, and in churches and congregations! And now I am waiting for the last solemn change to come to myself. I am living to prove that this is not my rest, because it is polluted. But there is a rest remaining for the people of God; and we which have believed do enter into that rest by precious faith.

But to return to my narrative. I have stated that the first seven years of my pastoral charge over this church were the most peaceful and the happiest time that I ever knew since I have been a preacher.

But lately I have had some changes, and have been much cast down, at times, through people failing in business, and their removal from this church and congregation. A great deal of this took place through pride, indolence and extravagance; and this has tried me much. And I am still tried respecting the carelessness and slothfulness of some men in business. When I was in business, after the fear of the Lord was put into my heart, I was obliged to work hard and live hard; and never spent one shilling unless I gave it away to the needy. I am sure that no man can get on through life in business without very close application. For many years I feared I should not be able to get through life honourably.

And there is another thing that I greatly feared – that I should live to be a burden to the Lord's dear people. These feelings and fears have sunk me very low from time to time. But my dear Lord and Master has opened His hand so bountifully to such a poor, blind, empty, vile sinner, that I can feelingly join Agur, and say, "Two things have I required of Thee, deny me them not before I die. Remove far from me vanity and lies, give me neither poverty nor riches; feed me with food convenient for me; lest I be full, and deny Thee, and say, Who is the Lord? Or lest I be poor, and steal, and take the name of my God in vain."

But my dear Lord hath provided such bounties for me, and given me more than I ever asked Him for. For many years I felt a desire to be in a position, and also in possession of a little money to give to the Lord's dear needy people; and the Lord has granted me my desire. When the dear Lord put it into the heart of my dear friend, Mr. Harrison of Leicester, to leave me the farm at Besthorpe, two good cottages and gardens, and between eighty and ninety acres of land, I thought it would have killed me. O how my soul cried day and night to the dear Lord to keep it out of my heart, and my heart out of that! And, bless His dear name, He has done so; for my dear friend died March 3rd, 1855, and now I am writing this on the last day of January, 1871. When the contents of the will were read to me, and I heard it: "I give and bequeath to my friend, Thomas Godwin, minister of the gospel of Woburn, my farm at Besthorpe, absolutely." O my dear readers, trust ye in the Lord for ever, and cast all your care upon Him, for He careth for you. And remember and forget not what a rich Father you have, who declares that the gold is His, and the silver is His, and the cattle upon a thousand hills are His, and the whole world and the fulness thereof. And is there anything too hard for the Lord to do?

Now that I am unable to walk, through increasing infirmities, to see the friends when sick who live at a distance (for ours are a very scattered people), the Lord has given me a four-wheel, so that I can drive to visit them. But my readers must remember that all this has not made a gentleman of me. No, I never felt myself to be such a poor, empty, ignorant creature in all my experience as I feel now, from time to time; groping and groaning about the house and garden. But I am as fond of work, if I could do it, as I was when I worked for one shilling per week, or when a milk boy and cut my own loaf, and used to put the knife down to see how long it would serve me. O Lord, what hast Thou done for a poor ill- and hell-deserving sinner!

And from the first entrance of the fear of the Lord into my heart, the Lord hath appeared for me in every trouble and strait. And many times, when I have had sums of money to pay, the postman has again and again brought me letters with £5 or £10 notes in them. And once at Woburn, after my first wife fell into that low state of mind, after we had removed from the rooms in the Market Place and I had taken a place a little out of town at £14 per year, and the first year's rent was due, I received two letters from friends – one had a £10 note in it, and the other a £2. So here was £12 towards the £14. This was a year before Mr. Harrison left me the farm and Mr. Holmes left me £20. And although my soul was then sunk so low, through the heavy affliction of my wife, yet my soul was like David's when he danced before the ark. O how my soul loved the dear Lord for opening His dear children's hearts to supply my need! So that He is a God of providence as well as a God of grace.

I have endeavoured to keep these things separate from the work of the Spirit of God in my soul, to show to my readers that God's divine providence towards His children is one thing, and the applications, manifestations and revelations in the soul another thing. These are everlasting testimonies from God the Father, through God the Son, and brought into the soul by God the Holy Ghost; and these divine things make poor fools wise unto salvation.

This concludes Mr. Godwin's own account of his life.

CHAPTER 11

We now include the little pieces Mr. Godwin afterwards wrote from time to time.

January 21st, 1869

A memorable day of bliss and blessedness, revealed and sealed home into my heart and soul by the anointing power of God the Holy Ghost, under which my soul has been as happy as I could well live.

I have been travelling through a painful path for some days of hard conflict and deep-felt sorrow under the power of darkness and temptation; and have had some heavy sighs and groans pressed out of my soul for another sweet visit of His great salvation.

My soul has been longing for a new year's gift, and wondering whether I should ever have another sweet visit of His great salvation this side of the grave. The latter part of last week, my soul was tormented with indwelling sin, infidel thoughts and the devil's temptations; so that the war was so hot, and the conflict so hard, and my faith and hope so low. But I felt like this: It may be to meet some of the cases of the poor tried children of God on Lord's day, the 17th. And truly I found it to be so. And last night, the 20th, I read these words for a text: "Lord, be Thou my helper"; and it was the very cry of my soul.

This morning, I felt life in reading and prayer, so that my faith and hope revived. "His mouth is most sweet; yea, He is altogether lovely. This is my Beloved, and this is my Friend, O daughters of Jerusalem" (Song 5. 16).

––––––

On December 9th, 1869, I lost my dear and valued friend and brother, Mr. Philpot, one with whom I had enjoyed sweet communion for many years. I went to Croydon to see his body well laid in the grave. Although dead, he yet speaketh by the many able works he has left behind him. "The memory of the just is blessed" (Prov. 10. 7).

———

February 10th, 1870

I had been asking the Lord to give me a new year's blessing; and, bless His name, on the 10th of February, after reading in the family part of the 24th of Luke, the word being so sweet to my heart and soul, I took it up again after prayer, and life and light sprang up in it. And the Holy Ghost shone so sweetly upon it that it began to enlarge itself in my heart; and my heart enlarged in that; and these words swelled in my heart like leaven: "He showed them His hands and His feet." And a blessed sight it is to my sin-oppressed and devil-tempted soul! And His precious love poured into my heart in such a blessed way and manner, so that my cup has been full and running over with love to the dear Lord Jesus Christ and His dear redeemed people.

The savour of this lasted several days. On the following Lord's day, I spoke from these words: "And for their sakes I sanctify Myself, that they also might be sanctified through the truth" (John 17. 19).

———

On January 18th, 1871 a heavy affliction fell upon me in my left shoulder, arm and hand. My soul was shut up in a state of darkness, hardness, death and sorrow; and Satan seemed to be let loose upon me; and the rebellion of my vile heart began to work within against the Lord for laying all this suffering upon me, until I felt more like a devil than a saint. This lasted until Friday morning, when the dear Lord broke my hard and rebellious heart all to pieces, and filled my soul full of love, joy and peace. And sure I am that "He stayeth His rough wind in the day of the east wind.

———

February 1st, 1871

A day to be remembered by me, notwithstanding all the suffering I have passed through for the last fortnight, and left my bed as full of pain as I could well bear.

As I sat by the fire, looking out of the window, feeling that it was a trying time for the poor, many suffering privation as well as pain, the postman came to the door with the letters. When I opened one, the writer said, "I have sent you a few of my *pills,* hoping they will do you good." And, dear readers, what do you think these pills were made of? Why, four ten pound notes, and two fives, which made £50. The Lord came into my heart, and I began giving to the poor. And I am sure that I received it freely; and this has made me give freely through the day. And I do believe that a few such pills as these would do thousands of God's poor tried children good.

Now you can see, my readers, that the Lord will supply my need. If this narrative should fall into the hands of any of God's poor ministers who are tried in providence, be as careful as you can not to get further into debt. And when you are preaching, do not try to preach money out of your hearers, neither tell your hearers how badly you are off; but lay all your debts and troubles before the Lord, and ask the Lord to bless the testimony to the hearts of your hearers; and the Lord will open their hearts, and you shall witness His dear hand in helping you. When I was in debt, I never opened my mind to any of my friends until the Lord had brought out by hard labour and hard living. He brought me out by littles – here a little, and there a little; and now I can look back with pleasure and profit, and see the hand that opened the way, and brought me through to this day. Then "seek ye first the kingdom of God and His righteousness, and all these things shall be added unto you."

———

February 1st, 1872

"Cast thy burden upon the Lord, and He shall sustain thee. He shall never suffer the righteous to be moved." This day was a day of days, not to be forgotten by me when the dear Lord visited my soul with the joys of His great salvation. O how sweet was His Word to my heart! And my faith laid firm and fast hold of my blessed Lord and Saviour, and held sweet communion and fellowship with the Father, and with His Son Jesus Christ, and felt as happy as I could live. But, alas! alas! I soon found that the Canaanites still dwell in the land, and will mar and disturb my peace; according to that word: "This is not your rest, because it is polluted."

January 20th, 1873

As I was looking into the fifth chapter of the Revelation, such a sweet spirit of meditation fell upon me and sprang up within me, and such an unfolding of the truth of that chapter to my soul; until my heart and soul were swallowed up in the great and grand truths therein recorded. I felt as happy as if my soul was about to enter heaven.

February 4th, 1873

The dear Lord shed abroad His precious love in my heart and soul in such a blessed way and manner, until my cup was full with these sweet words: "Having loved His own which were in the world, He loved them unto the end." How sure I am that every soul that God the Father loved with an everlasting love, that God the Son loved with an everlasting love and redeemed with an everlasting redemption, and that God the Holy Ghost loved with the same unchangeable love, will be loved unto the end! And His sweet comforting love now warms my heart, cheers my spirit, illuminates my mind, and works that assurance in my soul that I must endure unto the end, because my Lord and Saviour tells me that He loves His people unto the end. And bless His precious name for ever and ever,

"Whom once He loves He never leaves,
But loves them to the end."

And my heart loves the Three-One God in return. I love the Father for loving me and choosing me; and I love the dear Son for redeeming me, and paying my great debt for me; and I love the Holy Ghost for quickening my soul into divine life, and for sealing the killing power of the law home upon my conscience, and for taking the pardoning blood and justifying righteousness of the Lord Jesus Christ, revealing and sealing it home with power into my guilty soul, which made and still makes my soul rejoice in His great salvation.

In 1873 we found it quite necessary, from the bad state that the roof and front of the chapel were in, to see what we could do to it. But after so much had been done, it was a great undertaking for us to collect such a large sum as it would take to put a new roof and front to it. But however, the workmen commenced their work; but it was a long job, and they did not get on very well, which tried my faith and patience. Having to preach in the schoolroom for several months, it was so hot and inconvenient for the accommodation of the congregation through the warm weather, that I often wished it had never been begun.

But on the first Lord's day in January 1874, we re-opened it, finished and paid for, at the cost of £736 14s. 4d. All the money was raised among the people, with the exception of £100 given me by two dear sisters, to whom the Lord has given the hearts and means to help the needy. May the Lord abundantly bless them. I spoke from these words (Haggai 2. 9): "The glory of this latter house shall be greater than of the former, saith the Lord of hosts; and in this place will I give peace, saith the Lord of hosts," and had a happy day in my own soul. Truly we can say, "What hath God wrought!"

We now have a well-built chapel, good schoolroom and every convenience. During the last thirteen years, since I have been pastor here, we have spent in repairs for the chapel, etc., the large sum of £2,068 8s. 4d. And my desire is that during the few remaining days or months I may have to sojourn here, we may live together in love and peace, that the text may indeed be fulfilled in our experience. And when my work is done here below, may the Lord send the church a pastor, a man that shall go in and out before them, and feed the flock of slaughter.

[How blessedly God fulfilled this desire! Less than five years after Mr. Godwin's death, Joseph Oldfield accepted the pastorate.]

CHAPTER 12

A SHORT ACCOUNT OF MR. GODWIN'S LAST DAYS WRITTEN
BY HIS BEREAVED WIDOW

My dear husband had suffered for some years with feeble action of the heart. Dr. Brooks, who examined his chest, told me that his heart was in that state that any exertion might cause him to drop dead, and begged me not to let him work in the garden. This was quite a trial to him, for he was very fond of rising early in the morning to work in it. He said he often enjoyed sweet meditation in watching the wonderful works of God in creation. The opening of the buds, and the expanding of the leaves, often led his mind up to nature's God; and he would come in to breakfast cheered and refreshed. But after he was not able to work, he would walk about, feeling grieved, seeing so much to do, yet not able to do it. Being naturally of an active mind, he did not like to sit idle. And his weakness was such that he could write but very little for several months before his illness, his hand shook so much. He often said, "What a useless lump I am become! What a wonder the Lord bears with me!" At times, he sank very low in his mind, was often under a cloud, would burst into tears and mourn over his darkness and useless life. Yet the Lord helped him in the pulpit to speak to the tried and exercised.

The last time he entered the pulpit, he spoke from these words: "So will not we go back from Thee; quicken us, and we will call upon Thy name. Turn us again, O Lord God of hosts; cause Thy face to shine, and we shall be saved" (Psa. 80. 18, 19). He spoke with freedom, and in his usual way; and we little thought it would be the last time he would stand there. But the Lord's thoughts are not our thoughts.

———

From the "Gospel Standard," October 1877
"At one time, when a little water was given to him, he blessed the Lord for it, and said, 'There is not a drop of water in

hell,' and burst into tears at the mercy of the Lord in delivering him from hell. He asked me to read to him Psalm 102, which comforted him. But, at times, he sank very low under the hidings of the light of the Lord's countenance and the powerful temptations of Satan. He often said he wondered he could stand up to speak at all, but, at times, he was much helped to declare a free gospel; and under that text: 'Christ is All and in all,' he very sweetly entered into what it was to have Christ dwelling in believers the hope of glory. He lived upon the sweetness for many days.

"On the following Tuesday night he was much favoured on his bed, and held sweet communion for hours. In the family service, in the evening, he was much drawn out, and felt liberty, and prayed for us that the Lord would comfort us if He removed him. He also begged for another song in the night season. In the morning, he said to me, 'Yes, I shall soon be landed. The Lord has told me so. He has sweetly revealed Himself to me on my bed this morning, and brought me up from the low dungeon, and set my feet upon the Rock of eternal ages. I can leave all now.' Seeing me distressed, he replied, 'It may not be just yet. I am willing to stay the Lord's appointed time; and He will take care of you.'

"On July 28th I noticed a difference in his voice, and his memory failed him very much, and he did not eat his dinner as usual. I said, 'You don't seem quite so well.' He replied, 'No, dear; I feel very strange in my head.' After trying to sleep in his chair, I advised him to go to bed and try some remedies which had relieved him before. I read to him one of his favourite chapters (John 17), thinking I might read him to sleep; but after lying for about an hour, he got up, and said he felt better. But he had no sleep; but afterwards he fell asleep for nearly an hour. He then had a cup of tea, but no appetite to eat. On taking up his Bible he sighed very much. Being Saturday evening, I said, 'Now you want a text.' He said, 'I don't know what I want. I feel a very poor creature.'

"One of the members came in, and we noticed his voice was very feeble. The member read and prayed; to which he [Mr. G.] responded a hearty Amen. On his leaving, he said, 'You seem very poorly. Shall I call and send Mr. Lucas [the doctor] over?' He replied, 'O no, friend; I don't want a doctor, but the good Physician. Perhaps a night's rest will set me to rights.' At nine o'clock he said, 'Is my bed ready, that I may go and lie down to die?' I assisted him into bed, and watched by him. He was soon asleep, and slept until half-past eleven. He then got out of bed three times in about an hour; the last time I said, 'I should like to put your feet in mustard and water.' He said, 'Very well.' I got it, and put his feet in; and also held his hands in a basin of hot mustard and water for about a quarter of an hour. Then he looked wearily towards the bed. I noticed it, and said, 'Do you wish to go into bed?' He replied, 'Yes, yes, yes.' He soon fell into a doze for two or three hours. About five o'clock I observed he breathed very hard, and looked different. I then sent for the doctor, who, when he came, said he had been seized with a fit of paralysis, which affected the muscles of the throat. He lay in an unconscious state for hours.

"Being Lord's day, several friends came in after the morning service; but he took no notice of any. But after the afternoon service, when the deacons came, he knew them, blessed them in the name of the Lord, and said he was happy, quite happy, his dear face beaming with heavenly joy and peace.

"To another friend, later in the evening, he said, 'Prepared – ready. I am ready to depart and be with Christ.' I believe from that time he was quite sensible, but not able to converse, except a few words at a time. He slept very much; we had to rouse him to give him nourishment. The doctor said he would sleep on until the heart stopped from sheer exhaustion. He was in no pain.

"At one time, seeing me in tears, he burst into tears, and said, 'Poor thing!' At another time, he looked at me, and said, 'No wrath, no wrath; no terrors, no terrors.' A friend said, 'If you were able, would you not speak well of Christ?' To which he replied, 'I would. Yes, I would.' Shortly afterwards, he said, 'He scorns thousands and thousands; and He saves thousands and thousands,' and more words we could not understand about professors.

"On a friend coming in, he was asked if he knew her. He said, 'O yes!' and called her by name. She asked, 'Is Jesus precious?' He at once replied, with much emphasis, 'O yes! He is.' She said, 'Then you are happy.' He said, 'O yes! I am on the Rock, on the Rock. "Rock of ages, shelter me!"' He repeated several times, 'Shelter me.' At another time he said there was an eternal weight of glory laid up for him, awaiting him; his face beaming with joy and peace.

"Early on Thursday morning he awoke out of a nice sleep. Noticing him looking round the room, a friend went to his side, and asked what he was looking for. He replied, 'I am looking for union and communion'; and other words which we could not understand. After a brief interval, he said, 'I have had union and communion with the saints.' On a friend leaving him, who had sat up with him, he sent his love to his wife, and said, 'Bless her! The Lord hath blessed her with spiritual blessings in heavenly places in Christ Jesus.' On being asked how he felt, he replied, 'Very blessed. No wrath, no terror, no wrath.' When his daughter came, he knew her, burst into tears, and was much overcome at the sight of her and his son-in-law, and blessed them in the name of the Lord God almighty.

"On the Friday morning he seemed so much better that the doctor told him he believed he should see him about again. He replied, 'O no, doctor! I don't think so.' I said, 'Would you not like, dear, to stay with us a little longer?' He said, 'Yes, if the Lord's will.'

"The enemy, who had assaulted him all his life long, was not allowed to come near him on his dying bed. When asked by the deacon, on the Friday evening, if the enemy tormented him, he said, 'No; quite happy.' At another time, he said, 'Death is swallowed up in victory. O death, where is thy sting? O grave, where is thy victory? The sting of death is sin; and the strength of sin is the law; but thanks be to God, who giveth us the victory through our Lord Jesus Christ.'

"The last twelve hours he never moved hand or foot, and breathed out his soul to God who gave it at half-past nine on Sabbath night, August 5th, so entering into an everlasting Sabbath, leaving a sorrowing widow and many friends to mourn their loss. He was an affectionate, kind husband and father, and a faithful, loving pastor. His wish was granted him that, when his work was done, the Lord would take him quickly home to Himself.

"The friends were extremely kind in sitting up and assisting to nurse him; and everything was done that love and skill could suggest. He was attended by three medical men, who were very attentive and kind; but the time was come that he must enter into that rest which remaineth for the people of God. He is now singing, 'Unto Him that loved us, and washed us from our sins in His own precious blood'; while I am left to mourn his absence; for in him I have lost a kind, sympathizing companion and a wise counsellor. And as we saw eye to eye in the things of God, we could converse together on spiritual matters, and I often had my strength renewed and heart warmed while he related the glories of King Jesus."

"Mark the perfect man, and behold the upright; for the end of that man is peace" (Psa. 37. 37).

From the "Cambridge Express," August 8th, 1877

"GODMANCHESTER"

"It is with much regret that we chronicle the demise of the late Mr. Godwin, who had for a period of about sixteen years been the much-esteemed and beloved minister of the Particular Baptist chapel of this place. The deceased had been in failing health for the past year or two, but was enabled to prosecute his ministerial duties up to a short time of his death. He was seized with paralysis, and lingered about eight days, and expired at his residence on Sunday evening last.

"Deceased was held in considerable regard and respect by a very large circle of friends and a numerous congregation that sat under his ministry. He was of a kindly and generous disposition; but his charity was without ostentation, not letting his left hand know what his right hand did. The poorer members of his congregation have lost a great friend and benefactor, as his house was at all times open to them, and his charity dealt out with an unsparing hand.

"As a preacher he was popular, although, at times, eccentric; but his admirers were numerous, and many would come several miles Sunday after Sunday to hear the gospel from his lips.

"A few years ago, when the chapel was enlarged and restored, the deceased was foremost in the work, and contributed most liberally towards it.

"His remains were interred in a brick grave in the new burial ground appointed for the Nonconformists on Wednesday last. An immense number of people were present, and they came from all parts to pay the last tribute of respect to one whom they loved so well. A short service was held in the chapel, and the corpse was subsequently conveyed on a hand hearse to the burial ground. The obsequies were performed by Mr. Taylor, of Manchester, an intimate friend of deceased, and Mr. Gadsby's successor. Several hundreds of people witnessed the interment. The age of deceased was 74."

———

The following is a copy of the inscription on the tablet erected in the chapel at Godmanchester to the memory of Mr. Godwin:

THIS TABLET WAS ERECTED BY
THE CHURCH AND CONGREGATION IN
MEMORY
OF
THOMAS GODWIN,
WHO FOR SIXTEEN YEARS FAITHFULLY
AND AFFECTIONATELY PREACHED THE
GOSPEL IN THIS PLACE,
DIED AUG. 5, 1877,
AGED 74.
"I KEPT BACK NOTHING THAT WAS PROFITABLE TO YOU."[3]
—ACTS XX. 20.

---

[3] A boy at Godmanchester chapel was so impressed by this text on the memorial that he never forgot it. Himself becoming a pastor, he felt there could be no greater tribute paid to a minister than that the Godmanchester congregation paid to Thomas Godwin by applying this text to him.

A Tribute from A. B. Taylor of Manchester

In attempting to pay a tribute of respect to the memory of one so retiring, and yet so endeared, I fear lest, on the one hand, I may say too much or, on the other, too little about my worthy friend; but, should I err, I may perhaps be excused if the sorrowing of intimate friendship be considered. Man is apt to lean to the side he loves and more so in the case of a brother minister, who could not be known without being loved, yet one who did but little to make himself the property of the public; nevertheless one who was entirely the property of the church of Christ, and with the fondness of a kind heart breathed a true Christian spirit.

Brother Godwin was not a man of mere grammar, who could heap together in order words of scriptural truths, doctrinal, experimental and practical truths, all of which may be found in God's Word, but which, like the head of the axe the prophet caused to swim, may be borrowed. Alas! alas for all such! Not so Thomas Godwin. His matter, though somewhat rough, was worked out of his own system, and drawn out of his own well; as all who rightly knew him were and are willing to admit. Christ, the living Fountain, was the source from whence he drew all his supplies; and Christ being formed in his heart the hope of glory, he enjoyed much of Christ's Spirit. He was a man truly humbled, whose beginning and ending in the divine life ran one grand parallel. The grace of God had warmed his heart, and the fear of God regulated his life.

As a scholar, our brother stood on no high elevation, except in divine things. He had been at the best school, and was truly taught of God; and having learned of the Father something of God's most holy law, and the terrors of the Lord, as a perishing sinner he heard the sound of a great trumpet, and, drawn by the Holy Spirit, he fled for refuge to Him who says, "As soon as they hear of Me they shall run unto Me."

The uplifted Saviour was to him a wonderful sight. He learned that Christ received sinners; and, venturing, he felt the spirit of grace and supplication sustain him as he approached. Then, blessed with a sense of pardoning mercy, his mouth was opened amongst the people of God; and before he or the people well knew what he was doing, he was preaching Christ to sinners.

This was something dreadful and unpardonable, especially in high circles, where priestcraft rode rough-shod round the parish while the "Meetingers" were held up to ridicule and contempt. Our brother went on preaching Christ, and baptizing believers in the name of the Lord Jesus. Poor fallen nature around him, even where it might be called religious, could not see in him God's work, any more than the despising Jews could see in Jesus of Nazareth the eternal Son of God.

As a friend, Mr. Godwin was open and kind. There was much simplicity of manners and integrity of character in his whole bearing that endeared him to his friends. He was extremely fond of meeting with one whose eyes were being opened to divine things. He did, without design, mingle cheerfulness with sedateness and, pointing the anxious one beyond the future, could throw a handful of purpose, which often endeared him to the troubled soul. Even grace had not altered the character of his mind. It is true, much was changed; but the fragments of youth were visible to the last.

In handling a doctrinal subject, or any point of discussion, Mr. Godwin seldom succeeded; and sometimes the balance of his judgment seemed in danger, so anxious was he to get at what he called "savoury meat." His heart was warm; discussion seemed too dry for him.

The strength of his ministry lay in relating the operations of the Spirit of God upon the heart – times of refreshing, sealing times, heaps of stones, Ebenezers, Bethels, Hermons and Mizar hills; all testimonies. On these subjects he could revel with pleasure when his heart was warm. He would, at times, burst out in his own provincial dialect, and this was rich indeed when his congregation happened to be in the "wilds of Wiltshire," when the more humble of his hearers felt themselves enriched under a shower of what to them was the most powerful eloquence. When his heart was thus warm, he seldom failed to invest his subject with considerable interest.

Throughout his ministerial life, quietness was dear to him, and seldom indeed could he be brought on the foreground, except in the pulpit.

Christian humility was very apparent in his character; yet no extent of misrepresentation or calumny could move him from what he believed to be his duty in observing the weakness, errors and evils of his brethren. He was clear-sighted and firm as a rock in claiming respect for the servant of Christ, in honour of his Master; yet in things personal he was very retiring. To blame his friend was a task to his tender heart; yet he stood firm where guilt was plain. He stuck to his friend in adversity as in prosperity. He could soothe the bed of affliction; and many a child of sorrow has he beguiled into holy resignation by his peculiar method of opening up the treasures of God's love, grace and mercy, in a way suited to the case in hand. And thus, though, like other servants of Christ, and mankind in general, he spent his years as a tale that is told, there is an eternity of real enjoyment for the ransomed of the Lord.

Yours most truly
A. B. Taylor

ALEXANDER BARRIE TAYLOR:
1804-1887

An eloquent preacher and William Gadsby's successor at Manchester.

Usually known as "A. B. Taylor," brought up in formal Presbyterianism in Scotland, he was led to England to become an eminent and successful preacher of the gospel. Even while a small boy he became convinced that believers' baptism is according to Scripture.

As a preacher, apart from his grace, his venerable appearance and eloquent speech attracted many. It was said that it was worth travelling to Manchester to hear him majestically announce the hymn:

> *"Descend from heaven, immortal Dove,*
> *Stoop down and take us on Thy wings,*
> *And mount and bear us far above*
> *The reach of these inferior things."*

How often following the death of a famous preacher has his congregation been scattered, and his successor has had to leave in disappointment! Yet following William Gadsby's death in 1844, Mr Taylor enjoyed both peace and prosperity during his thirty-eight years' pastorate.

CHAPTER 1

EARLY DAYS

Alexander Barrie Taylor was born on October 18th, 1804, at Craig Hall, near Pittendynie, in the parish of Manaedie, Perthshire, on the banks of the River Shockie, which runs into the Tay, about three miles above the city of Perth. We continue with his auto-biography in his own words:

I well remember my father leading me by the hand to the lair of the roe, the den of the brock (badger), the covert of the tod (fox), seat of the mawkin (hare), and burrow of the rabbit, while the scream of the curlew and song of the lark roused my young attention into active enjoyment. And now, in my eighty-third year [1887] my memory is as good as ever, as regards things in early life. My fond parents tried to make me possess what is called "early piety," and taught me to repeat the 23rd Psalm and the three last verses of the 11th chapter of Matthew long before I could read. Dear parents, they meant well, and we should not despise good intentions. I now feel that I have reason to regard my parents as having been Christian people.

The first little view I had of wrong from right was when a youth told me he would kill me if I told what he had done. I did not then know that what he had done was wrong, but I never forgot that threat.

The marriage of an aunt, before I was four years old, I well remember, perhaps all the better because of the music and dancing, fiddles and bagpipes in the barn – a thing quite common in those days.

I can also remember being taught in those days about Christ being nailed to the tree. My little pity was stirred, and my young wrath kindled against such cruelty.

When my mother was leading me by the hand she told me that we all had to die some day, and this was to me most confounding. After some confusing thoughts, I said, "Must we be like the partridges and hares dada brings home?" Mother said, "Yes, but we shall not be shot." Then I was quite at the end of my little wits. Seeing my perplexity, she said, "But though we die we shall live again." This was still more confounding, and I remember saying, "Mother, if we are to live again, why should we die?" She then talked to me about a subject so profound to me then, that I could do nothing but listen, but this much I remember.

At six years of age I was sent from home to school to Mr. Thomas Dick. He was author of several works on astronomy. He was educated for the ministry, but he stepped aside, and was never restored. Perhaps the seceders of those days saw too clearly, "Be ye clean who bear the vessels of the Lord." I remained six years with Mr. Dick.

ALEXANDER BARRIE TAYLOR

About this time the Corn Laws wrought a great change in the county [keeping bread dear], and to make small holdings into one large farm, twenty-six families were removed from their happy homes where they had lived for many ages past. These families were cast on the world, my father's being one of them. They sought homes in the more busy scenes of human life. Only last year I visited the one large farm, and took with me my three daughters to show them the place where their old father was born, and where he spent his early years. I ought here to say that we were very kindly received and entertained by the present farmer, Mr. Young.

The next twelve years of my life have many and varied experiences in them, some of which would no doubt please a certain class of readers, but I do not think they would edify.

WORK AT GLASGOW

During my working life, it was my lot to be put to work in connection with the calico printing trade, and after filling several minor places such as tierer, worker in the bleach grounds, colour shops and printing table, it was finally settled that I should be an engraver. My employers kept a schoolmaster for their apprentices, who were taught free on week evenings during their apprenticeship, so I had the benefit of this boon. I ought to say here that my great pleasure in life was shooting, so much so that it was suggested that I ought to be a gamekeeper, but my good mother would not hear of that, and indeed she often hid my gun, which put me in a terrible fix.

In the year 1824, all the employees were turned adrift, the company at Ruthven-field being about to give up business. I went to Glasgow, got a situation, and had a heart as light as any fool God ever let live. My parents stayed at Perth.

I was then twenty years old, and a member of the church to which my parents belonged, the United Session [Secession?] at the little town of Methven. Mr. Jamieson was the minister. I took with me a certificate of membership, which I now possess.

Before I left for Glasgow, my poor mother appeared much distressed and was very spiritless, though naturally of a cheerful disposition. I began to fear that her reason was failing, and named my thoughts to my father, who said she was only distressed because I was leaving home. That I thought was very silly, because I considered it the best thing I could do. Dear mother! you had thoughts to which I was quite a stranger; for while I thought only of freedom and independence, you were fearing the consequences of freedom and independence.

On a cold morning in November, about five o'clock, three young men and I started on foot a sixty-four mile journey from Perth to Glasgow. On parting with my mother, she followed me to the door, gave me a kiss, and said, "Aleck, as soon as you can keep a wife, get married." This I thought complete evidence to justify my fears before-mentioned. Thoughtful mothers, what say you?

Thoughts about Baptism

I would now say something of my natural religion. It was common to me to go to the kirk with my parents, and so regular were they at the house of God that I do not remember their being absent. The ordinance of baptism was the first means of exercising my mind about the sprinkling of infants. In those days an infant of parents who were Baptists was put to nurse just near where we lived, and a little handsome cradle accompanied the child. I much admired the cradle and thought ours was a poor thing compared to it. I should then be about ten years old. I had some notion that the child must be different to other children, and I asked my mother if that was so. She smiled, but said the child was not different. After a while she said, "There is something different though about the child, and it is this: that child's parents have withheld what we have bestowed upon you." "What is that, mother?" said I. She very calmly said, "That child has not been baptized." I was dumb with wonder, scorn and contempt to think that the child's parents should be so neglectful. I could not master that case, and by and by I said to my mother that such parents

88

should not have children. She replied to me that I need not be troubled about the child as it was no worse for not being baptized. After a while I said, "If the child be no worse, am I any better for being baptized?" At this my dear mother smiled, and some time after told me that I had quite puzzled her.

At this time of my life I was compelled to read some portion of God's Word, and on one occasion I asked mother to show me where it said that children were baptized when Christ was here on earth. She said that when Christ was here, it was only those who confessed their belief who were baptized, but when those believers had children they were baptized according to God's Word: "The promise is unto you and to your children." This satisfied me then, as my mother's words at that time were convincing to me.

The wheels of time did not allow me to stop at ten years of age, and as I grew older, still reading to her betimes, my poor mother was compelled to hear what I read and my questions upon the same. On one occasion I was reading that very portion, before quoted: "The promise is unto you and to your children, and to all that are afar off, even as many as the Lord our God shall call" (Acts 2. 39). I remembered that to be the Scripture my mother had so convinced me with as regards infants' baptism, and my attention being fixed, I remarked that this promise is also to them that are afar off. I asked her to explain more of the words, but she did not, and I knew not why at the time, but do now. Finding that she seemed shy, I read on for myself, and found that there was not a word about baptizing children. I had not then seen a Baptist, but felt sure they were right according to God's Word. I thought I should like to see one, and being told where one lived, I went to look at him, but did not speak to him. When I told this at home, they had a good laugh at me.

FORMAL CHURCH MEMBERSHIP

As time went on, it was considered right to propose me for church fellowship. This was done by my father, though we differed about baptism. I was told to think what I liked, but not to trouble my parents with my thoughts. One Lord's day morning, on going to the kirk, father said, "Aleck, do you not think of joining the kirk?" I was so stunned that I stood still on the road while father went on. I noticed two trees cut down, and from the stumps I observed young shoots springing, and this led me to think that there should be something new about a Christian. When I overtook my father he said, "But you are a Baptist, and I don't desire that you should be what we are against your will. You have a right to join any church you please." I made no reply, and the matter dropped just then; but mother was of different mettle, and she insisted upon being relieved from her baptismal vows, which could not be until I had freed her by professing my faith in Christ and obedience to Him. I submitted, and offered myself as a candidate for church fellowship.

A quarter's training being the rule, I began in October and finished at the New Year. Nine of us made up the class, male and female. The last evening of the thirteen visits to the minister's house, which was three miles away, I had been shooting all the afternoon for a fat pig, and a lantern had to be placed to shine on the bull's eye so that we could finish. While at this work, a messenger came from my kind mother to ask if I had forgotten my engagement with the minister. I had not forgotten, but preferred the sport to the examination. This now seems awful to me, and indeed the whole system appears degrading, when one knows something of the teaching of God's Word. How dishonouring, then, must such a plan be to God!

When I got to the minister's house, most of my companions in tribulation were waiting. When called to the private interview upon the most important matter, viz. the call by God and translation out of darkness into His marvellous light, some one whispered to me that Kate —— had been put back another quarter for killing a cat. "O!" I thought, "if he finds out that I have been shooting for a pig, he will put me back a whole year." Even at that time my gun was hid in a coal-house that I might shoot by moonlight on my way home. When before the minister, I was asked to kneel, and he engaged in prayer in the most solemn manner. I was moved by the earnest appeals of the sober-minded man.

In a few minutes he said, "Alexander, you have answered all my questions in a proper manner, but did you ever feel any portion of God's Word to be a comfort to your heart as touching another world?" Now I was fast, for such an idea had never entered my head, let alone my heart. Placed as I was in a fix, I remembered he had preached thirteen sermons from the text, "Him that cometh unto Me I will in no wise cast out," and to free myself from the trouble, I repeated the said text. What a mercy it is that God is merciful to our unrighteousness! I was glad when he gave me a token for the Lord's table.

With all this sad formality I do now truly believe that that man – John Jamieson – was a real Christian, lived a life of godliness amongst men, and died in the faith.

I went to the table of the Lord, feeling no contempt for God's ordinances, but with a natural reverence for what I had been taught, and in some way thought it was right. But certainly I did not see things by faith, or in the light of God's countenance, though out of the Book of God I was taught the precepts of men.

CHAPTER 2

CARNAL SECURITY

Returning now to the days of my removal from home. The first night after leaving home we slept at Stirling. Our feet were blistered and very sore. We were kindly treated. It was well-known where we came from, as some hundreds had come the same way to Glasgow before we set off. One of the girls paid me kind attention by washing my feet and passing a needle and worsted thread through my blisters. I thanked her, and asked her why it was she was so kind to me? She only said, "I dinna ken!" This girl was a Highland lass, speaking only broken English beside her dialect. Such kindness is not soon forgotten.

We arrived at Glasgow, and parted company. I got work, and had one year and three months freedom from parental control. I had good wages, good health, light heart, and my aforesaid natural religion not much trouble to me. When I now look back to this time, I am more than astonished, and I must acknowledge that God kept me, when I did not care to keep myself. Were I to relate all that I passed through, or what passed by me, it would astonish you. I was at this time a vain and foolish fellow, mixed up with many things, the song and the dance, made smart with curled hair and fine slippers, albeit my good minister's certificate was at that time in my trunk.

About this time I remember one occasion, when we had £37 to spend on what in Lancashire are called "footings" – occasions when apprentice lads begin or end their term, and when it is expected that a certain sum will be given by each, and the whole is then spent mostly at a public house in eating and drinking. On the afternoon of this day I had a match on – a race on the ice. After the race the ice gave way, and I went down out of sight, and was thought to be drowned. The rest managed to clear. After a while, two young men sighted me struggling with the ice, and they got a rope, threw it to me, but it went wide. I saw this, and called to them to throw it over my shoulder, which they did. I then made it firm about me, and called, "Pull away now," and so got safely to land. I had then no thankfulness for my deliverance, but after a time of rest and refreshment I was ready for a dance, and went with my partner, who not long since was lamenting my death. See the delivering hand of Providence, and how "He is kind even to the unthankful." These are some of the things "whereof," Paul says, "we are now ashamed."

About this time I was proud to possess a valuable dog. I must, however, know its worth by trial, and so took it to a badger bait, and lay on a barn floor about two hours, until my turn came. Some sixty dogs were run at various animals that day, mine amongst the rest. I was satisfied with my dog's work in that line. After this was over, a ring was made for a dog fight, and various fights went on till dusk. This was my human life's pleasure at that time. That night I slept like a top, and had not a troubled conscience, but was quite proud of my four-legged deity.

THOUGHTS OF DYING

One very different instance I desire to relate now. In, I think, 1825, I was one night in my bedroom, and the thought of dying took possession of me, and I felt that should I die now, I should be lost. This pressed me very hard. I knew the word "repent," and thought I should like to repent, but knew not how. I threw myself on the bed, and in my way prayed that God would not send me to hell. I was in earnest, and sobbed my tears, but the thought left *me.* I always heard some one preach on the Sabbath, and amongst others I heard the great Dr. Chalmers[1] of Edinburgh, a mighty orator, but nothing that I heard impressed me for good, and all the above feelings passed away.

RETURN TO PERTH, AND A NEW COMPANION

The company I served, John MacGregor and Sons, of Keiness Hough, stopped work. I returned to Perth, and wishing to appear

---

[1]Thomas Chalmers (1780-1847) who led the Free Church of Scotland in the Great Disruption of 1843.

smart, walked about forty miles of the journey in a new pair of boots. When I took these boots off, some portion of my skin came with them. I then thought of the kind Highland lassie, but I was at home, so all was right for me. I had, however, now no companion, and wishing for one I looked about, but soon found more than I wished for, and therefore made a choice. Vile and low persons I never admired, and had no liking for drunkards, whom I thought not fit for society. I was naturally gay, and sometimes merry, but never half-drunk. When at Glasgow, I did not make use of my church certificate; on that subject I was at the time quite content. My parents at this time wished me to give up my business of engraver, but I could not consent, as I thought it was throwing away the time I had spent in learning.

Walking one day on the North Inch, I heard the sound of a gun. I made off and found a man trying a gun for a gentleman. I thought him an excellent shot, and after the trial I made myself known to him as being fond of the gun. This man was afterwards my companion whilst in Perth. I was now within six miles of my birth-place, which I often visited. I had nothing to do, a good home, indulgent parents, but myself careless and graceless. I passed my time in vanity with my new companion. He was a good shot – the best I had seen – and we had good practice on the North Inch. My fond mother found me pocket money privately. It is astonishing what some mothers will do in this way. I have known mothers who have ruined their sons by this fondness wrongly exercised.

My companion and I longed for the 12th of August [when shooting began]. We were within twenty miles of good moors. In those days the gentlemen went to the hill moors for about fourteen days only, and seldom went again the same season, so that the grouse were not protected as now. I mustered a licence, and by the end of August we were in good practice. But time went on, and I could not live always in this revelling happy state; my circumstances would not allow. It was determined that I should go to Lancashire to complete my apprenticeship.

ALEXANDER BARRIE TAYLOR

The Old Minister

During the above time, I had not seen nor wished to see my old minister, Mr. Jamieson. It became known that I was leaving for Lancashire. One day, walking along the Crief-road from Perth, I met Mr. Jamieson, and I should have been glad if I could have escaped him; but he came forward and smiled, gave me his hand, chatted in a kindly way and said, "Alexander, I hear you are going to England. How came it that I did not get back the certificate I gave you?" (I should explain that when a certificate is presented to a minister, he returns it to the one who gave it, so that a church member leaving a town can be found where he is by this practice.) I told him that the last firm I was with were not likely to last long, so I had not presented it. He said, "That is all right, but you will now require another certificate," when I replied that I had asked Mr. Pringle's elders for one. He now looked at me in the most solemn manner, and said, "I have a favour to ask before we part." I think I could have promised anything just then to get away, for I was sweating all over. I said I should be glad to serve him in any way I could. He said, "The favour I ask of you is, to read your Bible; you know not what God has for you to do. You are a child of many prayers; you know not what God has for you to do. Read your Bible." I felt I should drop to the earth, and wished he would be going.

The above words never left me for long together: I was ever puzzled about them, but they sank into my heart. When I recovered a little, I said to myself, "That is just like him – all Bible and Kirk." But I could not put away his words; they would often come and go. In the month of June in the same year (1826), sitting in a small chamber, I had a most strange and affecting sense of the sufferings of Christ for sin, though I dare not say for my sins. I was completely overwhelmed, and wept bitterly. I was a considerable time before I could recover from it. It came upon me again and again, until I felt exhausted and feeble. I cannot forget it, but still am not able to attach that worth to it that I should like. I highly esteem it, and will not let it go. At this time I knew nothing of the "new man" and the "old" in a gospel way, or under the teaching of the ministry; and yet I dare not say that I was "dead in sin." Surely "God brings the blind by a way they know not."

WORLDLY PLEASURE

The time now came for me to leave home again. My companion and I often talked over happy times with the gun, now that we were to part, and we resolved upon a last sally on a pheasant-roosting moor. This we carried out one night in November. We had watched the birds roost for several nights, and on this night we fastened the old gamekeeper in his house and set to work. In about thirty minutes we bagged twenty-three pheasants and left the place. The following morning we had the pleasure of seeing the gamekeeper with the bellman, offering £10 reward. I was close beside him. Paul says of some, "And such were some of you, but ye are washed, but ye are justified, but ye are sanctified." What cannot our Lord do?

Another branch of sport I was fond of was the killing of salmon in November and December, when they visit the rivers for spawning. Four are required for the work: two to spear, one to hold the torchlight, and the other to carry. To people not acquainted with these times and seasons, some of the things told will seem incredible, but many are possible. The present value of salmon was not known then. I also took delight in fishing with the rod in the River Tay. The fishing was my pleasure before I left home the first time.

WORK IN ENGLAND

The day came for me to leave Perth for England. I spent the first night at Auchterarder, the second at Stirling, and the third in Glasgow. I was in good spirits, without much fear or trouble of any kind. We sailed from Glasgow. The captain and I got friends, and I was sorry to part from him at Liverpool, where I stayed one night, and then took coach for Preston, where I arrived in the evening.

I stayed at the "Legs of Man" hotel. After supper, I asked the landlord to spend half an hour with me, and he kindly

· consented. I told him where I was going, and what trade I followed. I soon found that he took an interest in me, he also being a Scotchman. He began to tell me some of the customs of some Lancashire people, such as their drinking bouts, and their manner of fighting, kicking, etc. This made me to be thoughtful, and, I concluded that I had better keep aloof from such company.

"COMMIT THY WAY"

My new friend related many things which perplexed me, and I became anxious. I began to think of father and mother's advice and prayers, and my conduct in slighting the same. I thought, if God leaves me, I am lost. I knew I had been careless of His honour, and I felt very fearful. I thought of hell and then of heaven, and though I had a certificate of church membership, I did not see that I could expect to go to heaven. God's holy law condemned me. I went to bed, but not to sleep. I tried to pray, but could not. It was November, and a dark time too for my soul, but between six and seven in the morning I heard a voice saying, "Commit thy way unto the Lord, trust also in Him, and He shall bring it to pass." This I heard most distinctly. I got up and said, "What do you want?" feeling that some one had spoken to me. I got no reply, but waiting anxiously, the words were again given to me, but this time within me, "Commit thy way unto the Lord," etc. My fears were now removed, my heart was warmed, and I felt that my whole soul and body too were filled with a glorious something which I cannot well describe. That was the strangest thing that had happened unto me up to this time, but that I felt all this no power can now disprove.

I rose early in the morning, and walked past the Old Church at Preston. I sang, "The Lord is my Shepherd." I was up to this time ignorant of the ways of God with men. I believed in a Supreme Being, as I had been taught, but of the Spirit's work upon the heart, I do not think that I had heard of such a thing.

CHAPTER 3

MARRIAGE

Being partly engaged before I left home, I was soon at work at Foxhill-bank, near Accrington, where I served my time out, and engaged for twelve months as journeyman. Here I learned ways I had not before known, and I found myself acquiring the Lancashire dialect. I also found at this time the cares of the world beginning to touch me. I found mankind capable of using deceit against me, and many things I went through astonished me. I felt I was a fool, and I was certainly ignorant of many things that others about me were familiar with, and I was of course laughed at. I now think that God preserved me through that time.

At this place I saw a young woman I thought I loved, and in time asked her to be my wife. Her parents objected and behaved somewhat unkindly to me, but they afterwards regretted their conduct. We were however married at the Manchester Old Church (now the Cathedral) on the 6th day of October, 1828, and my wife proved a gift from the Lord. No man ever had a better wife, and after bearing six sons and six daughters, she died in the faith of the Lord Jesus on the 14th January, 1865, aged fifty-five years. Though, as I have said, cares and troubles began to press upon me at this place, I did not think to commit my way unto the Lord, but tried to do my best honestly. At Accrington I became acquainted with Mr. Harbottle,[2] a Baptist minister, a kind man, and I now think a good man, but I also think he was not quite clear on the doctrines of grace.

FURTHER CONVICTIONS

From Accrington I removed to Lower House, near Burnley, in 1830, in the April of which year my first son was born. I began

---

[2]Joseph Harbottle (1798-1864), minister at the old Particular Baptist chapel in Accrington.

to feel at this time that the world would not last for ever, and that it had to be burnt up. I certainly knew that from a child, but now began to feel it. One Saturday evening, after a day's shooting, the keeper and I were going along, when these words came to me, "What will ye do in the end thereof?" I tried to put them away, but they became all the stronger, and I was disposed to argue the matter, saying, "I am not going to talk about that yet; the end is a long way off." So I disposed of the case in that summary way. But the words came again the following morning, and again, till they became a burden I could not bear. I had not then a concordance, but I thought it was Scripture. Ever after when I went shooting, which I mostly did on Saturdays in the summer, the words were with me, and often on my tongue, so that my pleasure was marred. At this time I was called a Calvinist, and I saw the truth of believers' baptism, as all Bible *readers* do, but I was a stranger to divine faith. I sang at concerts and oratorios, and was one of the foremost to keep up the song. But despite all my resolves to hold the major key, I was forced, against my indomitable will, to take the minor. All my friends wondered what was the matter. I had told no one anything; indeed I did not know what to tell. I was observed and commented upon, but knew nothing of people's opinions.

The law of God now began to make sad work with me, and this I thought very strange, as all these things I had been taught from my youth up, and could repeat the commandments with ease. But I felt that now these commands were pressing me very hard, and that the law of God required a complete fulfilment; indeed Paul's words, "The commandment came and I died," were fulfilled in my case.

I was pressed to attend a gentlemen's concert, and the friend who asked me knew more about me than I knew of myself, as he afterwards told me. I sang, but with no comfort, and I felt my singing to be insipid and tasteless. That night I resolved to leave that part of the country and to take a situation where I was unknown. I wished to be properly religious, but I felt it was no use beginning where I was known, so I wrote to Scotland and got a situation. I passed through Manchester on the Tuesday evening, and I went to hear Mr. William Gadsby preach. His text was, "Say unto the cities of Judah, Behold your God." I remember nothing of his sermon, but the text sank into my very heart and remained there. I went to Liverpool in the morning, and slept at the house of a friend, a deacon of a Baptist chapel there.

A Dreadful Storm

The following day I sailed in the "City of Glasgow" steamship, and this proved her last voyage, as she was wrecked before we reached Greenock. The night (November, 1832) was a most dismal one – a storm broke upon us. The setting sun was most beautiful, and was admired by all on board; but it had not gone down above half an hour when we began to hear far distant thunder, and intense darkness set in. Lightning then began to flash, and we seemed enveloped in a great whirlpool, the sea roaring wildly, and altogether the scene was very fearful. When the hatches were put down, the screaming of the affrighted passengers was terrible. I and some others were on deck, and the horror that passed through my soul I cannot depict, but it was moved away by those sweet words, "Say unto the cities of Judah, Behold your God." I said, without reflection, "Lord, what does it mean?" No more satisfaction was obtained, but the words stayed with me all night, and a dismal night it was. I thought if the Almighty would but only cast me on a rock (and I knew He could), I should be thankful.

The old ship went beneath the waves many times, but rose again, and now and again we could hear the roar of the thunder above the noise of the sea. The storm abated and then increased. Our guns were fired while the powder was dry, but that was not for long. The storm lasted all night, but at daybreak the sea became calm, and the poor old ship was then seen to have been cleared of her deck fittings, etc. We had neither sails nor steam, and were drifting about till evening, when two steamers in search of us towed us, a complete wreck, to Greenock. As soon as we could speak to each other, I said, "Captain, we have had a terrible night." He replied, "I have been at sea thirty-two years, and I never saw the like before; nothing but Almighty God has preserved us." The calm way in which he spoke caused me to think he feared God.

Many times during the night of that storm I thought, What if I should open my eyes in hell? but, "Say unto the cities of Judah, Behold your God," was often springing up within me.

I got to the end of my journey, and began work at the very place where I served my apprenticeship. The first day I had a polite note from the manager asking me to take supper and spend the evening with him. How could I refuse – it was not in my nature. I went, and found myself amidst a most respectable company, amongst whom were some professional musicians, but there was not a good vocalist, so I soon found that I had to sing the most. There were other similar parties to which I was invited, but I could not go to all. I have said that I returned to Scotland to get away from my associates that I might become religious, and here I was no sooner clear of one lot than I found myself willing to join others. God's holy law did not now trouble me, and at the end of the month I found myself a worse man than when I left Lancashire. I resolved to return, so told my kind employer my purpose. He urged me to stay, but I had determined to go.

LANCASHIRE AGAIN

I took the coach at Perth to Edinburgh on the Saturday. The same evening I left for Manchester, where I arrived on Monday, almost frozen stiff. I had some refreshment and went to bed at the White Horse, Hanging Ditch. I then took the coach to Accrington, where I slept the night, and was soon after at work in my old situation, with Messrs. John Dugdale & Brothers, Lower House, near Burnley. I again found my pleasure in the fields amongst Lord Towneley's rabbits, and was not much troubled in my mind, but when I wished to be heart and soul in pleasure, God's law would throw some of its demands in my face and quite mar my pleasure. One afternoon, when alone resting in the wood, I felt that if I knew what to do I would do it, but I did not know what I ought to do. I felt quite certain there was nothing wrong in shooting rabbits and game of any kind. How easy to apologize for the things we are fond of, *but*, "What will ye do in the end thereof?" kept sticking in my throat, and I could neither swallow it nor get without it. I was led to think that I wasted valuable time, and did not read my Bible enough. I set to work to make amends, and I got a concordance. Whilst thus engaged, the words, "Say unto the cities of Judah, Behold your God," were again impressed upon me. I thought the cities of Judah were the churches of the world, and that the prophet was commanding that they should be preached to, but I also felt more than I dare speak about. About that time I was advised to go to Rossendale to hear a preacher, which I did; and many a long walk have I had to Ring's Row[3] since, to hear that man. I never got anything good from him, but I thought he was sincere.

I knew Mr. Harbottle, of Accrington, and Mr. Griffiths, of Burnley, but I did not think they could do me any good. I found that the law which so condemned me, they preached as a rule to live by, whereas I felt condemned in thought, word and look. I got Mr. Griffiths to preach at my house, but we soon had a different opinion about law and gospel, though I cannot say now how I took my stand. I felt sure the law could not save me, because I felt its condemning power. I had little knowledge of the different sects, and thought the distinction was mostly about the mode of baptism and the choice of minister. My eyes began to be opened on this subject, and as my reading increased, my past notions of salvation were scattered to the winds. I knew the Lord Jesus Christ to be the alone Saviour, but what to do with God's law I did not know, because of the words, "Cursed is every one that continueth not in all things written in the book of the law to do them."

I thought the preacher at Ring's Row might do me some good, and I left Lower House and went to Sunnyside, Rossendale,

---

[3]Meetings were commenced at a room in Ring's Row about 1825, the hearers being those who were dissatisfied at the old Baptist chapel at Goodshaw. At one time Daniel Whittaker (later of Redcross Street, London, and Hanover, Tunbridge Wells) was pastor. This cause had an unsettled history, and came to an end. Afterwards (in the 1850s) the present chapel at Goodshawfold was built.

to work. I took a house next door to the minister, who was then supplying at Redcross Street Chapel, London. When he returned, he brought back with him an invitation to become the pastor at Redcross Street, which he accepted. My plans were upset, as I had thought I should learn something by living next door to the minister, instead of which I had an empty house.

No Peace of Conscience

From being married till that time I had a form of prayer each night before retiring. I began to think I was mocking God, as I had read what the prayers of the wicked were in God's sight. I gave it up, for I felt that God might strike me dead. Without saying anything to my wife, I went upstairs, but she called out, "Surely you are not going to bed in that way; you have not made prayer!" I felt like a thief caught in the act. What passed between us I need not relate. It is to me now both painful and pleasant betimes. For a long time I ceased to pray in this manner, but I did cry to God in private. August (1833) was approaching, and with it my expectations of the shooting which, in my state of mind, were very troublesome. I thought, Are all who shoot damned? What about the gamekeepers? Are they all lost? And thus I tried to excuse myself in the thing that so beset me.

About that time I sang my last in public, at the Old Church, Haslingden. At the conclusion, I sang that fine old hymn of Martin Luther's:

> "Great God, what do I see and hear,
> The end of things created."

I felt a little of what Habakkuk says, "My belly trembled, my lips quivered, rottenness entered into my bones, and I trembled in myself." I was glad to get out of the place alive. Two much valued friends knew what ailed me, I believe, and watched over me in a quiet way. They lived to hear the stammerer speak some of the mysteries of the Son of God.

CHAPTER 4

A New Hymnbook

On the 11th of August, I got a hymn book (Gadsby's), and it proved to be a most wonderful book to me. On the 12th, the young squire asked me to get him a brace of grouse, and in the evening I went to the moor for that purpose, and beside my dog and gun I took the new hymn book. I sat down to read, and opened the book at hymn 238, which begins:

> "With melting heart and weeping eyes
> My guilty soul for mercy cries;
> What shall I do, or whither flee,
> To escape the vengeance due to me?"

When I came to the third verse,

> "But when, great God, Thy light divine
> Had shone on this dark soul of mine,
> Then I beheld with trembling awe
> The terrors of Thy holy law,"

I cannot describe the new things that opened up to me; my mind was empowered to look at, take hold of, and remember in a new light things I had long known, without any application of their truths. Darkness coming on, I had to leave the grouse for another day. The more I read of the hymn book the more I was surprised.

The next evening I went again for the grouse, and as I lifted my gun to my shoulder, I felt as if I saw down the barrels, between me and the birds: "Cursed is every one that continueth not in all things written in the book of the law to do them" (Gal. 3. 10). The words seemed words of fire to me. After re-loading, I picked up the bird, and said, "Poor thing, you are dead and done with, but if I should die now, I shall be damned." I returned home to find my poor wife distracted about me. I tried to soothe her, and told her about the hymn book, what a wonderful book it was.

ALEXANDER BARRIE TAYLOR

Manchester, and Gospel Liberty

In January 1834 I removed to Manchester. I then went to hear Mr. Gadsby. Much was said about him, and I continued to go to hear him. I had no settled opinion at that time of his preaching, but there was something that drew me. He visited London for six weeks, and the supplies I heard in his absence were Mr. Warburton, Mr. Tiptaft and Mr. Hitchcock.[4] The latter was a hard preacher; that is he insisted much on the awful justice of God. I was then a trembler, and his ministry added greatly to my fears. I felt one morning that I could not walk home. In the evening, however, he somewhat relieved me by the way in which he spoke of the "vessels of mercy afore prepared unto glory."

My health now began to decline, and I seemed doomed to be a victim to that fell disease [consumption] that carries so many away in this country. I told Mr. Gadsby of my condition of mind and body. I was truly at my wit's end and in real distress of soul, feeling myself to be a lost and undone sinner. Whilst in this misery, Mr. Gadsby in his prayer implored the Almighty to help any such characters as I then was, and I felt the stream of God's mercy coming to me in warm, eternal love, "Who forgiveth all thine iniquities, who healeth all thy diseases," etc. I had not time to say words but burst out in song, "Bless the Lord, O my soul." I said to myself, "I'll sing if I die." I soon found I was observed, so I sat down as quietly as I could, when the following words burst from me, "Who is a God like unto Thee, that pardoneth iniquity, and passeth by the transgression of the remnant of His heritage?" I felt there was not one unpardoned sin in my soul, wave after wave of blessing rolled over my spirit, and I felt redemption and salvation to be mine. What Mr. Gadsby said in his sermon or what text he preached from I knew no more than the absentee. I indeed rejoiced in Christ Jesus. I thought this indeed is being born again.[5]

---

[4]Roger Hitchcock, the seceding minister who baptized William Tiptaft.
[5]Mr. Taylor obviously means that he now possessed the clearest marks of being born again.

Yes, thank God for ever and ever. What I then experienced I cannot tell, neither can it be imagined by any.

BELIEVERS' BAPTISM

In consequence of my declining health I removed to the neighbourhood of Accrington, where I was well-known by worldly friends. I set my mind on a little cottage with a garden to it. In my earnestness, I said if God would let me have that little cottage to live and die in, I would ask no more on earth. To my astonishment, when I was looking for a house the said cottage was empty, so I took it, lived years in it, and many blessed prayer meetings and preachings have we had in it. My little cot became a centre for prayer and worship. My old friends looked on with amazement, but were dumb before God. I grew in grace, despite all who silently wished me brought back to my senses.

From this little cottage I walked to Blackburn every Lord's day morning, mostly in company with one or more dear friends of that time, whom I consider to have been the best divines I ever met with, and I have met not a few excellent ones, both in person and in books. My friends referred to were John Bury, Joseph Hanson, Robert Hindle, James Duckworth and some others. At Blackburn I was baptized in the name of the Father, Son and Holy Ghost, a believing sinner hoping for mercy through the blood of the Lamb. Before being baptized and received into the church, I related my experience in a short, simple and truthful way. I did not know what was expected of candidates, so untutored was I at the time. What I said was well received; but just then I was unmindful of others, for I seemed to be living above all human law or rule.

CALLED TO PREACH

The above-named friends took me by the hand, led me into all truth known by them, and tried me in all ways. I learned by every correction, and God blessed their instruction. Though I did not know it at the time, I feel that they were carrying out what Paul enjoins Timothy to do – "The same commit thou to faithful men, who shall be able to teach others also." At this point our churches are at fault. I state it fearlessly.[6] I had not then told my friends much of what I had experienced of the "Cities of Judah" before referred too, but they found me out, and pressed me to try to speak in the Lord's name. I promised, and the day was fixed a month before the time.

I did not tell my wife, but some one else did, and on the Friday afternoon before the appointed Sunday she met me with a very angry look, and said, "Are not you going to preach at Blackburn on Sunday?" I tried to evade the question, but her indignation increased so much that she lost all control, and finally threw the tea-pot at me, and left me. This was hard to bear, but I was enabled to keep outwardly calm. After a while I went in search of her in the house, and found her lying on the bed in tears, feeling sorry for what she had done. Some readers might think that this household circumstance should not be brought out, but, as it afterwards proved, it was the beginning of a work of grace upon the heart, and the end of that work has been already referred to, even the salvation of her soul.

I preached my first sermon at Blackburn in great anxiety. I took for a text: "But we will not boast of things without our measure, but according to the measure of the rule which God hath distributed to us, a measure to reach even unto you" (2 Cor. 10. 13). I spoke for about twenty minutes. I was often asked to preach, but it was not, after this first attempt, till the July of 1837 that I obtained strength of heart to try again, and then it was in much weakness.

ACCRINGTON

Feeling it to be a long walk to Blackburn, we began to think and wonder whether we could not form a church at Accrington,

---

[6]Very often in former days a church would ask one of its members to preach, feeling that the Lord had blessed him with ministerial gifts. The first step lay with the church. If the member himself was exercised, and his preaching acceptable, he was then sanctioned to preach by the church. Mr. Taylor felt this was so in his case, and thus 2 Tim. 2. 2 was fulfilled.

where there was not any preaching that suited us. This was in 1835. Our minds brooded over the matter warmly, but tenderly, as we felt that the Blackburn church must suffer if we left them. We, however, resolved to name the matter to the minister of the church, after making known our requests to the Lord. When the subject came before the church there was silence for a considerable time, which was broken at last by the old deacon, brother Miller, who said it was a reasonable thing we were asking. The question was well considered at several church meetings, and in the end it was resolved that the friends in the neighbourhood of Accrington would do right in attempting to plant a church there.

We, therefore, began to look out for a place, a large room, a chapel not being thought of then. Our prayers went up to God and our minds were known amongst men. We tried diligently to get a place, but for a long time were not successful, till at last there seemed to be an opening. We found a large upper room occupied by a widow, and we suggested to her that if she would remove to another dwelling we would pay her expenses and give her money besides. She agreed to our terms, and we were beginning to think all was right, but when the time came for her to remove she would not go. She said she had been told that we were a sad lot, and she had been advised not to let her room to us. This we were told on the Saturday night, and we were very discomfited. Some said it was evident that the Lord was not with us. We were together in the street opposite the Old Church gates, and a gentleman passing observed Mr. Bury, and called out, "Oh, Bury, what are you doing here? but I see, you are all one sort." After a few remarks, Mr. Bury said, "If I must tell you what we are here at this time of night for, Chadwick, we are looking for a place to worship in, where we may bring the truth into Accrington." "O, indeed! that's like you; no truth but what you bring. Well," said Mr. Chadwick, "if you will come with me, I will find you a place in ten minutes." (We ought to say that Mr. Bury and Mr. Chadwick had known each other from their youth.)

Mr. Bury looked at us, and said, "What do you say?" We replied, "Go," and in about quarter of an hour he returned and said he had taken a nice little chapel. In this chapel we enjoyed a preached gospel many years. We knew the place was to let, but up to this dare not think of such a venture.

These things may appear small to some, but small things have their meaning.

We opened our new chapel in 1836, and we had a minister whom I loved as I had never loved a man before [William Hatton, father of Joseph Hatton of Redhill].

———————————

CHAPTER 5

THE WORK OF THE MINISTRY

The work of the ministry was now growing upon me every day, and in the following year the church desired me to preach before them, which I did, in our minister's house, but in his absence. In a few weeks I was again asked to preach in a similar way, this time in the house of a member of the church – Joseph Pimlott. I took for a text, "And the daughter of Zion is left as a cottage in a vineyard, as a lodge in a garden of cucumbers, as a besieged city" (Isa. 1. 8).

The church now gave me authority to speak in the Lord's name wherever I might be invited. This was a strange time to me; I felt as if I had not a will of my own, but was quite passive. I was indeed humbled, but hopeful. I felt it was right, though I could not see how the thing was to be done. My prayer was, "Lord, hold Thou me up and teach me out of Thy law; be my light and my strength." The brethren saw my state of mind and seemed wishful to carry me over all the things I feared.

If ever a poor mortal had Zion's prayers I had at that time.

I now began to find many portions of God's Word crowd upon my mind, scriptures that had been with me before, but to which I had paid only passing attention as I did not understand them, though they made their mark. Now they returned with immediate effect and told me what to do. The portions were mainly: "Say to them that are of a fearful heart, Be strong," etc., "Take up the stumbling-blocks out of the way of My people," and that chief scripture so often alluded to, "Say unto the cities of Judah, Behold your God."

It would be impossible now to give all the portions of God's Word that then fell powerfully upon my mind and heart; but, "The name of the Lord is a strong tower: the righteous runneth into it, and is safe," also "Ho, every one that thirsteth, come ye to the waters," were much impressed upon me, showing now the purpose for which they were sent.

READY TO TURN BACK

I received an invitation to preach at Sabden, where there was a church formed, but they had no place of worship. They met in each other's houses. I promised to go, but when the time came I felt so loaded with anxiety and responsibility that I felt I could not go, though I left home for that purpose.

It was a fine summer's morning, but I was so oppressed that I lay down under the hedge on Moor Head Fields, just above Accrington, and there stayed till all the places of worship had commenced their services. I then went back to Accrington in great horror of mind. On my way I passed a place of worship, the old Methodist chapel, and I went in. Behind the minister, on the wall, these words were written, "Take heed how ye hear." I said, "I will," and to my thinking, both then and now, I never heard a man make so many errors in preaching in all my life. To finish with, he said, "The Lord Jesus is standing holding off the stroke of divine justice to see if you will come. If you will not, He will remove His love and mercy, and the stroke of justice will damn you for ever. Now only is the accepted time."

This poor man was sweating and broiling like a lunatic striving to get loose from chains. I cannot forget that morning. What with my own side of the subject, and that poor man in the pulpit, it was a dreadful time to me. I must say, though, that I never before saw so clearly man's plan of salvation in distinction to God's as I did that morning.

The following week was a very trying one to me. Sunday came round again, and this time the friends sent an escort, who saw me safe to Sabden.

I was in much trouble of mind all the way, and my prayers and my tears were the outcome of my feelings.

We met Mr. Thornber[7] (who died at Bedford) on his way to Accrington. He was a fine, big man, who wore a cloak with tassels

---

[7] John Thornber (1803-1875) pastor at Providence Chapel, Bedford, for nearly thirty years. About this time he was minister at Sabden.

hanging. As we came near to him, my heart sank within me, and I could scarcely look at him. Putting his hand on my shoulder he said, "He must increase, but I must decrease." We parted. I know not how.

I had a text on my mind, such an one as I have seldom dared to touch since: "Great is the mystery of godliness: God was manifest in the flesh, justified in the Spirit, seen of angels, preached unto the Gentiles, believed on in the world, received up into glory" (1 Tim. 3. 16).

I used foolishly to say, in the days of my ignorance, "If I am to be a preacher, I should like to be a good one." Well, I had a good text, whatever sort of a sermon I preached, and that text, now in my old age (eighty-one), I can say has served me in some way in almost all my sermons I have preached, and it is not exhausted yet. I knew I had not spoiled the text, though I made but little of it, as I then thought, in my small sermon.

In the afternoon I preached from these words: "For with my staff I passed over this Jordan; and now I am become two bands" (Gen. 32. 10). I felt I was strangely helped, enjoyed what I said, and well understood my own view of the matter. The people appeared to have heard to profit, for the whole church accompanied me part way home, and the same persons who came for me in the morning brought me back at night.

When I retired to rest my sleep was sweet to me.

LIBERTY AT RING'S ROW

I went on the Sunday following to Ring's Row, and the people there received me kindly, but I got away as soon as I could, not caring to be spoken to by the friends.

I preferred to dine with my old friend, George Hudson, though he lived some distance away. He it was who built the little chapel at Goodshawfold, then and now used for worship by those who love the truth.

In course of time I preached for the friends at Accrington. We had for our stated minister Mr. Hatton, who came from

Macclesfield. He was father to the Mr. Hatton[8] who was the editor of the *Gospel Standard.*

My visits to Ring's Row were now frequent, and when I had been some four times my mind was disturbed by the thought that I had been taking the poor people's money, when I was able to make at my trade more in a week than they possibly made all together. I thought, "Is this preaching a free gospel?" I found myself pronouncing my own guilt. I felt I would not have my conscience troubled with this matter, and I determined to return the money, so on a Monday morning I went to Ring's Row, taking my oldest son with me. I called on the deacon, friend Atkinson, and told him I had brought the money back, as I had been upset in my mind. I also said, "You must not expect me again, for I shall not come. I have suffered enough." He at once called his wife, and told her to send old Betty, at the same time saying, "Aleck says he won't come again." When Betty came, she took me by the coat breast, and looking me straight in the face, she said, "God bless thee, Aleck. See, see, I have been twelve years in bondage and soul trouble about my salvation, and while you were preaching yesterday afternoon about a precious Christ, He was made precious to me." After that I was broken down, and promised to come again the next Sabbath.

Some time after this I met a person, who stopped me and said, "Aleck, are you going to preach?" I replied, "I can scarcely call it preaching, but I do speak a little." He said, "You have begun among the wrong sort. It will not last long. Nobody suits them long." I replied, "I shall not try to suit them." Then he said, "You will soon have to give up." "Well," I replied, "I must leave that; but I shall never try to suit anybody with my preaching."

This conversation moved me a little, and set me thinking. I watched the people's ways; but their attachment increased, and their love abounded more and more. I had been pressed to go

---

[8]Joseph Hatton (1821-1884) pastor for many years at Smallfield. He was baptized at Accrington during his father's pastorate.

amongst them, and I was feeling that I loved the people. Portions of God's word rested on my mind then, and do now; and often have my sermons been brought to a close when I felt the absence of the power of the Spirit, by those scriptures: "Keep thy foot when thou goest to the house of God, and be more ready to hear than to give the sacrifice of fools, for they consider not that they do evil. Be not rash with thy mouth, and let not thine heart be hasty to utter anything before God; for God is in heaven, and thou upon earth; therefore let thy words be few" (Ecc. 5. 1, 2).

They knew that I was fully employed all the week, and that I had to leave home early on Sunday morning to be in time for worship; and one dear man (George Hudson), now in glory, came often to meet me with a horse, on which I rode, while he walked beside me. This man knew me in degenerate days, and could the better see the change wrought in me by God's grace. They continued to send this horse for me about twelve months, when they put their moneys together and bought me a horse, saddle and bridle, and sent them to me. They also paid me for the horse's keep, so long as I continued to go. Many blessed seasons, and many conflicts, too, have I had on that horse's back.

After this they gave me a call to become their pastor, which I did not feel I could entertain. I had a large growing family, and I now feel that the dear Lord kept me in the right track.

OTHER PULPITS – AND ACCRINGTON

I had at this time much communion with the Lord, or as the Scripture saith, fellowship: "Truly our fellowship is with the Father, and with His Son, Jesus Christ."

I supplied other pulpits at times, and I saw something of the state of the churches. I was asked to Blackburn, Rochdale and Manchester. To go to any one of these places was a trial, but especially Manchester.

I remember on one occasion at Manchester I was constrained to remark that all God's people had their trials, but I had a great one, for I felt that I had Mr. Gadsby on my back, and could not get him off. However, the Lord helped me, and I forgot that dear servant of Christ.

The time came when the Accrington people were without a minister, and as they said they had a claim on me, my services were divided between that place and Ring's Row, though I dare but say that the warm side of my heart was at Ring's Row.

The church at Accrington after this gave me a call to be their minister, and they seemed determined that I should be with them. Two of the deacons already named waited upon me and said they would not accept my refusal unless I could give some Scripture reason for the same.

I felt I was their debtor in such ways as God can only know; but I felt also that I must decline, and I quoted those words of Paul's to Timothy with much savour: "Meditate upon these things: give thyself wholly to them; that thy profiting may appear to all."

One said to the other, "John, we cannot resist that." I said further, "You know all about me, and with my large family, I cannot give myself wholly to these things, and my mind is that I will not take charge of a church until I can give myself wholly to the ministry."

Friend John said, "Well I did not think you could get out so clean"; and looking at brother Hanson, he said, "Joseph, we must take off our pressure."

"Now," I said, "I will tell you what I will do. I will give the Accrington church power over my Lord's days, if they will agree to let me go to Ring's Row frequently." They seemed pleased, and the matter was laid before the church and accepted. But it was a trying case for me and the people at Ring's Row, and unpleasant feelings were experienced on both sides.

CHAPTER 6

I now occasionally supplied at Manchester, and in 1843, through Mr. Gadsby, I was asked to supply at Zoar Chapel, Great Alie Street, London, for the three last Lord's days in October. The appointment was fixed, and I well remember the evening before the day I left for London.

The whole church, pretty much, came to my house to hold a prayer meeting, to plead with the Lord on my behalf, and I believe prayer was heard and answered.

Mr. Gadsby did not go again to London. He died in January 1844.

My labours went on at Accrington and other places. I now also went to Liverpool to old Mr. Medley's[9] people. After his death a scattering took place; but a good man, Mr. Bennett,[10] continued the cause. A friend agreed to help him with money, but failed to do so. However, friend Bennett went on and the Lord prospered him, "for them that honour Me I will honour," and friend Bennett was honoured in life and death.

It was during one of these visits to Liverpool that my friend James Knight's[11] soul was set at liberty; and he then felt: "Whither thou goest I will go, and where thou lodgest I will lodge: thy people shall be my people, and thy God my God."

I now went yearly to London, Zoar, and this church gave me several calls, but I could not see the leading of the Lord, but continued to visit them yearly. I also went to Gower Street, at which place I received an invitation to Leicester, where I went yearly for some 37 years to Alfred Street Chapel.

---

[9]Samuel Medley the hymnwriter (1738-1799).
[10]There is a memorial tablet to John Bennett in Shaw Street Chapel, Liverpool.
[11]One of the original Gospel Standard Committee in 1872.

MANCHESTER

The church at Manchester was without pastor a little over four years, during which time I supplied along with others.

I always felt a great timidity at Manchester, and sometimes a slavish fear, which brings a snare. I had to forget Mr. Gadsby before I could get into my own line of things, but often the Lord led me away from the fear of man.

I remember well my feelings when Mr. Gadsby died. It was Lord's day. I felt as if all good things had gone now, and seemed to forget that the Lord liveth; but the words, "The Lord liveth, and blessed be my Rock," etc., came to me with living power, and I was enabled to speak from them, with much sweet confidence in the living God.

The friends at Manchester, with Mr. Gadsby, were experiencing great trouble; for some portion of the people, being dissatisfied, opened another chapel in Oldham Street, where they were supplied for a time with some clever preachers. The church at Rochdale Road still struggled on through deep waters, and while in these troubles they gave me a call to be their pastor. Prior to this they had given Mr. Godwin a call, but as he told me afterwards, he saw too much of the spirit of battle to go amongst such a people.

A CALL TO THE PASTORATE

When I received this call, I thought the people must have poor judgments to ask me, and for a long time I took no notice, only to say that I thought they had acted foolishly. After a few months the invitation was renewed, and I was urged very much. I had not then made it a matter of prayer, for I did not think such a thing could be.

At this time I had a nice little engraving business, and the church at Accrington paid me twelve shillings a week. I owed no man anything, and I felt to be in my right place, for I had many friends at Accrington. But one especial friend I had in Mr. Henry Bury, whose goodness to me I could not name. I felt I could not leave such friends without showing the basest ingratitude. Besides, I did not feel a desire to go to Manchester.

Mr. Gadsby was regarded on all hands to be the best preacher of that day, and a man of extraordinary ability. He had been pastor for 38 years, and for me to follow such a man seemed impossible, so I said, "No!" in my haste, and answered accordingly.

In a while I had another letter, pressing me to accept their invitation, and I received several private letters of encouragement, but felt no desire to undertake such a charge.

Mr. Kershaw, of Rochdale, had an interview with me, and we had much talk over the matter. I said, "Mr. Kershaw, I feel no desire to go, and indeed have not made it a matter of prayer." He said, "You surprise me." I said, "Well, it is so." He told me many things at the time, which I did not understand so well as I do now.

Many weeks passed over and I continued to supply occasionally, but though I had not prayed over the matter, I often thought of it.

One Saturday, on going up Rochdale Road (St. George's Road then), when just opposite the chapel, I looked at it across the street, when these words fell on my mind: "There the glorious Lord will be unto us a place of broad rivers and streams" (Isa. 33. 21). I stood still a while and pondered on these words. I moved on towards my lodgings in Livesey Street, but from that time I was compelled to call upon God in much anxiety and ask what I must do. Day and night this care filled my thoughts, and like Jeremiah of old I objected, urging that I was not fit for the place. I said, "Lord, let the people fix upon another. I cannot undertake such a charge." Many thoughts pressed hard upon me. I thought of my large and increasing family, the giving up of a good business and leaving Accrington, the home of my divine life. But above all the state of the church troubled me.

DIFFICULTIES AT MANCHESTER

Mr. Gadsby had been dead some four years, and before his death the church passed through a very furnace of trial, which caused Mr. Gadsby seas of trouble and sorrow up to his death. All these things were before me, and they sometimes drove me from prayer on the subject. A great scattering had taken place, and I thought sometimes the sheep looked at each other anxiously. Mr. Gadsby several times talked with me, and on one occasion he said, what grieved him the most was the thought that some sheep had gone with the others.

The separatists had opened a large chapel and obtained a regular minister. The latter published a book[12], setting forth that God had set before him an open door, that no man can shut. All these things, I thought, were against me if I went to Manchester, and whatever others thought of me, I had a very poor opinion of myself. As the subject became pressing, I sometimes trembled, and on one occasion I was much cheered by these words: "When Ephraim spake trembling, he exalted himself in Israel."

One of our deacons at Accrington (Mr. Henry Bury) was much troubled about my going to Manchester. One evening he said to me, "If it would be right for me to bind you to us while I live, I would do it." He was a worthy man, and a kind man both to me and others. God had given him both hand and heart, and I think if I had wanted any help, even to hundreds of pounds, he would have given it.

Strange as it may appear to some, the Lord took him home before I had concluded to go to Manchester. In his will he left £550 for a new chapel, besides giving the site.

Mr. Kershaw again talked with me about my invitation to Manchester, and very kindly asked if I had made up my mind. Before I replied he named another church, and asked if I would go there if they gave me a call. I thought a while and said, "Did that church ask you to put that question to me in that way? or is it your own act and deed?" Thus was I perplexed and knew not what to do.

---

[12]The reference here is almost certainly to John Corbitt's *The Lion Slain and the Lamb Exalted*. The separatists met in a few different places but within a few years the cause expired.

The man who most sincerely wished me to stay at Accrington, while he lived, was now dead. I had many advisers, and there was I, sometimes crying to the Lord, and sometimes feeling that "He shutteth out my prayer."

THE MATTER SETTLED

One Saturday evening, in my lodgings at one of the deacons at Manchester, I had been pleading with the Lord for direction, when the words: "Not by might, nor by power, but by My spirit, saith the Lord of Hosts," came upon me; I was held fast and let loose at the same time. I thought, It is "by My Spirit, saith the Lord of Hosts." Then "the place of broad rivers and streams" came up again, and all was to be done by the Spirit of the Lord of Hosts. O, what a sight I had of the hosts the Lord can marshal when He gives command! I did not sleep much that night, for there came also before me all the imaginary battles that might have to be fought at Manchester; but I thought of the Lord of Hosts, before whom all human might and power would have to give way and the Lord alone be exalted.

After this I accepted the pastorate, and began my ministrations on the first Lord's day in December 1848. I did not expect to have everyone's good will, but feeling that the Lord had bid me go, I went. I also thought that time would prove the right or wrong.

If I had at this time faith to go to Manchester I had also some unbelief, for I kept my machinery for twelve months, lest I should fail in my preaching and so be in trouble with my large family. Here was unbelief in exercise, and what shall I say? It is the truth, and that only shines bright.

THE MANCHESTER PASTORATE

My first text was, "The glorious gospel of the blessed God" (1 Tim. 1. 2), and from that day I have not shunned to declare the same with all my heart and soul, as God the Spirit has enabled me. I have never shunned to declare the whole counsel of God, so far as knowledge has been given to me. I have imparted that knowledge to all who came under the sound of my voice, and I had many seals and souls who have borne clear testimony to the same; and as the Holy Ghost is a witness in the heart of the saint, so God is my witness.

In respect of the members of the church at Manchester, and many who were not members, I was treated with all kindness, favour and tender love. I felt ashamed, and thought this cannot last; but it has lasted, and is now as lively as ever after thirty-six years have passed away. Many old friends have died; all the deacons who then held office have gone home; and during that 36 years, I have laid in the grave 295 bodies, not all my own people, but mainly, and thus we move on.

At the end of the first twelve months after I came to Manchester, I thought about my business which I had given up, and my machinery. I thought I would just look at the church book and see how many names had been added in the year. I found the number to be 39. I thought of David numbering the people and shut the book.

There lay my machinery. The very next day my last employer, Mr. Thomas Simpson, of Foxhill Bank, near Accrington, sent a man to enquire if I had sold it. If I had not, he was prepared to take all at the original cost. The reader may think how astonished I was. He took all and paid me a cheque for the money. This was to me a most astonishing circumstance. The hand of God I saw clearly in it. There are other circumstances I could relate with prudence, but I forbear. I do not like the way some people have of readily attributing every minute circumstance of their lives to the one power or the other – God or Satan. Such people must know more of God and His doings than any prophet or apostle that ever lived. Watching God's hand in providence and grace is a profitable employment, when exercised with that caution – "Swift to hear, slow to speak."

When I was walking up to the place where I first spoke in God's name, those words before alluded to met me, "Keep thy foot when thou goest into the house of God, and be more ready to hear, than to give the sacrifice of fools: for they consider not that they do evil." Many sacrifices have thus been offered and many a fool has lighted the fire from the sparks of a heated imagination, and the enthusiasm of an educated mind, who could never say "the angel of the Lord did wondrously while they looked on."

The kindness of the friends at Manchester was all but unbounded. I was often put to the blush by their conduct. I saw God's hand, and was humbled while rejoicing.

WILLIAM GADSBY'S WIDOW

The late Mr. Gadsby's family were extremely kind. Mrs. Gadsby was then alive. I visited her on her death-bed. She had been long mentally afflicted, and I was anxious to know if that affliction had affected or changed the religion of her youth. To me it seemed like looking for something that had once been there. She saw my anxiety, and said, "Mr. Taylor, when sacrifices were offered under the law, no doubt the beasts were dragged by ropes; but when Christ was sacrificed for me, He laid down His life Himself. It could not be taken from Him. He laid it down of Himself."

I said to myself, "Blessed be God, for ever and ever; the work of the Holy Spirit cannot go lunatic." Thus that dear woman died leaning on the atonement of the God-man.

We have now finished Mr. Taylor's own account, but continue with some particulars about the rest of his life.

CHAPTER 7

Throughout his 38 years pastorate at Manchester, Mr. Taylor's ministry was made a blessing. When the religious census of 1871 was taken on the third Lord's day of June, there were 950 persons present at the service at Rochdale Road Chapel, Manchester. He also preached extensively throughout the country.

One of the Manchester newspapers wrote:

"Gifted with a form of magnificent proportions, a face that photographers loved to study, a voice of remarkable beauty and power, and a nature ever frank, hospitable and manly, it will be readily understood how he was loved almost to idolatry."

It was said that free willers who gnashed their teeth at his preaching of predestination went away charmed with the way that he read the Scriptures. But the secret of his success was the power of the Holy Ghost.

We have been able to find out very little concerning the latter part of the life of A. B. Taylor. His own account, though written when he was an old man, ends about the time he commenced his Manchester pastorate. The account in the *Gospel Standard for* 1887, following his death, merely mentions his last days and gives an account of his funeral. There are, of course, numerous references in old memoirs and magazines, but no continuous account.

During the thirty-eight years of his Manchester pastorate there was an unbroken round of preaching, both at Manchester and throughout the country. Blessed with health and strength, he scarcely missed an engagement. And his ministry was made a blessing to many. It was when he was once taking the Anniversary at Southill that Alfred Dye (later of Rowley Regis) was wonderfully blessed. This is interestingly told in Alfred Dye's remarkable autobiography, *Sovereign Grace O'er Sin Abounding.* The text was: "Fear not, little flock; for it is your Father's good pleasure to give you the kingdom." Mr. Dye relates with what beautiful simplicity Mr. Taylor opened up his text. First, the flock. Then, they are a *little* flock – little in the eyes of the world, little in number, little in their own esteem. But they have a Father, and their Father is in heaven. He has a kingdom, and He is going to give it them; and He is *pleased to* do it. Therefore, *"Fear not,* little flock; for it is your Father's good pleasure to give you the kingdom."

Many of Mr. Taylor's sermons were published as *The Manchester Pulpit,* while several appear in old volumes of the *Gospel Standard.* A sermon of special interest is the one he preached (when over 80) at the Jubilee Services of the *Gospel Standard* magazine in 1885. His text was: "He must increase."

He was particularly happy in administering the ordinances, and seemed specially helped in his funeral addresses. Those delivered at the funerals of John Kershaw (1870) and Thomas Godwin of Godmanchester (1877) were published.

Throughout his pastorate, there was a large church and congregation at Manchester. Congregational singing of a high standard was maintained. Having been a well-known singer in his early days, Mr. Taylor took a keen interest in the singing during the services, and it is said that any mistake would bring an appealing look from the pastor in the pulpit! He was strongly opposed to the use of an organ in the house of God, describing it as "praising God by machinery."

After his death, 200 of his poems were published, along with his brief memoir. Some of the poetry is excellent, but some is mediocre. It would appear that he often jotted down little pieces in rhyme, but it was foolish to publish them. His best poem is undoubtedly "Star of Bethlehem." During his pastorate a collection of hymns for Sunday schools was issued by the Committee of the Sunday school at Manchester. This is still used there, and has recently been republished.

Mr. Taylor's wife died on January 14th, 1865. On the Lord's day morning before she died, her husband said, "Well, my dear, I must go once more and say something to the people about the Lord Jesus." She answered, "Yes, you must," adding, "O! I wish I could tell them what He has done for me, sinful me. He has redeemed me from death and hell."

Of their twelve children several died in infancy. He lost a grown up daughter in 1857 and his oldest daughter (who was married) in 1864. The husband also died, so the children were brought up by their grandfather.

Apart from these sore trials, Mr. Taylor had a more comfortable life than many of God's people. He was quite well to do financially, and was blessed with much peace in his church and congregation. His son, John, was one of his deacons.

In many ways the home life of A. B. Taylor must have been different from that of almost any well known minister. When he first came to Manchester in 1848 he took a cottage, Collyhurst Cottage, that stood in its own ground. Here he was able to keep his own cow. However, in walking with a friend in the lanes near Middleton (a few miles from Manchester) in 1851, he saw a little farm house that took his fancy – Moss Cottage. There he removed and carried on a small farm, the rest of his life being spent there, whilst he rode down to Rochdale Road Chapel for the services. The Sunday School outing each year was always to Moss Cottage.

We give an interesting account of a visit to Moss Cottage paid by one of the Lancashire ministers, William Whittaker of Stubbins *(Friendly Companion 1891):*

"We went one Friday nearly ten years ago (i.e. in 1881). On enquiring at Middleton Junction station, the porter said, 'You mean Mr. Taylor's, the minister, don't you? See, it's yonder; the white-washed house just across there.' In about ten minutes we were near 'Moss Cottage well,' reading the inscription on the stone above it, taken from one of his sweet poems:

> 'Rest, traveller; drink and be refreshed;
> But know
> The journey's short!'

We looked in the well and found, as he says in his poem, 'Moss Cottage well is sometimes dry.'

"On reaching the back gate we had rather a noisy reception: dog after dog kept barking, and the angry-looking turkeys kept clucking. Their horrid howling was, however, as useful as a bell, for soon the old man came, as he oft did ministerially, and delivered me out of that dilemma.

"How bright, clean and cheerful our old friend was! True, his long, light brown overcoat reaching to his ankles, together with his ruddy face and fair complexion, gave him somewhat the appearance of a farmer; but when you looked in his face and at those small, deep-set and determined looking eyes, beneath one of the broadest brows I think I ever saw, and at that mouth, soon sweet and soon severe – friends felt the former and opposers feared the latter, and which also proclaimed the mildness of the gospel and the majesty of the law –

> 'By him the violated law speaks out
> Its thunders; and by him, in strains as sweet
> As angels use, the gospel whispers peace,'
>
> (Cowper)

you felt you were in the presence of one whose equal is seldom found. When he took hold of my hand and said, 'Come in,' the barking ceased and all was quiet.

"He took me into the kitchen and said, 'Just sit there, and I'll come for you in a while.' The 'while' was just a few minutes, during which I had time to look at the walls and what was on them. On one side was a case of birds, about which creatures he knew almost everything; on another side was a large map of the human frame, with other small pictures; whilst over the fireplace were photos of special friends. What interested me most was some writing on the desk at my left hand. How could I help but look? It was a poem, in its raw state, on 'Time':

> 'Time is fleeting, skimming, flying,
> Ever on its whirling wing;
> Heeds no scene, however trying,
> Moving on at nameless swing.'

Before I could get through it he was heard coming. I am glad it is in his book.

"'William, come this way,' he said; so we went upstairs together. But what stairs! Creak, creak, creak, step after step. We felt safer at the top than in the midst. We turned to our left and found we were in his study. I never saw anything more like a library than Mr. Taylor's study was. There was shelf above shelf, I think, nearly all round the room, filled with books, and every one numbered, as libraries are, and on the side table he had a catalogue, so that any book could be readily found. The window was an old-fashioned one, sliding to the right and left. As we sat there we could count no fewer than forty factory chimneys in the neighbourhood of Hollinwood and Oldham.

"We were soon settled down for a two hours' chat about men and things and, if I remember right, Rossendale, in which is Goodshawfold, was about his first inquiry. It was at Rings Row that the truth was preached in his early days, but it is now Goodshawfold, and he had a kind regard for us there. . . .

"At 1.30 he said, 'Come on, the dinner's ready,' so we went down into where there was a large round of beef; but before he touched it he asked the Lord's blessing. What a prayer that was! I never heard one like it before or since! He spoke to God with that reverence and deep solemnity as if he had never spoken to man. He repeated the verse:

> 'When all Thy mercies, O my God,
> My rising soul surveys;
> Transported with the view, I'm lost
> In wonder, love and praise.'

There were only our two selves at the table, but we were enough. To me it was one of the principal pleasures of my life to spend a day with him alone."

***

CHAPTER 8

This account of Mr. Taylor's last days was written by his son-in-law, and appears at the end of his memoir.

We now come to the days of decline. Mr. Taylor often said that he would like, if the Lord would grant his wish, to die in harness, and the present writer has often heard him say that he preferred to wear out than to rust out. For a long time Mr. Taylor's friends observed a bodily failing, but he took care of himself, and by a wise use of his remaining strength he was able to accomplish much. His preaching of late years was remarked by some to savour of a mind solemnly impressed that the end was not far off.

He continued to preach each Lord's day, with some exceptions, both morning and night up to the day when he preached his last sermon; and when he was taken ill, he then had some appointments pending, London and elsewhere, which he would have fulfilled if spared.

His last sermon was preached, June 26th, 1887. He spoke for about half an hour from Matt. 15. 13: "Every plant, which My heavenly Father hath not planted, shall be rooted up."

It was evident to some that he was speaking with great difficulty, and he was compelled to give up, remarking that he felt quite beaten. He told me that he had enjoyed his text much during the preceding week, and felt that he could see through it, all round it, and to the bottom of it, and could preach from it then, if he had strength.

After he was at home a while, it was quite plain that he was very poorly, and he allowed his doctor, Mr. Kershaw of Middleton, to be sent for. On the Thursday following he would go to town, feeling that he had some urgent business, and though not at all fit, he went, his grandson driving him in the gig. On his return he called at the Middleton Junction station for his daughter Sarah (my wife) and drove himself to this house. He said, "I shall not get over this, Sarah. I have felt myself go weaker and weaker for four years, and could not regain my strength. I can see the end is approaching. Ah, but the Lord has been good to me. When I think of all He has done for me, a poor little 'prentice lad to start with, I am astonished and confounded." When they got near the Moss Cottage, he said, "This has been a nice, little retired spot for me." This circumstance was so solemn that my wife says it will never be forgotten by her. In the evening he was placed near the door for air, and he said, "Commit thy way unto the Lord."

The next day he also went to Manchester, which seems almost incredible, but his determination was to go, and the boy took him. This was his last visit. It might be noted here that his yearly contract ticket for the railway expired on the very day that he made his last journey. His breathing was very bad, but he was very cheerful, his conversation was savoury, and his faith anchored firmly on Christ. He looked forward to "the glory which shall be revealed." That night was the time for the church meeting, July 1st. He sent a very kind message to all, telling them that he would help all he could in getting suitable supplies [i.e. ministers to take his place].

He was now ordered to bed by his medical man till he saw him again. This he did not like, but he obeyed. All was done for him that was ordered, or that love could suggest.

Early on Tuesday morning, July 5th, he repeated that verse:

> "Let me not murmur or repine
> Under this trying stroke of Thine,
> But bow beneath affliction's rod,
> Be still, and know that Thou art God."

On the Monday, Mr. Chandler [minister, Accrington] and Mr. Moxon [minister, Bury] called and were permitted to see him, though against the doctor's orders. When Mr. Taylor shook hands with them, he shook with emotion, and began to tell them of his last text, saying he never had such a view of a text in his life. They did not stay long, as he could not bear much talking.

He repeated on one occasion that part of the metrical version of the 23rd Psalm:

"Goodness and mercy all my life
Shall surely follow me,
And in God's house for evermore,
My dwelling-place shall be."

In his own writing he alludes to his being taught this Psalm by his mother at an early age.

Feeling it desirable that a physician should be called in, his son Alexander brought Sir William Roberts, and a consultation took place, which was so far satisfactory, that we were told that all was being done that could be.

During the tossings of the night he said,

"Though painful at present, 'twill cease before long,
And then, O how pleasant, the conqueror's song!"

"Do not let me repine, Lord –

"Did Christ, my Lord, suffer, and shall I repine?"

Another time, he said, "Patient in tribulation, continuing instant in prayer."

During this part of his affliction he suffered much, the heat being oppressive. Those about him had constantly to use the fan.

Once, when a little calm came over him, he said, "All the days of my appointed time will I wait till my change come." "Is there not an appointed time to man upon earth? are not his days like the days of an hireling?"

It must be remembered that Mr. Taylor was very deaf, and that many of his sayings were not addressed to any one, but were the spoken meditations of his heart. Truly, his meditations of Him were sweet.

On the 12th July, he said, "How a tempting devil hunts about for the precious life, but he can't find it! It is hid with Christ in God."

A little after breakfast he said,

"Thy mercy, my God, is the theme of my song,
The joy of my heart and the boast of my tongue;
Thy free grace alone, from the first to the last,
Has won my affections, and bound my soul fast.

"Thy mercy in Jesus exempts me from hell,
Its glories I'll sing and its wonders I'll tell."

He repeated these lines quite firmly, but he was exhausted, and said, "But I must stop." Later on, the same day, he said,

"Plagues and deaths around me fly,
Till He bids I cannot die."

His daughter near to him said, "Well, father, you have often repeated that verse:

"Hail, blessed time! Lord, bid me come."

He replied, "Ah, yes, I have –

"And enter my celestial home,
And drown the sorrows of my breast
In seas of unmolested rest"

During the early morning of the 13th, he repeated the former part again, but when he got to the third line, he said, "But I have no sorrows; they are all gone."

After a hard struggle, caused by paroxysms of the heart, he said, "When Christ was suffering, they gave Him vinegar to drink. O, they were hunting the Lamb of God then."

He seemed to recover a little, and we began to think he might rally. He left his bed each day, and went into his reading room. He wrote several letters and indited others.

To make his time as pleasant as possible, the doctor proposed a bath chair, but this he declined, saying he would use his own gig; so on Saturday morning, July 16th, he was with great trouble got down stairs, and being placed in his chair, he was drawn through the house and down the garden path, and with great difficulty placed in the gig. He was driven a few paces up and down the lane, but he soon had enough. It was plain that this must not be repeated. He was never as well after, as he seemed to take a little cold.

One morning in his study, he laid his hand on his left side, as if to stop the hard beating of the heart, and said,

"And when this heart and flesh shall fail,
And mortal vigour cease,
I shall possess within the veil
A life of joy and peace."

Mr. Carr, of Leicester [Edward Carr, later of Bath], was supplying at Manchester on the 17th July, and at Mr. Taylor's request, I took him to Moss Cottage. It so turned out that the interview had to be very short, as Mr. Taylor became agitated and could not talk, so we retired. Mr. Carr just went to say goodbye, and Mr. Taylor then spoke a few kind words to him, saying if he had to speak again, he should declare the same glorious truths that he had done in the past.

On Wednesday the 20th, the deacons visited him, by his desire. They were received very affectionately, and having asked how they were getting on with supplies, he expressed his satisfaction with their report. He exhorted them to be kind to the ministers supplying, and said, should anything be said by them that did not appear quite right or consistent, they, the deacons, were not to be in haste to speak, but if a private opportunity offered, to use it becomingly, remarking that the Lord would set all right.

Being asked if the truths he had so long preached were able to support him, he answered, that if they did not, nothing else would, adding, were he to live another fifty years, he would preach the same Christ and the same covenant of grace. He then said very solemnly that he had not shunned to declare the whole counsel of God, so far as the Lord had taught him. He mentioned particularly that the doctrine of the Trinity was very precious to him, and that the Lord had led him to see the coequality of the Three glorious Persons in the Godhead very clearly. He remarked that he did not think many ministers were led to think and speak of the wonder and beauties of the Trinity much. We are assured that this meeting of minister and deacons was a very solemn one, and one to be long remembered.

On Thursday the 21st, he said, "What a thing it is to see Calvary's cross with its love, mercy, atonement, justification and sanctification!"

"Dear dying Lamb, Thy precious blood
  Shall never lose its power,
Till all the ransomed church of God
  Be saved to sin no more."

"How sure and full the recompense, when a poor, struggling sinner arrives in glory! Affliction is but for a moment. What the enemy of souls would do if he could; but there is a guard of heavenly warriors waits and keeps him back."

During this night and following morn he was very poorly, and he said he felt very lifeless in body and soul. But, he said, "I have felt grand." His daughter-in-law said, "Yes, father, and you will again."

His son John was also with him, but not just then, as he was resting a little. He was called, when his father began to talk solemnly to all around him, and said, "Man goeth to his long home, and the mourners go about the streets. Yes, yes, yes. Men rest in their beds and sleep together in the dust."

Rousing up a little, he said,

"Soldiers of Christ hold fast,
  The war will soon be past,
  When victory comes at last,
    We'll meet in glory;
And O, what joys shall crown that happy meeting;
We'll bow before the throne, each other greeting."[13]

He was unable to say more; his emotion was so great, his whole frame shook.

---

[13]Part of Joseph Harbottle's farewell hymn.

His will was that Mr. Chandler should bury him; he also said others might speak too, but he said, "They must not talk about me, they must talk about Christ. I have talked about Him until I have been hoarse, haven't I? and I shall see Him soon as He is, not as He was – as He is."

On Friday morning, the 29th, he was heard to say – "Yes, solid peace."

> "When thou canst no deliverance see,
> Yet still this Man thy peace shall be."

On Saturday he asked the doctor what word he might send to his people. The doctor replied that he might say he was better, and had had several good days, but the affliction was so changeable, he dare not say what tomorrow might do. This was remarkable, as on the morrow he was worse, the right lung being congested. From that time we saw the end approaching rapidly. His left hand was now swollen.

On Monday the 1st August he was last in his study. Those who helped him out will not soon forget it. On reaching his bedroom, being seated in his chair, he said, "Ah, Sarah, I shall soon be landed on yonder shores of bliss. It is all right – it is all right. God Almighty knows it is all right."

Tuesday he was very ill; all his children came to see him, thinking it might be their last look. He was not able to say much, but he remarked, "It will not be long. Watch me closely." After a while, he was seen as he was often, when in prayer in the pulpit, with his right hand raised, his lips moving, and from the little that could be gathered, it was evident he was meditating on Christ, for he said, "They all forsook Him and fled."

He was also heard to say, "'Judah must first go up to battle,' that is Christ again. 'Judah is a lion's whelp, from the prey, my son, thou art gone up; he stooped down, he crouched as a lion.'"

On the Thursday he said at the dawn of day, "It will soon be a grand dawn for me." On the day after he was just heard to say, "Dying, dying." His last words of better things were, "Far more precious to the soul the Rock prepared of God."

On the Saturday two friends, ministers[14], were allowed just to see him, and in speaking to one of them, he drew him close to him and said, "It is well, it is well." When they were leaving, he lifted his left arm, and pointing upwards, he whispered, "I am going."

It was my lot to be in the house on the Saturday night, and I was called out of the next room to assist, as he had just got out of bed. When we had guided him into the chair, and were just holding him up a little, we observed his lips moving, and one of his daughters, Mary, who was in front of him remarked, "He is dying," and so it was. He passed thus peacefully away at a quarter to four o'clock the dawn of Lord's day, 7th August, 1887.

-----

[14]William Whittaker of Stubbins, and H. M. Hinchcliffe, later pastor at Uffington.

CHAPTER 9

THE FUNERAL

A full account of A. B. Taylor's funeral appeared in the *Gospel Standard* for 1887, page 381. We give just a few details.

There were upwards of 800 people in the chapel at Rochdale Road, Manchester, when Mr. Robert Moxon of Bury occupied the pulpit at half past one. After hymn 468 had been sung, Mr. Moxon read 2 Kings chapter 2, and prayed. Hymn 470 was then sung and Mr. Moxon addressed the people. Of Mr. Taylor's ministry he said:

"His abilities to set forth these truths were such as few are endowed with. Order ran through every discourse; choice, chaste language characterised every sermon, solemnity and deep feeling pervaded every subject, and all was prefaced and supplemented with earnest prayer to God. He contended for an experimental religion and an apostolic worship. He was a real lover of Zion, and rejoiced in its welfare. He was a friend to the poor, a sympathiser with the afflicted and distressed; and his praise is in all our churches."

The service closed with hymn 466, during which the body was taken to the hearse.

There were about fifty carriages to convey the people to the cemetery, about two miles away, and also the trams, omnibuses and waggonettes which run regularly along the road were quickly filled. Hundreds of people lined the road to the cemetery, and when the carriages arrived there, there were some hundreds already assembled. Police were present to prevent confusion.

At the cemetery chapel, Mr. John Standeven of Patricroft addressed the gathering.

The committal at the grave was taken by Mr. George Chandler of Accrington, who gave an address to the friends gathered there. In his remarks he said of Mr. Taylor's preaching:

"Perhaps the leading feature in our friend's ministry was the Person, work, sufferings, blood, righteousness and offices of the

Lord Jesus Christ, knowing full well that a sermon without Christ is only as a cloud without rain. It was also an instructive ministry, informing the judgment of those who sought knowledge as well as food for the living. He was a true expositor of the Word, and used no strained interpretations to make it fit some ideas of his own, nor did he keep back those discriminating doctrines, such as special redemption and electing love, so that we may say as Paul did to Timothy, "Rightly dividing the Word of truth." He had no novel views or private sentiments, but was open, honest, faithful and affectionate, seeking God's glory and the good of souls, illustrating his subject with chaste and suitable figures, often throwing in some beautiful original idea, which gave fresh interest."

Hymn 466[15] was then sung, and the service was closed with prayer.

Tea was served in the schoolroom for some hundreds of visiting friends, and in the evening a meeting was held at which various addresses were given.

---

[15]We give the hymns exactly as in the 1887 *Gospel Standard.* It will be noticed that hymn 466 appears twice.

FRANCIS COVELL: 1808-1879

The stammerer who was made an able minister of Jesus Christ.

No Strict Baptist minister of the last century was more loved and esteemed than Francis Covell. A tradesman in the town of Croydon, he stammered so badly that sometimes his customers could not tell what he said; but by the power of God he was made a successful minister. The first time he preached, his stammer disappeared.

Preaching first in his own home, his hearers built a large chapel, which soon was filled to capacity, in his native town.

When the eminent J. C. Philpot retired from his pastorates, it was Croydon where he chose to live, not least so that he could sit as a hearer of Mr. Covell – "Brother Frank," as he delighted to call him.

A wonderful pastor, Francis Covell's loving, genial, generous character made an impression on all. "Always kind and cheery, like a ray of sunshine, shedding a warm, bright influence around him," was the way one of his hearers described him.

This account of his life was written by Ebenezer Wilmshurst, who from 1892 to 1906 was minister at Tamworth Road Chapel, Croydon.

CHAPTER 1

EARLY DAYS

Francis Covell was born on December 8th, 1808, at Croydon, Surrey, in which parish his ancestors had lived for upwards of two hundred years. His father carried on the business of tinman and brazier in the High Street. Francis, rather singular to relate, was sent to a school, the playground of which formed part of the ground upon which Providence Chapel (the scene of his ministerial labours) was afterwards erected.

Mr. Covell, in an address, thus refers to this period of his life:

"When I consider His great goodness towards me in the helpless days of my infancy, in giving a kind and tender mother to nurse me, to succour and take care of me, and a kind and good father to provide for me, and support me when unable to take care of myself – I might have been thrown out a helpless babe without friends, neglected, despised, unknown, and uncared for; when I think of His good hand towards me during my boyish days, correcting me for many evils, checking me in my conscience, and thus keeping me from lying and swearing and many other things that I might have done, but for His restraining power in smiting my conscience; He also brought me through various sicknesses until I arrived at youth and manhood – O the forbearance and long-suffering of God! How He followed me, guarding me by day and preserving me by night, as I lay unmindful of that eye that was upon me, that heart that was toward me."

His father was a very hospitable man, and fond of company, which, as Francis grew up, he much enjoyed, and became an eager follower of so-called innocent amusements. He was especially fond of dancing; and in this he became so proficient that others were glad to receive instruction from him, which he willingly gave them; not for remuneration, but from that kindness of disposition which was through life such a marked feature of his character.

EARLY CONVICTIONS

When a boy at school, he was the subject of convictions for sin, and when conscience accused he would seek some secret place to pray, and would vow never to do the like again, but only soon to become once more entangled. But his convictions becoming stronger, he became very strict in his attendance at the parish church, watched over his words, gave money to the poor, and set about a general reformation; but in these he found no salvation, and he used to say that he "was glad to part with a better righteousness than many hoped to be saved by." His anxiety of mind at this time was so great that he would stand during the sermon that he might hear better, and he at length believed that his religion was so pleasing to God that if only two persons in Croydon went to heaven, he should be one of them.

It was his custom at set times to retire to his bedroom to say a set number of prayers. Accordingly one Sunday he retired as usual, and began to read his prayers. He had not read far before the Spirit of God opened his heart, and he was filled with horror at the evil he felt within. Terrors seized upon his mind, so that he feared the boards would crack asunder and let him drop straight into hell. As all his secret sins passed in review before him, he cried and groaned for mercy. He now used to wander in the fields and lonely places, praying, "God be merciful to me a sinner," and shedding thousands of tears of sorrow. He had none to teach him and take him by the hand, but the Lord was leading him in a way that he knew not, and bestowed upon him many tokens that encouraged him still to seek after Him.

DELIVERANCE AND TRIALS

About this time, in order to improve himself in the knowledge of his father's business, he went into a large manufactory in London. One day, feeling himself a lost and ruined sinner, he fell down at the foot of his bed in the apartments where he lived, feeling if God did not have mercy upon him he was lost for ever. But the day of love was come, and the Lord made such a discovery of the Lord Jesus to his soul that he was filled with joy and peace in believing; and in this sweet enjoyment he walked for some months.

The Lord having now delivered his soul, he found the preaching at the parish church did not suit him. This brought him into great trouble, for his father thought it unpardonable that he should think that he knew better than the parson, and, as all the family were Church people, he would not allow him to continue to come to his home as formerly, unless he would conform to family custom. This was a bitter trial, for he loved his parents dearly, but like Moses of old, "he chose rather to suffer affliction with the people of God."

But if Mr. Covell found it impossible to get on at the Church, he also found it difficult to find anyone to understand his feelings amongst Nonconformists. He went one Sunday morning to the seven o'clock prayer meeting at the Congregational Church, Croydon, and told some of the people there that God had pardoned his sins and saved his soul; but they told him that he was an

Antinomian. What that meant he could not tell, any more than he could understand Arabic; but nothing could strip him of the hope of salvation God had given him.

At this time he often had to be satisfied with a very scanty meal, his dinner frequently being made from a few dried sprats and bread; but such was his enjoyment of the Lord's presence, that he would walk about the City of London, and feel his portion was infinitely better than all the possessions of merchant princes.

But this season of estrangement, through his father's displeasure, was brought to a close in an unexpected manner, for his father's health began to fail, and his affection again ran towards his son, and he therefore sent for him to come home to assist in the business. His father was shortly afterwards removed by death, and by his will left the house and business to his son Francis.

A few months afterwards, he married his cousin, Elizabeth Turner, who proved a true helpmeet to him for nearly forty years, and during the whole of that period she never slept away from home a single night.

Mr. Covell had five children, two of whom died in infancy. The eldest son, who was afflicted from the age of two years, was a source of great trial and anxiety, and it was Mr. Covell's prayer for years that, if it was the Lord's will, he might see the end of his afflicted son; and God graciously answered his petitions, by taking the son to Himself a few weeks before his father.

HIS FIRST GOSPEL SERMON

Mr. Covell never heard a clear gospel sermon until after his marriage. He was one day talking to a friend of his wife's about the way the Lord had led him, when this friend observed, "There is a man comes to preach in London sometimes that I think would suit you; when he comes next, I will let you know." He did so. It was at Gower Street Chapel and the minister was William Gadsby. His text on that occasion was, "And we know that all things work together for good to them that love God, to them who are the called according to His purpose," (Rom. 8. 28). When Mr. Gadsby came to describe what sinners are called from and what they are called to, Mr. Covell found great difficulty in restraining himself from calling out in the chapel, "I am called! I am called!" After this he sought opportunities of hearing such ministers as Gadsby, Warburton, Cowper, etc., as often as he could, and tried hard to get the people with whom he worshipped at Croydon to have such men to preach, but in vain. He therefore left the chapel and met with his wife in their own house for reading and prayer, and in the course of four or five years they were joined by ten or twelve others.

CONCERN ABOUT PREACHING

Mr. Covell had long been exercised in his mind respecting the ministry, feeling such a desire to tell of that Jesus who had saved him from the burning pit, and such was his anxiety that, for seven or eight years, his mind was full of tossing up and down respecting this great work, both night and day, but the great obstacle in the way was an impediment in his speech, causing him to stammer and stutter. O, how he cried to the Lord with tears to loose his tongue! At length the Lord operated so powerfully on his heart that he felt, unless he did say something of the Lord's mercy and goodness, he should be cut down as useless. Therefore, with fear and trembling, he determined to make the attempt, feeling a secret persuasion the Lord would remove the impediment in his speech. On July 18th, 1844, when the few friends who met at his house had concluded their meeting for prayer, he felt he could not let them part without repeating the text which had been impressed upon his mind (Titus 3, 3-6): "For we ourselves also were sometimes foolish, disobedient," etc. Upon these words he began to make some remarks, and immediately his tongue was loosed; lo, the impediment was gone, and he spoke to the friends for fully an hour, and from that time he never failed or faltered in his speech! The next Sabbath evening, when the friends met for reading and prayer, one of them said, "You have not finished your subject of last Sabbath," so he preached again from the same words, and continued it also on the following Sabbath.

We might here refer to the fact that the late Mr. John Kershaw, of Rochdale, was one of the first to distinguish that Mr. Covell had gifts that were likely to be useful to the church of God.

Mr. Kershaw occasionally came to Croydon to preach, and when he did so, he stayed at Mr. Covell's house. One evening, as he was sitting somewhat apart from the others trying to meditate upon the Word previous to going to the service, he could not forbear hearing Mr. Covell's conversation with some friends in the room, which impressed him so much that when walking together to chapel, Mr. Kershaw asked him if he had not been exercised about the ministry. Mr. Covell put off the question, saying, "We are going to chapel now; don't trouble about such things as that"; but Mr. Kershaw at a later period renewed his question saying, "The matter so rests upon my mind that I feel if I am wrong in my impressions upon this point, I may be in others." When so pressed, Mr. Covell had to acknowledge that it was so, but pledged Mr. Kershaw to keep the secret. When Mr. Kershaw came again and found that Mr. Covell had not gone forward in the matter, he threatened to tell the people, but Mr. Covell said, "You dare not, because you are bound by your promise." One of the greatest obstacles in the way was the affliction Mr. Covell had of stuttering when he spoke, which was at times so bad that it is related that when serving a lady in his shop on one occasion, he had so much difficulty in replying to her questions that she told him he had better go and call his master, not thinking she was speaking to the master.

In God's own time the attempt was made to preach, as already related, and at the conclusion of the discourse one friend observed in astonishment to another, "Why, he didn't stutter" – neither did he from that time forward.

Soon after he had commenced to preach, Mr. Covell had to go on business to Beddington, and called on the mother of the rector of the parish. She, having heard that he had commenced preaching, asked how he could do so, as he had never been to college. He replied, "I have not been to college, but for eleven years I have diligently studied the Scriptures." Doubtless that eleven years' study of the Word, under the teaching of the Holy Spirit, was the best training he could have had, and laid the foundation of that wonderful knowledge of the Scriptures which was such a marked feature of his ministry.

CHAPTER 2

PREACHING IN HIS OWN HOUSE

The Lord having now loosed the tongue of the stammerer, and caused His servant to put his hand to the gospel plough, he looked not back, but from that time to within a few days of his being called home, he continued to preach the unsearchable riches of Christ as he had tasted, handled, and felt them. For some time the services continued to be held in his own house, but presently the room would not contain his hearers, and then *two* rooms were devoted to the purpose, and Mr. Wallis, who led the singing, was asked by the speaker to stand between the two rooms to pitch the tune so that all might the better join in the hymn; but it soon became needful to place forms in the shop to accommodate the increasing number of hearers; and, said Mr. Covell in after days, "We did not mind the steam (occasioned by the breath of those assembled) getting on the kettles."

But Mr. Covell's preaching soon became noised abroad, and he used to say in after years that "he was the talk of the town, from the hotel down to the little pot-house." Moreover, many of his customers began to expostulate with him, asking him if he thought he knew better than many who had attended the parish church all their lives, and strongly advised him to give up his preaching and not pretend to know better than his superiors; but this, of course, he was unable to do. They then began to threaten him with withdrawing their custom unless he desisted, and ultimately many did discontinue their custom. This in some measure tried him, and worked peevishness and fretfulness, and he thought the Lord dealt hardly with him. This rebellious state so prevailed one day that he threw off his working jacket, and he said in his mind he would go out into the fields and have it out with the Lord; and as he poured out his complaints, it seemed as if the Lord drew near, and said, "Now, what is the matter? Have I been a barren wilderness? Would you like to change with your persecutors?" This so sweetly broke the snare that he went back

145

to his home blessing and praising the Lord and seeking for mercy and pardon, and was delivered from the fear of man.

One of the hearers who attended the services in Mr. Covell's shop, and who knew the preacher well, has given the following reminiscence of these early but memorable days of his ministry:

"I remember Mr. Francis Covell from about the year 1840; he was always of a cheerful and pleasant disposition, and kept a tinman and brazier's shop in the High Street, Croydon. He worked at his trade, and employed some three or four hands; he was a friend of my father's, and used to visit our house occasionally. I used to observe that he was ready to assist every good work and to show kindness to the poor. In July 1844, I was calling upon one of our customers in Croydon, when he informed me that Mr. Covell had begun to preach. I felt surprised to hear this, as he used to stutter in speaking, and was moreover so cheerful and, at times, jocular in his manner that I had not thought him at all likely to become a minister. Upon my arriving home, I told my father, and he said, 'Well, we will take an opportunity some Sunday evening of hearing him.' At that time my father attended the chapel at Beddington Corner, where we had supplies, and Mr. Covell also sometimes attended.

"In a few weeks my father and other members of the family went over to Croydon to hear Mr. Covell, and my father said afterwards that while hearing him preach, the words came to his mind, 'Arise, anoint him, this is he!' and I felt myself, after hearing him preach, that this kind of ministry was what I should like to sit under. He was solemn and discriminating, and yet most encouraging to seeking souls. He was also very practical in his discourse, and moreover such power attended the Word that his sermons were not easily forgotten. I heard one countryman say, after hearing him, 'Mr. Covell seems to get inside of you.' Another person who came to hear him said 'he should not come again, as it was too hot for him.'

"I had a favoured season on one occasion while hearing him preach in his shop. His sermons in those days were very long, and often occupied one and a half hours in their delivery; indeed, sometimes he was so led out that I have known him to exceed that time.

"Mr. Covell was one day travelling in the train, and fell into conversation with a fellow-traveller, and the subject turned upon religion. Presently Mr. Covell's name was mentioned by his fellow passenger, who began to find fault with him, and spoke against him as a bad kind of man. Mr. Covell agreed with him in this, but added, 'I believe he means well, and that he is an honest man.' Mr. Covell afterwards related the incident to a friend who knew the passenger aforenamed, who asked him if he remembered the conversation in the train. He said 'Yes.' He then informed him that his fellow-traveller was none other than Mr. Covell of whom he had spoken such hard things. The poor man, on hearing this, was much confused and put out with himself for speaking as he had done, which no doubt had been prompted by jealousy as he was a preacher living about two miles from Croydon, and some of his hearers had left him, feeling they could profit more in hearing Mr. Covell.

"In February 1845, Mr. Covell began to preach once a month on Sundays at Beddington Corner, and continued to do so for twelve months. Many of his Croydon friends came to hear him there, and the chapel was filled whenever he preached. The other Sundays in the month he still preached in his shop; but the place soon became too scant for them, and they were anxious for a more commodious meeting-place; and it so happened, in the providence of God, that a chapel – 'Ebenezer' – in the old town was at liberty, and was hired by the friends. When Mr. Covell commenced his ministry here, he took for his text the last eight verses of the seventy-eighth Psalm, and preached three or four Sundays from these words.

"It soon became evident that a still larger and more suitable chapel was needful for the increasing congregation; therefore the friends determined to build a new chapel in West Street. When the plan of the proposed building was shown to Mr. Covell by a friend, he said, 'It is too large.' The friend replied, 'Is it too large for your faith?' 'No,' replied Mr. Covell; 'it is too large for the people's pockets.' 'Then,' said his friend, 'it shall not be one inch smaller.' The people had such a mind for the work that the chapel was completed quickly, and was opened on the second Sunday in March 1848, and was called Providence Chapel. The cost of the building, with the ground, was £1,460. Towards this amount £560 was raised and paid; the remainder was borrowed at a moderate interest, which by degrees was paid off; but it took some years to accomplish this task.

"The chapel at first was about half filled; but the congregation slowly increased, and for a few years previous to Mr. Covell's death it was most difficult to find seats for the hearers.

"Mr. Covell was always ready to counsel those young in the way against anything that he thought might injure them. I remember once that I was about joining a literary society, but he advised me not to do so, but to keep at home, observing, 'You will get more into society than will do you any real good, and these are little foxes that will spoil the tender grapes.' I followed his advice, and have often been glad I did so.

"Mr. Covell was once walking in a lonely lane, and he met two men that he felt sure were after no good. He began at once to consider what he should do, and decided that it was his duty to speak to them, which he did in a very serious manner, speaking to them of the solemnities of death, asking them if they ever thought of their dying day. The men seemed very uneasy, and were glad when the opportunity occurred of getting away from the stranger who spoke to them so pointedly and solemnly.

"I was a close observer of Mr. Covell's life from the commencement of his ministry till his death, and I can testify that the following Scripture was fulfilled in his career, 'The liberal soul deviseth liberal things, and by liberal things shall he stand' (Isa. 32. 8). He was always kind to the poor, especially to the household of faith. He seemed to live for the cause of God and the good of His people. His words and actions showed that the salvation of sinners and the honour and glory of God was his sole aim. He had a single eye to the glory of God. For some few years he took nothing for preaching, but when the friends found out how his circumstances had changed through his business falling off, and his liberality to the needy, they showed their love to him by supplying his needs."

BAPTISM

Mr. Covell was baptised on July 2nd, 1850, at Eden Street Chapel, London, by Mr. Tiptaft in the presence of a crowded congregation. Mr. Covell spoke at the pool for a short time before going into the water; and the next day and the following he felt so favoured in his soul that he said, "To realise this would make the weakest go through the ordinance."

[The unusual procedure of being baptized after preaching for some time was, of course, due to the unusual circumstances. Mr. Covell was not brought up a Baptist, and at first preached to a gathering of hearers, irrespective of any denomination.]

CHAPTER 3

A TRIED PATHWAY

Mr. Covell was led to give up business in June 1851 and throw himself upon the providence of God, giving himself wholly to the ministry of the Word.

The following year, 1852, began under a cloud owing to a bad gathering on his hand and the failure of his general health, so that his medical attendant said that he could not say what the end might be. Having passed through several days and nights in great pain, he earnestly begged of God to heal him, and he felt a persuasion in his soul that God would answer him. A day or two after he told the doctor he believed he should get better. The doctor replied, "Time will prove that; but if you do, you will not be able to use your hand for some time." But so rapid was the cure that in a fortnight from that time he was able to write a letter.

Mr. Covell's providential trials drove him to a throne of grace, and help came in answer to prayer. He used to say, "The Lord has suffered me to come into a low place to enable me to speak to the profit and comfort of exercised business men, and others in like circumstances. Ah, my friends, you little know how I have walked the fields, crying, 'Have pity upon me, Lord! What will men say of Thy truth? How Thy name will be blasphemed! What will become of Thy faithfulness? Where will Thy love and power be seen? Good God, do help me! pray save me from impending ruin which I see before me.' I have stood in the pulpit in times past without a sovereign in my pocket with which I could say I was going through the next week; but His watchful eye and loving heart and bountiful hand appeared for me again and again, causing me to acknowledge His goodness, testifying that I had a God that cared for me, who would hold me up, and see me through every strait and every difficulty."

HIS MINISTRY MADE USEFUL

In the *Memorials of James Boorne,* of Greenwich, there is a particularly interesting account given of the great blessing that he received under Mr. Covell's ministry in the year 1856. Mr. Boorne had felt to be in a backsliding state of soul, but on Sunday, May 10th, he heard Mr. Covell from Hebrews 10. 21, 22. During his discourse he took up the case of one who, through sinking into a backsliding state, could not draw near to God. He said, "When such a man is retiring to rest, Satan will say, 'You are not fit to go to God tonight; put it off till tomorrow morning; get into bed and meditate over a few things there.' But," said he, "as sure as you get into bed you will go to sleep, and Satan will rock you to sleep too; and, God only knows, there may be a poor soul here who has been in this case, and gone on in it week after week, week after week." These remarks came home to Mr. Boorne with a "Thou art the man," and the tears began to flow.

Then Mr. Covell went on to show that though a child of God – like king Asa – might be drawn aside by the power of Satan, yet the Scripture declares the heart of Asa was perfect all his days. "Therefore, poor soul, Satan's sieve may turn thee this way and that way, but thou hast at the bottom a true heart amidst all the rubbish – thou knowest that thou hast." Again, Mr. Boorne's eyes overflowed with tears, and he felt, "O, how marvellous! a true heart to be in me!" This sermon led to a very gracious revival of the work of grace in his soul, the full particulars of which are recorded in the interesting volume of *Memorials of James Boorne.*

MR. PHILPOT AND MR. COVELL

During the year 1864 the beloved J. C. Philpot, owing to failing health, found it needful to resign his pastorate over the churches of Stamford and Oakham, and he was led to choose Croydon as a suitable locality to reside in, especially as he would be able to enjoy the ministry of Mr. Covell. The two ministers, known to each other before as lovers and preachers of the same gospel, now, owing to frequent opportunities of converse, became warm and attached friends. Whenever health permitted, the gracious scholar loved to sit at the feet of the gracious "tinman," and whenever the scholar could be prevailed upon to take the pulpit, the "tinman" was equally delighted to sit at his feet for instruction.

It was Mr. Philpot's dying wish that Mr. Covell should conduct the service at his funeral, with which request Mr. Covell complied, and his address upon that occasion was a masterly one; and we cannot pay it a greater compliment than by saying it was worthy of the memory of the gracious, talented man whose body he committed to the silent grave. In speaking of Mr. Philpot as a friend, Mr. Covell said: "I can bear testimony, from a long intercourse, to his courteous and affable manner, and it must ever be a source of satisfaction to me that he declared that he enjoyed my ministry; again and again has he expressed how thankful he was to God for bringing him to Croydon."

SANCTIFIED AFFLICTION
In October 1865, Mr. Covell ruptured a blood-vessel and lost a considerable quantity of blood. This alarming event caused much consternation and anxiety to his wife and family, but Mr. Covell seemed to be kept very quiet in his mind during the occurrence, and when he reached the top of the stairs leading to his bedroom, he said, evidently for the comfort of his family,

> "All things for our good are given,
> Comforts, crosses, staffs, and rods;
> All is ours in earth and heaven,
> We are Christ's, and Christ is God's."

As he lay in bed, forbidden to speak or to see anyone, God blessed his soul and shone into his heart in a wonderful manner, and when allowed to speak a little, he said, "For some time past I have been putting up many cries to God, and He blessed me with many little tokens and manifestations of His favour; but since I have been on my bed, I have found they were only foretastes of what was to follow. I have indeed proved the truth of what the psalmist says, 'He that goeth forth and weepeth, bearing precious seed, shall doubtless come again with rejoicing, bringing his sheaves with him.'"

CHRISTIAN SYMPATHY
On June 18th, 1870, his loving and devoted wife died after a short illness, of whom her husband could say, "I believe she is

now in heaven." Mr. Covell, having so recently known the trial of losing a good wife, could feelingly sympathize with others in a similar bereavement. The following letter he wrote to a friend some time afterward:

"My dear friend, – How true it is that 'man is born to trouble,' and that 'few and evil are our days.' How the good Lord has cut away the strings that were likely to hold you here, and speaks to you by them, 'Behold, I come quickly,' that your heart may respond in the sweet feeling, 'Come, Lord Jesus! for what wait I for? Truly my hope is even in Thee.'

"As to your dear wife, it were almost cruel to wish to keep her here in such continual pain and sickness. O the blessed change, to be swallowed up in life and love! O, the child of God has got the best of it; and now she reaps a harvest of joy, and of the blessedness of it there will be no end. You may mourn, but she rejoices. I trust you may see and feel a Father's hand in it; and this will enable you to say, 'Not my will, but Thine be done!' O, what a mercy it is when our will is swallowed up in His! How true we find it, that every good gift is from above! We can see what is right and good, but we cannot reach it. All our strength is in Him; and the Lord is pleased to make us know it. May He be pleased to help you at this time, that you may feel the Lord is good and a stronghold in the day of trouble, and have another token for good that the Lord loves and cares for you; for sometimes it is by terrible things in righteousness He answers us; and so we prove that all things, dark as well as light, work together for good.

"Accept of my best wishes and sympathy in this trial, and may you have to say, 'I was brought low; but the Lord helped me.'

"Yours truly,

"Croydon, December 27th, 1871."   "F. Covell."

Mr. Covell used occasionally to preach at Cranbrook, and he did so in 1873, soon after the death of our dear father, Mr. James Wilmshurst. Before leaving the town he called on our mother to sympathize with her; this visit was a model of brevity and point. He shook hands, inquired after her health and that of her family, and then, in his striking manner, quoted the lines of Berridge:

"If sick, or blind, or poor,
Or by the world abhorred,
There's not a cross lies at thy door
But cometh from the Lord."

Having repeated the verse he at once said, "Goodbye," and was gone, but the brief visit and the lines quoted were felt to be most helpful, and were never forgotten by those who heard them.

MR. COVELL AND THE PRIEST

Mr. Covell was always of a particularly friendly disposition, and would speak freely to anyone he came in contact with, however much opposed to them he might be in his views of truth; he would do so to Father David, who was for many years the Roman Catholic priest in Croydon. On one occasion, Father David was telling him of his new house, which he said was beautifully furnished. "No," said Mr. Covell, "it cannot be." "Indeed it is," said the priest; "you come and see." "No," replied Mr. Covell; "there is one thing lacking, you need a wife." And all true Protestants will agree with Mr. Covell that the priests' homes would be better if their vows of celibacy were removed, and their homes brightened by the presence of a good wife, which is from the Lord.

On another occasion the Baptist minister and the Romish priest met opposite a new church in Croydon, in which extreme ritualistic practices are carried on. Mr. Covell said, pointing to the church, "They (the worshippers) will soon come over to you." "No," said the priest, "we do not want them." But however Father David and his fellow-priests may repudiate the ritualists, there is little doubt that the statement of the Baptist minister is according to the truth, for the way is now well beaten by the feet of the thousands who are continually passing from the ranks of ritualism to those of Romanism.

A FEW MEMORIES

One day Mr. Covell met a man that, when he was following his business vocation, he had worked with. The man was in a poor and wretched condition, having given way to drink. The man solicited help from him. Calling him by his name, Mr. Covell said, "You do serve your master well; he is a hard master; he does pay you badly, yet you serve him faithfully. How thankful I am that I have a better Master, who pays me good wages!" Mr. Covell closed his admonition by relieving the man's needs, as he had done on previous occasions.

One Sunday morning two men of respectable appearance came into Providence Chapel. As the service proceeded, they appeared by their actions to have come to make game of the preacher. Mr. Covell observed their proceedings, and in the course of his discourse he looked straight at them, and said, in his solemn and impressive manner:

> "Fools make a mock at sin,
> And with destruction sport;
> But death will stop their simple grin,
> And cut their laughter short."

The arrow evidently hit its mark, for the two men at once rose from their seats and left the chapel – we would hope, sadder but wiser men.

We now give an extract from a letter received from a friend, which will give expression to the deep affection felt towards Mr. Covell by his constant hearers:

"The loss of Mr. Covell's ministry to his regular hearers was indeed heavy, and is still deeply felt. What a father he was to his people! and whatever his own griefs might be, always kind and cheery when one met him, like a ray of sunshine, shedding a warm, bright influence around him. How he watched over his flock with earnest desires for their salvation, and noted if any were absent from chapel! Never can they find such another. 'I've got the best,' he said, in allusion to his departure and unknown successor, 'and you can't have first love at the end.' His prayers were remarkable – just like himself – such fervency, such tender pleading, as one never hears elsewhere, except from his brother, who had a similar gift, though not quite in the same degree.

"Towards the close of his days, dear Mr. Covell ripened very fast; and I well remember, one Wednesday evening a few months before his death, being greatly disappointed on going into the chapel at seeing him in the desk, while another minister occupied the pulpit; but can never forget the solemn and pathetic manner in which he gave out that hymn of Berridge's, 'If Jesus kindly say'; and when he came to the last verse, with what emphasis and feeling it dropped from his lips, as if his heart was in every word:

> 'A soft and tender sigh
> Now heaves my hallowed breast,
> I long to lay me down and die,
> And find eternal rest.'

"Years have softened our grief, but the loss is as great as ever, and there seems to be no one who can in any measure supply his place."

CHAPTER 4

A GLANCE AT THE PAST

It being the custom only to have annual collections at Providence Chapel, Croydon, Mr. Covell used frequently on these occasions to give some interesting reminiscences, which made those addresses interesting and valuable.

On March 12th, 1876, being collection day, he made the following remarks at the close of his discourse:

"It is twenty-eight years since the chapel was opened. What has held us together? Prayer. I believe many of you have come up praying for God's blessing – 'Lord, bless him that we expect to hear,' so you have been delivered from all pick-thank feelings, finding fault with the weakness that has been displayed. As you have come up, so I believe I have come up – 'Lord, bless the people; smile upon them; do them good.' So this tie between us has been a better one than man could have invented. We have no handsome place to draw you to; you are not likely to increase your business by coming here; it has not been the excellent singing, or the splendid tones of an instrument that has attracted you; nor has it been the silver eloquence of the preacher. If anything has reached your hearts, it is because out of his weakness God has perfected strength.

"When I look round, what faces I miss that I was wont to see twenty-eight years ago! Where are those faces that used to meet in my own house, that wended their way to the little chapel in the old town, and who, with heart and hand, helped to build this place? I have no doubt that some are singing of that grace which saved sinners like them. What fears and shakings I have had, what puffings from the devil that I should not hold out and hold on, and that you would be tired of me! But notwithstanding my fears, God has multiplied us. We have had no Penny Readings to get you together, no concerts; we have nothing else to attract you but the truth that you are sinners, and must be saved by the grace of God.

"When we opened this chapel, I thought the forty-eight pounds collected on the opening day was a wonderful sum; but He has since opened your hearts to such an extent that your praise is in all the churches. If this year's collection does not come up to what it did last year, I shall not think your affection towards me and the cause of God is in the least diminished, but that it is your circumstances have brought you to do what you have done. Whatever you give, whether two mites or more, God enable you to feel, Lord, prosper Zion."

The total sum collected on this day was £462 15s. 7d. [a remarkable sum a hundred years ago].

HEART PRAYERS

Mr. Covell, in one of his sermons, said, "When I went to church, I am not aware that I ever pleaded for mercy in the whole of my prayers, yet I was good in my own estimation, and other people thought so too. But while upon my knees one day, going through my wonted prayers, God shone into my heart and showed me the evil, sinfulness, devilishness and abominations therein, and feeling that I should sink into hell, I cried out in earnestness, 'God, have mercy upon me.' Mercy has been my plea from that day to this. The night that God blessed my soul, pardoned my sin, and made me as happy as I could hold, I dropped at the foot of my bed, and cried, 'Lord, save me; Lord, have mercy upon me; Lord, do save me'. In His love and pity He heard me. I do not mind saying there was a good man I was made useful to, I trust, before I began to preach. When he came to lodge at the house where I did (as he desired it), we used to kneel together in prayer. I used to say, 'You speak, Ned.' For three months he never went farther than this, morning and night, 'God, have mercy upon me; Lord, do save me; Lord, have mercy upon me.' He lived for some years to prove the goodness of that God whose mercy he sought; he made a blessed end, he went to heaven, and is now singing, I have no doubt, 'to Him that loved him, and washed him from his sins in His own blood.'"

"LOVE AND GRIEF"

"When God was pleased to pardon my sins, and to give me to realise that I was saved with everlasting salvation; when His love flowed into my heart, and I felt Christ was mine, then how I hated my sins. I felt that my sins would never damn me, but of all the filthy wretches under heaven I was the worst. How I loathed and detested myself on account of my sins, while I felt Christ had put them away by the sacrifice of Himself; I washed His feet with my tears, and grieved because I had put Him to such a shameful death by my sins."

TRUST IN THE LORD
"I know this to be true, 'It is better to trust in the Lord than to put confidence in man.' Once in my life I put a deal of confidence in a friend of mine, but I was deceived. I have often trusted in my heart, and that has deceived me. Again and again I have been brought to trust in the Lord, and never was disappointed or deceived. Therefore I will speak well for God. I know His name; I have found Him to be a Refuge; I know Him to be a God of power, a God of mercy, a God of wisdom, a God of love. Though I desire to bless God for many kind and good friends I have, yet my trust is in the Lord that made heaven and earth."

O, MY SIN, MY SIN!
"Nothing will make a man's knees bow like this, 'O, my sin, my sin!' 'Enter not into judgment with Thy servant, for in Thy sight shall no flesh living be justified.' As a father, I have known something of trouble; as a husband, I have known something of trouble in the loss of a wife; as a man of business, I have known what trouble is in losses, crosses and disappointments; as a man, I have known what it is to lose friends; but nothing has brought such tears out of my eyes, nothing has made me droop, or sent me upon my knees, like my sins. I know a little of what dear Hart says:

'O thou hideous monster, sin,
What a curse hast thou brought in!'"

GODLY FEAR IN THE HEART
"Sometimes I have such a desire to run after the things of the world. Then I bring myself to this, 'Now, if you were in India, America, or anywhere where you were unknown to any soul,

could you do it then? Would you do it?' 'Good God, I could not, though none knew it but Thee and me.' Thus the Lord is seen over us, to preserve us from the world and from the power of sin."

GRATITUDE A GIFT FROM GOD

Mr. Covell, in one of his discourses, said:

"God has made me prove that 'every good and perfect gift is from above.' You can no more work gratitude in your heart than you can faith or love. If it will redound to the glory of God, I am willing to tell you simply how He made me prove it. I was driven hard for £200. As I walked the fields I said, 'Good God, if Thou wilt help me, how I will praise, love and bless Thee!' I could no more see the way in which I was to have it than I can see my way to the throne of England. I thought if God helped me, if I did not praise Him the very stones would cry out; I felt I must, I could not help it. I said, 'O Lord, I will believe and trust in Thee as long as I live, and never doubt Thy goodness any more.' I thought I should make the hedges ring and echo.

"My friends, God gave me the money, and as I had it in my hands there was no more thankfulness in my heart than there is life in this cushion. When I went to pay it, my heart was as cold as the ground I walked on. I thought, 'What a wretch I am! Did you not say how you would praise God?' But I could not do it. I did say with my lips, 'Lord, I thank Thee,' but there was no heart in it. I thought, 'Perhaps when I get the receipt that will do it.' I came home as cold as I went out. I could no more bring my heart to gratitude than the devil.

"I remember, a few days afterwards a little circumstance transpired in which I saw somewhat of the finger of God moving towards me, and my heart broke, and my eyes ran out with tears. That is the way God will teach us the riches of His grace."

MEMORABLE SEASONS AT GOWER STREET CHAPEL

Mr. Covell once gave the following relation of blessings he received at Gower Street:

"Some years after hearing Mr. Gadsby the first time in Gower Street Chapel, I went to preach there, and a good man waited on me after the service and said, 'Do you remember any particular time here?' I said, 'Yes, I have been many times blessed here when hearing different good men.' 'But do you remember any time in particular?' 'Yes, I do,' I said; 'I was very much blessed at one time when hearing Mr. Gadsby.' 'That was the time I mean,' he said; 'I sat close to you, and you could not sit still, and I thought, "That man has got something; he has got a blessing," and directly you got into the pulpit today I recognised you.' I had no idea but that I sat quietly, although I was feeling so much.

"Some time after that I was going to preach there again, and my poor afflicted son had been very trying, and had caused me some tears and sorrow. As I was going down Gower Street in the evening, very low in mind, I cried out, 'Have pity on me, O Lord!' God seemed to bring these things to my mind, 'Are you not the man that was willing to have any trouble, and pass through anything some years ago, knowing that all things should work together for your good?' I said, 'Yes, Lord, I am.' Then these words dropped in my heart, 'The Lord taketh pleasure in His people; He will beautify the meek with salvation.' That turned my sorrow into joy, and made me go singing to preach."

———————————

CHAPTER 5

THE LOCAL NEWSPAPER

Not long after he died, the *Croydon Advertiser* made reference to Mr. Covell:

"The church and congregation to whom Mr. Covell ministered was probably the most regular in attendance in Croydon, and for devotion to their pastor are unsurpassed in any quarter. While their minister and spiritual adviser, Mr. Covell was also their friend and counsellor in temporal matters, and his congregation seemed to look upon him as much in the light of a father as in that of a pastor. The recipient of numberless confidences, his advice was always kindly given, and invariably accepted and acted up to. . . . As a preacher, Mr. Covell was most earnest and original; under the apparent solemnity of his manner there lurked an abundance of the milk of human kindness, and there will be many persons who have to acknowledge acts of charity and large-heartedness, which Mr. Covell studiously avoided proclaiming, and would, perhaps, have repudiated any credit for."

WORDS TO THE YOUNG

Although Mr. Covell had no Sunday School, he would occasionally speak to the young from the pulpit, and always with much kindness and solemnity. In reading the first chapter of Job he would stop at the fifth verse, and tell the young who had godly fathers and mothers what a good thing it was to have parents who prayed for them. Also he would sometimes say, "Listen, children!" and then would relate the call of Samuel. Once, when reading 2 Kings 22, he made the following remarks:

"How young was Josiah to have it recorded of him that he took an interest in the house of God! There are many young people here; how many of them love God's house? You are never too young to die, you have no lease of your lives; if you look in the cemetery you will see the names of many younger than you. A week today, for aught you know, your friends may be saying over you, 'Dust to dust, ashes to ashes,' and while they were saying it, would they have any reason to believe that you were singing in heaven? Would they be able to say that, though you did not observe it, they had watched and seen you go by yourself and pour out your soul in prayer to God? Would they find any leaves in your Bible turned down? Would they have ever heard you say that you liked this or that servant of God for his earnest manner of setting forth God's Word? You would like to be in heaven; but if you do not walk the way that Josiah walked on earth you will never be with him where he now is."

"THEY SAID, 'HE IS A METHODIST'"

Mr. Covell once gave the following relation of how he was enabled to show his colours amongst his fellow-workmen:

"Without wanting to speak with egotism, I may say, when I was working in a shop in London, my father one day came into the shop, but the men did not know him. He said, referring to me, 'What sort of a young man is that?' They said, 'He is a Methodist.'[1] They could see a difference between me and them in this: at mealtimes I read the Bible; I had moral courage enough. It is not everyone that has that. I could say to them at night, 'I am going to chapel. Which of you will go with me?' I have never repented that I made an open profession of what I was. God made it manifest that I was His in a shop of sixty to eighty men. I would have got tipsy, lied and sworn as they did, but for the grace of God."

FEARS AND FAITH

"When I was in business I had a persuasion that God would take my soul to heaven, yet I had many fears whether He would enable me to pay my debts and bring up my family. I have walked about for an hour or two, and argued, and have not made one hair white or black to my advantage. Praying is better than arguing, and committing our way to God is better than planning and scheming.

---

[1]Years ago this term simply meant someone who was separate from the world.

"At one time, when sorely pinched, sharply squeezed, and in fear how the matter would end, I ran to a secret place and dropped on my knees before God, crying, 'Help me, Lord.' God dropped these words into my heart (what golden words they were to me!), 'Seek first the kingdom of God and His righteousness, and all other things shall be added unto you.' 'Good God, I shall be helped!' I said. I knew what Hannah felt when she went away with her countenance no more sad. Nor was mine either."

BEGGARS AND THEIR PLEAS

"What pleas men will make when they come begging! I have plenty of beggars at my door. How the various pleas they make give them a claim upon me, they think, and entitle them to get something from me. They come to the door; when I go, they say, 'I hope you will help me, sir.' 'I do not know you,' I say. 'Why, I have been living in Union Street all my life.' Along comes another: 'I wish you would help me, sir.' 'Why did you come to me? Who sent you?' 'Well, sir, I heard you were charitable and good-natured, so I thought you would give me something.' Another comes, 'Do, sir, help me. I have sat under such a minister, and I know such and such people you may know.' Along comes another: 'I don't know you,' I say. 'Why sir, I come to your chapel at times.' They think that is quite enough. They conclude these things are all claims, and that I have a right to assist them, though, you see, there is no claim in the least; yet, for the life of me, when they come with these pleas, I cannot send them away. Now, what I want to show is this: In going to the Son of God you have got a claim, you have got a plea. He has encouraged you to come. It is declared by the Holy Ghost, 'Behold the Lamb of God, which taketh away the sin of the world.'"

PRESENTATION ON HIS SEVENTIETH BIRTHDAY

On December 8th, 1878, Mr. Covell completed his seventieth year, and the members of his Church and congregation availed themselves of the opportunity to express their affection towards their pastor. The presentation consisted of an oil painting of Mr. Covell, a timepiece and stand (valued at £50), one hundred and thirty-one new sovereigns, and an illuminated address. The birthday being on Sunday, the presentation was made on the previous Friday evening. On the following Sunday morning Mr. Covell preached from Joshua 23. 14, "And, behold, this day I am going the way of all the earth: and ye know in all your hearts and in all your souls, that not one thing hath failed of all the good things which the Lord your God spake concerning you; all are come to pass unto you, and not one thing hath failed thereof." The sermon was a most impressive one, and the address that Mr. Covell gave on returning thanks for the expression of his people's kindness towards him was of a most interesting character, in which he made reference to many incidents already referred to in our narrative. Therefore space will only now allow us to give a brief extract from the address:

"Love and gratitude to the God of all my mercies, and to you, my friends, for your kindness, affection and liberality, constrain me to speak. None can tell, *none can tell*, but those who have been placed in the same pleasing position, the feelings of that man whose friends shower down blessings upon him, while he feels so unworthy and undeserving; it will sink him into nothingness. This obligation you have laid me under – and a sweet obligation it is, too – has brought me in debtor to you, never to cease lifting up my heart to God in prayer that your souls may be comforted, that He may bless you heart and soul. May God so lay me upon your hearts that you may never bow the knee in prayer but His poor servant, and your servant for Christ's sake, may be remembered by you. May you cry, 'God help him, God be with him, and assist him continually; make him faithful and affectionate. God make him a blessing to our souls.'"

A DREAM AND ITS FULFILMENT

A good man living in the country was some years ago passing through a season of trial and great exercise of mind, during which time he had a dream in which he thought himself near a palace, when a summons was brought him to go and speak to the prince. On hearing this his mind was filled with fear, feeling that he was utterly unable and unworthy to go in and speak with the prince. Just then he thought he heard Mr. Covell's name announced, which greatly relieved his anxiety, for he felt, Mr. Covell can go in and speak to the prince for me. Here his dream concluded, but a short time afterwards, while still under this exercise of mind, an opportunity was offered of going to hear Mr. Covell preach at Tonbridge. While Mr. Covell was speaking in prayer in his usual powerful manner, the good man was so overcome and favoured in his soul that he felt his dream was fulfilled and that Mr. Covell had indeed gone in and spoken to the Prince for him.

A Reminiscence of Mr. Covell

A friend has supplied the following:

"I well remember Mr. Covell telling me of a sweet visit he had from his Lord while walking in Addington Park, the grounds attached to the palace of the Archbishop of Canterbury. He said it was in his earliest days, when 'the poor tinman' (a frequent signature of his in his letters to Mr. Crouch and Mr. Pitcher) was in much trial with regard both to his business and his ministry; he walked out one evening to try to relieve his burdened soul in prayer. While in the park, pleading with God, the Lord broke in upon his trial, made it sweet, and gave him to realise more blessedly than ever before his personal interest in His covenant promises. Those who knew Mr. Covell will well understand that I am unable to convey to paper the power and sweetness with which he concluded this narrative by quoting the words, 'The righteous is more excellent than his neighbour.'

"It was chiefly in prayer that Mr. Covell excelled. He said once to me, 'I shouldn't dare to tell my people what tears I have shed over them in this chair. They talk about hearing me to profit. Pooh! I wish they would come to hear wet-eyed. I have had both hells and heavens in this room about my ministry, and the people don't know half of what it costs me.'"

Mr. Covell on the Supply System

March 9th, 1879, being collection day, Mr. Covell gave, as was his wont, an interesting and characteristic address:

"I needed no memorial of your kindness, my friends; but I have one at home (referring to his testimonial) that, when we have all passed away, and are mouldering in the dust, my children and my children's children will be enabled to look upon in proof of the union that existed between pastor and people at West Street chapel. There is a union between us that no casual supply minister can ever feel towards a people to whom he speaks only occasionally. Supplies who visit a people once in two or three months, as the case may be, cannot feel towards them, nor they towards him, as a stated minister and people feel towards each other. The supply does not yearn for them as the pastor does; he does not carry them on his heart as he moves from place to place all the year round; he cannot present them to God continually – 'Lord, bless the people.' It is not possible that the thing can exist in the heart of supplies as it does with the pastor, who tries to feed them with knowledge and with understanding, to build them up in the truth, having them on his heart and affections.

"The supply system, is therefore a bad system at the very root. I know that in some places it cannot be avoided, but in many places, I fear, the real prosperity of Zion does not lie at the hearts of the people. And something else I am almost ashamed to say – the supply system is thought by some a cheaper system. God Almighty root out such a sordid spirit. Is it likely, if cheapness be the order of the day, that real soul prosperity can exist in such a place? But I have not to say this of you, my friends. When other ministers have spoken to me of our large collections, I say to them, 'I cast my eye over your congregation and that of others, and see as much money in those congregations as in mine.' It is not the amount of money, but being willing to part with what they possess. Where there is love in the heart, it needs no exhortation to give. It is not the amount of money given, but the heart that prompts it."

CHAPTER 6

MR. COVELL'S AFFLICTED SON

In September 1879, Mr. Covell lost his eldest son, who had been greatly afflicted from childhood, and had formed a heavy burden upon the heart of his loving father for forty years. The *Gospel Echo* for February 1892 gives the following interesting narrative in reference to this afflicted son, arising out of a visit that Mr. Crouch[2] once paid to Mr. Covell. The writer says:

"A minister was preaching in London this evening, and having occasion in his remarks to refer to the thorn in the flesh, as recorded by the Apostle Paul, he named the following incident in the life of the late honoured servant of God, Francis Covell of Croydon.

"A friend called upon him during a brief visit to Croydon, and the two ministers had an enjoyable conversation upon divine things. It is well known that Mr. Covell was much favoured of God, and that he lived very near to Him in his daily life. During conversation the friend remarked that he should think his (Mr. Covell's) a very happy lot. 'You have a loving people, all you can desire in this world, and an abiding assurance of eternal blessedness in the world to come. You can have little or nothing to give you any sorrow.'

"Mr. Covell made no response to this at the moment, but before bidding his guest farewell, asked him into an adjoining room, and showed him his imbecile son, totally unfit for employment. This sad sight needed no emphasis of words to convince the visitor of the mistake he had made in his estimate of Mr. Covell's lot in life."

SERMON ON HIS SON'S DEATH

The first time Mr. Covell preached after his son's death was on September 21st, 1879. His text was: "To them who by patient

---

[2]William Crouch, pastor at Pell Green from 1818 to 1861

continuance in well-doing seek for glory and honour and immortality, eternal life" (Rom. 2. 7). In the course of his sermon he said (speaking with great feeling), "Just to show how God answers His people's prayers, although He often sorely tries their patience first, I must touch upon something in my own case. I mean my poor boy's death, though I cannot say very much about it, for it is a very tender point with me. I feel myself so weak when speaking of it that I know if I talk much about it I shall be overcome; but I must mention it to show God's great goodness and forbearance. No one knows the many petitions I have put up that God would spare me to see the dear boy's end, for I knew that nobody would care for him, and bear with him as I did, neither could anyone be expected to; but I have often kicked against it till the last three months, when I have felt such submission to the Lord's will, and that if He did take me first all would be well. And now His time was come to deliver him, and to answer my three petitions, which were – that I should be with him at the last, that a medical attendant should be also present at his death, and that he should be spared much suffering."

A Touching Interview

Mr. Wileman, in his little tract entitled, "The Dying Pillow," gives the following interesting account of his farewell interview with Mr. Covell. He says: "The last time I saw this favoured man of God was three weeks before his death. After referring to the death of his afflicted son, with his face beaming with holy joy, he said, 'And now God has answered all my requests, and I have nothing to live for but to enjoy Him. I think of a morning when I get up, if the Lord were to come and say to me, "Now, Covell, I have come," I should reply, "Here I am, any minute, Lord." It is not that I want to die to get out of trouble, not that, for I have every earthly comfort; but O to see Him! O to be near Him! O to be like Him! O to get at Him! O to bask in His smiles! O to get at the Fountain! O to have a look from His eyes, and a smile from His face! What is all below to this?'"

MR. COVELL'S CLOSING SERMON

When Mr. Covell, in his address to his congregation on the anniversary Sabbath in March 1879, said, "The end is not far off," probably neither he nor any of his hearers thought how near it was. On Wednesday evening, November 19th, 1879, he preached his last sermon, taking for his text those striking words in Psalm 120. 5, "Woe is me, that I sojourn in Mesech, that I dwell in the tents of Kedar!" The discourse was characteristic and impressive, and seemed to be uttered by one evidently on the threshold of heaven, longing, sighing, panting to be there, freed from sojourning in Mesech, no longer obliged to dwell in the tents of Kedar, but as he would often say:

"Bid a farewell to evil – a final farewell,
Shut in with my Jesus for ever to dwell."

Being reminded on his death-bed of this sermon, he said, "O, I felt as if I wanted to get through the tents, to *get through them! through them! to get to Him!*"

HIS LAST ILLNESS

On Friday, feeling great pain, he sent for his friend Dr. Evans, who at once saw the dangerous nature of the malady (intestinal displacement, causing obstruction of the bowels), and advised an operation, to which he submitted, and which was skilfully performed the same night. Just previous to the operation he clasped his hands, and raising them, offered a most fervent prayer that wisdom, skill and judgment might be given to the surgeons, and that success might follow the operation; and if not, the will of the Lord be done. But the appointed time was come, and not all the surgeons' skill and not all the people's entreaties, could turn the Lord from His purpose. He was about to fulfil the prayer of the Lord Jesus, "Father, I will that they also whom Thou hast given Me be with Me where I am, that they may behold My glory." Yet, his family and friends watched, and prayed, and hoped, but the doctor, who was fearful of the issue from the first, found his worst fears were confirmed, and that his patient was gradually sinking.

FAREWELLS

On Tuesday, November 25th, it was deemed advisable to let him see his family and other members of his church and congregation. He spoke very affectionately to each individual case. He then gave instructions as to his private affairs and funeral, and what he should like placed on his tomb. He then prayed for his people, and exhorted those around him to tell them to be kind to one another, and bear with each other's infirmities, and to take care that they fell not out by the way. "Tell them I have the comfort of it now; I never tattled from one to another." He also said, "If anyone should like to say anything about me, they might speak from these words – if the Lord should lead them to it; I have no wish to dictate to anyone: 'Remember them which have the rule over you, who have spoken unto you the Word of God: whose faith follow, considering the end of their conversation: Jesus Christ the same yesterday, and today, and for ever.' I love a private religion more than making a show, but if it will encourage any, and honour God's dear Son, and His grace and truth, they might speak a little about me, and may some poor sinner be comforted by it. Give my love to the people; tell them to bear and forbear one with another, and remember them that have the rule over them." He spoke lovingly to his deacons, giving them excellent pastoral advice. To a friend he said, "Well, Mr. M——, you've come to see a poor sinner die. What a good God mine is! You know something of Him. Seek His face, seek His face, cleave close to Him; follow hard after Him. Give my love to friend Smart [Daniel Smart of Cranbrook]; tell him I thought he would go first, but I've got the start of him. 'The last shall be first.' Good-bye. God bless you."

CHAPTER 7

Dying Sayings

Many were the sweet and precious expressions that fell from his lips during the last few hours of his life, amongst which were the following, although not given quite in the order in which they were uttered:

"The Lord is so good; I am so blessed. 'No horrors make me weep,'

> 'But now I stand where Moses stood,
> And view the landscape o'er,
> Not Jordan's stream nor death's cold flood
> Can fright me from the shore.'

I had a sight of it, a fortnight or three weeks ago, in the chapel, and I thought my body would have dropped in the pulpit then, and my soul have gone to heaven. I am a poor sensible wretch, and have nothing to rest on but the finished work and obedience of the Christ of God, and I fall into His arms, who, I believe, is taking me to heaven to sing His praise."

"Take me sweetly, lovingly; don't leave me now, Lord; the waters are ankle deep; it is hard work going up the hill; Lord Jesus, pull me into heaven. O that I were there to see Him as I have longed to see Him, and serve Him, and know Him better. I am a poor sinner, Lord; grace alone is of any use to me now. I have loved to speak of and exalt grace, and was never more happy than when encouraging sinners to trust in Thee."

"O the many blessed, happy hours I have spent with my Jesus alone – Him and me, Him and me. O the sweetness and blessedness there is in Christ Jesus."

"I would not exchange this dying bed with the Queen of England. Why! when she comes to the same place, she can have no more than I. The Queen upon the throne, the beggar in the poorhouse, and Frank Covell only want the same – that is, to have some one to wet their lips with a feather; that's all."

"What heavenly hours I have had with God in His house, in the fields, in this room! I have had a Triune God in my heart."

"I've often talked of the palm and the crown, and now I am going to have them."

"O, what a great thing to be right! What is honour, wealth, or mirth? Sooner have Paul's grace than an emperor's crown."

"I long to be with Him. I see Him behind the cloud."

"The waters are so low I can go over dryshod and without fear."

"'Say ye to the righteous, it shall be well with him.' Here's a proof of it; you can all say you have seen a proof of it. You can say you have seen a man upon a dying pillow who has nothing to do but to die."

"All is settled, and my soul approves it well."

"Safe, safe, safe! 'Saved in the Lord with an everlasting salvation.' Hallelujah, hallelujah, and now all earthly objects, however fair, farewell!"

When he moaned, being asked if he was in pain, he said, "O no, I am so happy, so happy, so happy; honour Him, praise Him, magnify Him; good God, good God; O so happy; glorious, glorious, glorious!"

After trying for some time to sleep, he said, "God so fills me with His glory and blessed presence that I cannot sleep. Queen Bess said, 'The half of my kingdom for an inch of time'; but I say, 'Make haste, my Beloved, make haste!' What a difference! and she a queen, too, while I'm only a poor sinner."

To those who stood around his bed he said, "All you have had your meals today, but I have only had my lips moistened with a feather, yet I've had the best. Is there a fire in the room?" "Yes; do you wish to see it?" "No, I've done with earthly things. I've had a sight of Jesus, and that has tarnished all, and I shall soon be gone." (His eyes were closed most of the time during his illness.)

"Just and righteous are all His ways; He makes all things work together for good. He has granted every wish of my heart; I've been dead to the world many months."

"What a hard thing it is for old nature to die! Death is a struggle – such a hill, such a hill, a long hill. Death is a penalty which all have to bear. Abraham, Isaac, Israel and the prophets had to go through it, and why should I be exempted? What a burning desire I have had for the people's welfare; what a desire to speak well for God, to encourage His people, and how often I have had God's testimony in my heart! It was not said, 'Well done, good and *successful* servant,' but 'Well done, good and *faithful* servant.'"

"I long to be with Him. I see Him behind the cloud. 'Tis hard dying, but for the many precious promises."

"All saved on the same footing. Grace, free grace, shall have all the glory. Happy man, happy man; 'Saved in the Lord with an everlasting salvation.'"

THE CLOSING SCENE

As he drew near to the end, the doctor whispered to a friend, "Pulse very low." Mr. Covell said, "What, doctor?" "You are nearing home now." He replied, "Hallelujah, Hallelujah! Grace, grace, honours to grace!"

After an interval he said again, "I'll struggle to the last to tell about grace. I've tried my voice, it tried my voice, but I did it as well as I could." The doctor said, softly, "Any conflict?" Reply – "No; a little in the night, but it was soon over; I was enabled to stand fast, the Lord was my stay. I told the enemy what the Lord had wrought in me and for me, and that will stand."

He now sank rapidly. At 10 a.m. the words could just be caught, "I'm so happy, so happy – it's all ordered well! all ordered well!"

After this he was evidently engaged in prayer. His lips moved, but no words could be understood, and at 11.15, Wednesday morning, November 26th, 1879, in the seventy-first year of his age, his soul took its flight to that happy abode, where he had so long desired to be.

> "A solemn yet a pleasing sight
> To see believers die;
> They smile and wish the world good night,
> And take their flight on high."

The church and congregation worshipping at Providence Chapel, Croydon, were filled with deep sorrow when they learned of the decease of their beloved pastor, and knew that his earnest voice, speaking words of counsel and comfort, would be heard by them no more.

MR. HAZLERIGG ON MR. COVELL

Mr. Hazlerigg preached at the chapel shortly after the beloved pastor's death, and he thus described the secret of the power which was so conspicuous in his ministry: "Your pastor," he said, "is only gone to heaven, where his heart was before. We read in the *Pilgrim's Progress* how the pilgrims came to the place where they were so ravished with the sweetness of the gardens that one felt sick of love; now it appears that your pastor felt that love sickness. Mark your late pastor. What a great deal of private religion the good man had; how much of soul communion with God; and what a man he was in prayer! It is no irreverence to say of him, that it seemed as if he would pull down a blessing from God upon his people; he was truly a mighty man in prayer; secret communion and private prayer were the secrets of his ministerial power. What a mighty man he was in the Scriptures! Then, what a blessed experience; what an experience of the plague of the heart! I have heard him speak many things about the discoveries of his heart. Then, what a heaven of pardoning mercy, righteousness, and the love of God shed abroad in his heart, he enjoyed at times. His life and conversation manifested three sweet gospel characteristics – humility, love and peaceableness. In him we have a religion before and with God, manifesting itself in a blessed gospel walk before men."

LETTER FROM THE VICAR OF ADDINGTON

Some four miles from Croydon lies the churchyard of rural Addington, where for two hundred and fifty years the Covells have had a family vault, and here it was determined to deposit the remains of the late beloved pastor, and an application was made to the Vicar that he would allow the Rev. W. L. Rolleston, Vicar of Scraptoft, Leicestershire, an old friend of Mr. Covell's, to conduct the funeral service in the churchyard.[3] To this request the Vicar forwarded the following courteous reply:

"Addington Vicarage, Croydon,

"To Mr. W. G. Covell.   November 29th.

"My Dear Sir,

In writing to you yesterday, I did not at the time associate the death of your father with that of the minister whose life and labours I have always heard spoken of with such deep respect. I should be glad to give expression, as far as I am able, to my veneration for a life devoted to the Master's service, and propose therefore, if it should meet with your wishes, to take some part in the service on Tuesday next. I shall, of course, request Mr. Rolleston to take the more solemn part at the grave itself, but if you should prefer for any reason that he should take the whole service, I trust you will not hesitate to say so. I should regret extremely that anything should be done contrary to your feelings in the matter.

"I remain, dear sir, yours very faithfully,

"Erskine W. Knollys."

THE FUNERAL SERVICE AT CROYDON

The mortal remains of Mr. Francis Covell were deposited in their last resting-place on Tuesday, December 2nd, 1879. Signs were everywhere visible in the town, throughout the forenoon, of the deep respect in which the deceased gentleman was held. All along the High Street and South End many shops were partially or entirely closed, and everybody who had known him seemed anxious to testify to the reverence in which they held his memory. Although the preliminary service was announced for twelve o'clock, in the chapel in which Mr. Covell for so many years presided, long before the hour appointed the chapel was crowded in every part. The scene was indeed mournful and oppressive; there was hardly a person present who had not attired himself or

---

[3]At that time a burial service in the church or at the grave could not be taken by a nonconformist minister.

herself in black, and the drapery round the pulpit was of the same sombre hue.

Owing to a delay through the inclement weather, it was nearly half-past twelve before the funeral procession arrived at the chapel. The coffin having been placed in the front of the pulpit, Mr. Hazlerigg commenced the solemn service. His voice was broken with emotion as he spoke of Mr. Covell as being a man whose prayers had been mighty with the Omnipotent, and the whole family of God had sustained a great loss by his death. He then read a portion of the fifteenth chapter of the first Epistle to the Corinthians.

Mr. Hull, of Hastings, offered prayer, seeking the Lord's blessing upon the sorrowing family and the mourning church and congregation.

Mr. Hatton, of Redhill, next occupied the pulpit, and in the course of an address marked with much earnestness he spoke of Mr. Covell; he alluded to his dislike and hatred of all praise, and said he felt sure that if he were listening to his words, and heard him say friend Covell was a good man, he would reply and say, "Don't say it a second time; 'by the grace of God I am what I am.'" Speaking of his charity, he said Mr. Covell was in the habit of giving away something like a pound every day of his life. He did not, when appealed to for aid, ask, "Do you come to our chapel?" but he gave away the means with which he had been blessed. He also said, I do not say, Look at our friend Covell; no, I say, Look at the grace of God in him. It is not every man that has a praying heart as he had. It is not every man who preaches the gospel and will stand for it as he did, and sacrifice things for it as he did. The Lord grant you and me more of that grace. This grace will make a good man, or a good woman, or a good child. And now we follow the remains of our dear, departed friend; his works will speak for him in this town amongst professors who would probably despise his religion. Let me tell you, to do this is to despise the cause in which he died, and by which his light shined when alive, in the presence of his God and in the presence of his people.

A favourite hymn of Mr. Covell's was then sung to a favourite tune, "Martyrdom." The hymn commences:

"At length he bowed his dying head,
And guardian angels come;
The spirit dropped its clay and fled –
Fled off triumphant home."

Mr. Hazlerigg then pronounced the Benediction, and the coffin was removed from the chapel to the hearse.

THE JOURNEY TO ADDINGTON

The crowd assembled in the street was very large, and when it was increased by those leaving the chapel, must have numbered considerably over a thousand. Two mourning coaches, filled with relatives and friends, followed the hearse, and immediately behind came about sixty vehicles, comprising carriages of all kinds. In addition to these, several hundred persons walked the entire distance. The weather was bitterly cold, and snow covered the ground, but the friends toiled determinedly along the frost-bound roads, and breasted the slippery hills and vales of the route. All honour to those who were thus zealous to brave all difficulties to show their respect for their late pastor. The mournful procession reached Addington at half-past two.

CONCLUDING SERVICES AT ADDINGTON

The pretty little church was filled to overflowing, very few of the many mourners being able to enter, Mr. Knollys, the Vicar, conducting most of the service in the church. The coffin was then taken into the churchyard and lowered into the vault. The coffin plate bore the following inscription: "Francis Covell, died November 26th, 1879, in his seventy-first year."

The service at the grave was read by Mr. Rolleston. The clergyman having concluded, many hundreds went down one by one into the vault to take a final look at the coffin in which reposed all that remains on earth of one of the most simple-minded and blameless men that ever lived in Croydon.

THE FUNERAL SERMONS

The following Sabbath funeral sermons were preached by Mr. Ashdown at Providence Chapel. The text for the occasion was the one chosen by Mr. Covell on his death-bed, Heb. 13. 7, 8,

"Remember them which have the rule over you, who have spoken unto you the Word of God: whose faith follow, considering the end of their conversation. Jesus Christ the same yesterday, and today, and for ever." During the discourse, Mr. Ashdown referred very feelingly to the loss the church had sustained, giving them wise counsel, and related many particulars of their late pastor's life and peaceful death.

Our labour of love in recording briefly the life story of Francis Covell is now finished. We regret that the details of his useful life are somewhat fragmentary, but we feel sure what has been recorded of his godly life and happy death will be commended to the hearts of spiritual readers. May the great Head of the church raise up and spiritually endow many such men as pastors in His church, and in appointing them to their spheres of labour, may one be given to fill the pastorate at Providence Chapel, Croydon, rendered vacant when Francis Covell was taken home.

EDWARD SAMUEL: 1812-1896

The most remarkable story of a converted Polish Jew.

Edward Samuel was brought up as a strict Jew but, having to flee from his native Poland, was in the providence of God led to England. During his journeying he had a few amazing escapes from death. An interesting sidelight of his account of his early days is the view we are given of Jewish life and customs.

Brought to know Jesus as the true Messiah, led to know the doctrines of grace, and convinced of believers' baptism, he became a preacher of Jesus of Nazareth, the Son of God. For many years he was a minister at Sleaford in Lincolnshire.

Sadly his account only reaches the time when he was 33 years old, and it has been difficult to find much about him during the next fifty years when "Samuel of Sleaford" became a well-known name in Strict Baptist circles.

CHAPTER 1

EARLY DAYS IN POLAND

I was born in a small town called Vinooty, in Russian Poland, on the borders of Prussia, on the 14th of the month Nisan, 1812, on the evening before the Passover. My parents were Jews, who were strictly observant of their religion, as were all my ancestors.

I have a perfect recollection of my maternal grandfather. He held the rank of Rabbi over twenty or thirty thousand Jews and, as his office and position required, was notable as a learned student in the Rabbinical writings and traditions. Among other details of his official duty was that of a judge as to things ceremonially clean or unclean, and to him was referred the decision as to alleged violations of the Sabbath. The Jews referred to him many purely civil questions as to frauds or debts and, indeed, he was so respected by the magistrates that if contending Jews and Gentiles had a cause in dispute and took it to them, they were accustomed to depute their authority to my grandfather, leaving the matter for his opinion and decision. His study was near the synagogue, and there his time was almost completely occupied.

One incident connected with my boyish history impresses the habits of my conscientious grandfather strongly upon my memory. His residence was fifteen miles from that of my parents, and I went to visit him. His study was about ten minutes walk from his private dwelling, and I proceeded thither. He had not been at home during the previous night, a circumstance which created no uneasiness, inasmuch as he had been accustomed to spend three nights in each week in that solitary retirement. It was early in the morning when I went to him to have, according to custom, his hands laid upon my head, and to receive his blessing. Instantly I perceived there was something the matter with his nose, and on inquiring what accident had befallen him, he replied, "Last night while reading, I fell asleep over the candle, burnt my nose, and set my cap on fire." Such was the zeal of my dear grandfather that he fasted two days in every week, Monday and Thursday, and every other day during one whole month in the year, the sixth month Elul, which corresponds with the latter end of August and the beginning of September. On the day of Atonement, which is a fast day, he used to deliver an oration to the congregation, clad entirely in white, wearing no shoes that day – not leaving the synagogue the whole day. His oration was so affecting that the whole congregation was in tears. I remember once witnessing it and, although only a child, not more than eleven years, was equally affected with the rest.

The day before Atonement the most respectable families used to bring their children to my grandfather that he might bless them. His custom was to visit our house once a year and spend a week, including one Sabbath, and preach on that day. Every day during his stay the Jews used to bring their little children that he might lay his hands on their heads, and bless them. In this manner I understand the words of Christ, "Suffer little children to come unto Me." Not to sprinkle, nor baptize, but to bless them.

EDWARD SAMUEL

A STRANGE PROPHECY

I remember another incident, which made such an impression on my mind that I never forgot. I was not more than nine years of age when my eldest brother, two sisters and myself were on a visit at the aforementioned grandfather's. Sitting at the dinner-table, I did something to displease my grandmother, and she, being naturally not very amiable, as I sat opposite her, stretched out her hand across the table and with great vehemency said, "Nisan" (which was my Jewish name), "as sure as I am born you will kick the bucket." This is a phrase which, though known to Englishmen as a vulgarism synonymous with death, is employed seriously by continental Jews as strongly and solely significant of what they consider to be apostasy from the truth, or a disgraceful adoption of the profession of Christianity.

My grandfather, understanding the phrase, although I did not – methinks I see him now before me – turned his face towards her with a look of the greatest disapprobation, although he was a mild and most amiable man, and whispered something to her which I did not hear. Thus she prophesied the truth. Caiaphas prophesied that there was a need for one man to die that the whole nation perish not; Balaam that there should be a star rise out of Jacob; and my grandmother that I should become a Christian. All was true, and all was accomplished, although spoken by ungodly persons; and I bless my dear Redeemer for the fulfilment of all these things. On my return home, I related the circumstance to my mother who, bursting into a flood of tears, exclaimed, "I would rather die, or follow you to the grave, than live to see that." Hearing these words, and seeing my mother so affected, I was anxious to know the meaning. At my first inquiry I met with a denial; but after many entreaties she told me, with the tears still trickling down her cheeks. Finding the meaning, I began to cry, saying, "Mother, I will never become a Gentile. No, no, not I."

SMUGGLED GOODS

My grandfather on my father's side was also very religious. He had a farm which he let, and the rent supported him. He used to sit in a house every day, close to the synagogue built for that purpose, where the learned Jews met together for the study of the Talmud and to ask each other questions. I am inclined to think that where we read of Christ meeting with the doctors, hearing and asking them questions, the allusion is to the same kind of place.

My father and mother were very young when they were married. They had twelve children, eight of whom were living when I left my native country. My father was a wholesale woollen draper. The goods were all smuggled from Prussia, as in my country it was not considered any disgrace, or contrary to the Jewish religion, as all the towns on the Prussian territories did the same. My father went four times a year to Memel and Konigsburg, seaport towns of Prussia, to purchase his goods, from thence conveying them to Peterburgh and Moscow. He was generally from home about two months at a time, and sometimes longer. We kept four fine horses, and a man as driver, for some years. My father was very prosperous and accumulated a great deal of money; but, before I left home, we were reduced in circumstances. He was taken in Russia by the Kossacks (who are on the look-out) with the smuggled goods, lost all, and it cost a great deal of money beside to set him at large again.

BLIND EYES OPENED

I was the fourth child. When an infant, I had the smallpox and measles together, through which for a time I lost my sight. I remember my mother saying that the doctor who attended me said I should not recover, and if I did, I must remain blind; which I did for twelve months. One summer's day, the servant took me out for a little air. As she was walking in the street with me in her arms, an old Gentile woman, as she passed by, cast her eyes upon me; she stopped and asked the servant what was amiss with the child's eyes. The servant replied that I was blind through the smallpox. The old woman said, "I could cure him." The servant replied, "If you can, you will be well rewarded," but also told her that she doubted her ability, as her mistress had had many medical men, and they could do nothing for the child. "However, if you will go with me, I will hear what my mistress says."

When my mother saw the girl coming and the old woman behind her, she was rather frightened, as the Jews in my country consider that many of the old Gentile women are witches. The servant told her what had passed in the street between the old woman and herself. My mother then asked the old woman how this cure was to be effected, whether by magic or witchery. If that was the way, she would have nothing to do with her. She replied, No, that she would use simple means in her presence. My mother told her to call again in three or four days. Her motive for this delay was to write to her father to ask the lawfulness of it. The answer she received from her father was to this effect that it was lawful, providing that the woman did not kneel down to pray, or use any form of words, and my mother took good care to follow her father the Rabbi's counsel.

On the third day, the old woman came, and my mother told her if she could cure me, she should be handsomely rewarded. She affirmed she could. If it will not be too tedious to my reader, I will relate the means the woman used, whereby the cure was effected. She asked for a pewter plate, a piece of clean linen rag and a lighted candle. She then took the piece of linen rag in the presence of my mother, set light to it, and put the lighted rag upon the back of the pewter plate. After the rag was consumed, it left on the plate a kind of yellow moisture; this she took with a feather and applied to the skin which was grown over my sight, and continued the same once a day for about a fortnight when, at the expiration of that time, I could see, although it left a great weakness behind which I expect to carry to my grave.

This weakness of sight the Lord left to remind me of the superstition of the Jewish religion – the goodness of my covenant God in directing the means – His knowledge of past, present and future. He knew what He intended to do with me – to call me by divine grace, to send me to preach the everlasting gospel, which requires much reading; therefore, in His infinite mercy, He was pleased to restore my sight. Often I am overwhelmed with gratitude to the dear Lord in reading the Word, and especially since writing this little work, discovering so much weakness in my sight, for His goodness in blessing me with the little I have – knowing that, if He sees fit, He can strengthen it still more. It has many times brought me to a throne of grace, to thank Him for the past recovery and to pray for a continuation of the same.

The circumstances of my case I remember my mother relating many times.

RESCUED FROM DEATH

One Sabbath morning, going to the synagogue by myself, clad in my best, there was a lime pit full of water with a plank in it, and being but a child, I began to play with it and tumbled in. I could not cry for fright. I struggled until my strength was exhausted, and at last sank down. The water again brought me to the top, when an old Jew with a long beard, a neighbour, going to the synagogue, seeing some one in the pit ran to it as I was just sinking the second time, and took me out for dead and conveyed me home. All thought I was dead; the usual remedies for persons apparently dead from drowning were resorted to, and I recovered. Here was a brand "plucked from the fire," as well as literally from death by drowning. Had I died, what would have become of my soul? I must have eternally perished.

O the watchful eye of a covenant God over His dear children, even when in nature's darkness! He watches them in a peculiar way, as soon as they come from the womb of their mother. He follows them up step by step to preserve them, because they are a people whom He has chosen to show forth His praise; and this they do when they are taught by the Spirit of God. They praise Him for electing and adopting love. O for a heart to love Him, for a tongue to proclaim the riches of his grace! Here I have another Ebenezer to erect; first, He restored my sight and after that my life.

CHAPTER 2

A Remarkable Escape

It is a custom among the respectable Jews in my country at the Passover and Feast of Tabernacles to have a number of poor Jews out of the hospital, according to their circumstances, to celebrate with them those festivals. It was the day of preparation for the Passover; my father being from home, my mother went to the hospital to select three poor Jews, and brought them home with her. She asked one of them to go to the garden and dig up horseradish for bitter herbs to eat with the paschal lamb. I was very delighted not having to go to school; also, with it being the Passover, I made myself very busy, as on that day they clear out all the leaven from their premises. Generally two persons are engaged. One has a lighted wax candle, and the master of the house has a wooden spoon in the one hand and a quill in the other, searching every corner for leaven crumbs. Previous to that they put small pieces of bread in various parts of the house, which are gathered up with the spoon and quill. They then tie them up carefully in a piece of clean white rag, and kindle a fire purposely to burn the leavened bread, spoon and quill together. The reason the fire is kindled purposely is that it is not to be used for anything else. It was very pleasing to me as a boy to see my dear father search for the leaven. In case of my father being away from home, another male must take his place; he was away on the occasion I am alluding to. Our holy apostle speaks of "leaven" of a different nature, the "leaven of malice and wickedness." This leaven the Spirit of God only can remove.

But to return. Overhearing what my mother said to the man about digging the horseradish for bitter herbs to eat with the paschal lamb, which is a piece of lamb roasted, I went to the man and asked him whether he would allow me to go with him, which he did. The snow lying on the ground, he took a shovel and axe, went to the garden, removed the snow, and with the axe was going to loosen the earth, it being at that time very hard. I was about to

187

take up a piece of the horseradish when he let down the axe on my head. Seeing what he had done, he ran off and left me insensible and wallowing in blood. My grandfather saw me from the window, ran out and brought me in, thinking I was dead. A medical man was immediately sent for who, when he came, gave little hopes of my recovery; but, should I recover, to all probability I would be a lunatic. Here again I was plucked like a brand from the jaws of corporeal and eternal death. Little thought I then what the paschal lamb and the bitter herbs shadowed forth! Blessed be God for an experimental knowledge of both! The great Apostle of the Gentiles explains the meaning: "Christ our Passover is sacrificed for us," and the herbs are the sufferings for the profession of Christ. "He that will live godly in Christ Jesus shall suffer persecution. If so be that we suffer with Him, that we may be also glorified together."

RABBINICAL TEACHING

I was educated from a child in the Mishna and Talmud, and also read the Old Testament, but this was only a secondary consideration; the former was the principal. When seven years of age I could repeat from memory the whole book of Psalms and the Song of Solomon. I deliberately repeat this in the face of the fact that I have reason to believe there are individuals who have ignorantly expressed their doubts of its truthfulness. No well-informed Jew would stumble for a moment at such a statement. Every Jew knows, or *ought to know,* that the Jewish youth (at least on the continent) are NOT interdicted from *reading* the Song of Solomon. But my ignorant critic is thus far right, that the teachers of youth in the schools are prohibited from taking that book in its due course for exposition until the age of thirty is reached. A similar incredulity has been manifested as to what I have said respecting the Book of Psalms. I would desire those, who doubt the possibility of such a thing, to ask any intelligent Jew as to the ordinary recitation of the long 119th Psalm by the women of the Jewish community at certain periods in every married woman's history.

I proceed with my history. At nine years of age I had daily to learn three or four pages of the Talmud, which consists of questions and answers of the various Rabbis. At my grandfather's annual visit, he always examined us boys to ascertain what progress we had made through the year. I recollect that once in my presence he told my father that I should become a Rabbi. My father expressed and manifested his pleasure at the thought. However, it was rather an unfortunate remark for me, for it served as the reason for keeping me more closely to my lessons. But God had something better for me in store. He has raised me to a higher dignity than that. He has made me a king and priest unto the living God, and put me among His family, although unworthy of the least of His mercies. O! the depth of the riches of His divine grace!

LEAVING HOME

I continued at school until I was about sixteen, when a circumstance transpired in providence that I left home. The cause of my leaving home was fearing that I should be forced to be a soldier.

When Alexander, the Emperor of Russia, was on the throne, he took no Jews in the military service; he was rather a friend to the Jews than otherwise. After his death, Nicholas, his brother, succeeded him. After his coronation he issued a law compelling Jews to serve in the army and navy. This law was a terror to all the Jews in his dominions. The reason was that they must eat and drink those things which were prohibited by the law of God to them as a nation, break the Sabbath day, violate other festivals and, indeed, deny their whole religion. They would rather die, or even follow their children to the grave, than see them turn from their religion. This I had painfully to know when called by divine grace. The law obliged them to serve from fourteen years of age; they were sent to academies, where they were trained for the army or navy according to their abilities. The method they had of taking the Jews was so many from a thousand, and the heads of the synagogues were obliged to return the numbers. At first they took the lower order but, as already said, the town we lived in was small; therefore they were soon picked out. I witnessed at sundry times, when these young men were sent away, that the cries and lamentations of their parents and relations were most distressing, and almost heart-rending. I remember on one occasion being so affected that I fainted away. They rend their garments on these occasions as if mourning for the dead.

After the lower class were picked out, it of course came to the more respectable families, which was done by casting lots; and, knowing that sooner or later it must come to our turn, my grandfather advised that I and a brother, a little younger, should quit the country. My eldest brother, being married, was exempt, and the other too young. When this law was issued, there was also another law passed, not to give any passports for males from fourteen years of age to twenty, to prevent them leaving the country. I have known fine young men chop one and two fingers off from their right hand to disable them from service.

At length it was resolved that we should leave home for the purpose of going to Konigsburg in Prussia. As there were no passports allowed, we left in the middle of the night – a banker's son, myself and brother. It is a night much to be remembered by me, my grandfather and grandmother, father and mother, brothers and sisters, all weeping. My grandfather, who was seventy years of age, with a long white beard, placed his hands on our heads and, with tears trickling from his eyes, pronounced a blessing. Some of the words I have not forgotten, although so many years since. The words were these: "May the God of our fathers Abraham, Isaac and Jacob bless and preserve you, protect and defend you from all harm, keep you in His fear, help you to study His laws, strengthen you to obey Him, nor suffer you to forsake Him." The last words were these: "If you forsake the Lord, He will forsake you; but, if you cleave to Him, He will cleave to you." They then kissed us all affectionately, wishing us the presence of the Lord, and bade us farewell.

Now began the prophecy of my grandmother to be fulfilled, that I should forsake the Jewish religion. My spiritual birth was appointed by God to be in London: place, means and time are all by His divine appointment. His will cannot be counteracted, nor His counsels disannulled: "My counsel shall stand, and I will do all My pleasure." As London was to be the place, so death and hell could not obstruct the way. "O! the depth of the riches, both of the wisdom and knowledge of God! How unsearchable are His judgments, and His ways past finding out!"

CHAPTER 3

ESCAPE FROM POLAND

We left home at midnight in disguise, a banker's only son, my brother and myself. A kind of chaise, with two horses belonging to the banker, and four men were waiting outside the town to convey us to a village, fifteen miles from the town, joining the Prussian territories, to the house of a Gentile, where were waiting twelve men with guns and pistols to escort us into Prussia, which at that place is separated from Russia by a deep valley. This valley was watched by Cossacks; about every five miles there was a cottage or kind of station, from which stations they rode to and fro. The people of the village had a perfect knowledge of the movements of these patrols; when one had passed, there was about a half hour's interval, which time we embraced for crossing the valley. Here time might not be lost as the danger was very great. If these patrols overtook any person and resistance was made, they were allowed to shoot them dead on the spot.

From the cottage before mentioned we prepared to encounter the danger of which we were sensible. As we advanced towards the valley, two men of our company were previously placed on the lookout when, at their signal, we had to run as fast as possible. But we three boys, with fright and fatigue, could not run as fast as the rest; therefore we were sometimes carried, and sometimes dragged. After we had crossed the valley, there was a small mountain to climb. When arrived at the top we were safe – which we scarcely reached, when we saw a patrol galloping on his horse after us as fast as he could, but he was just about three minutes too late.

On the Prussian side there were six men waiting for us with a waggon and fire-arms. When they saw us on the top, they all cried with one voice, "All right"; and great was our joy, as it was the first time we had heard a voice since we left the cottage, being compelled to cross the valley without speaking. While writing, methinks I can see myself in the valley running; sometimes falling down, sometimes dragged by one, and then by another. Thus my pilgrimage began with danger, and is still encompassed with the same. Being in an enemy's land, I had to watch then; but much more now, as the danger is greater, the greatest enemies being within. Well may the Son of God say, "What I say unto you, I say unto all, Watch." It is no small mercy to be kept from carnal security and false peace. That covenant God who has delivered me doth deliver and I trust will continue to the end. Thus, dear reader, I have traced the cause of my leaving the land of my nativity, not to return again, and my arrival on the borders of Prussia.

We will now proceed on our journey to Konigsburg. We remained that night at the first village in Prussia, in the house of one of those Prussian men who were waiting for us. It is true, we all three went to bed in one room, but we had no sleep; there was a candle burning in the room, and we were talking during the remainder of the night. Now and then a secret tear stole from our eyes; again one would burst into a flood of tears, and the others follow. On the one hand, we were leaving affectionate and weeping parents and friends, and on the other we had to face an unknown world. These things would alternately pass, and repass in our minds; sometimes we encouraged each other by saying, we were young, and we will go to England, and make our fortunes. Thus passed the first night.

The next morning we were conveyed to a small town. The man took us to an inn where my dear father was accustomed to put up, and was well known. We had letters of recommendation from my father and grandfather; so also had the young man with us from his relatives. This little town was a place where the Russian and Polish Jew merchants used to resort, it being situated on the borders of both kingdoms. At this inn there were two merchants going to Memel. Seeing us youths respectable looking, they enquired from whence we came, and where we were going. We told them, and showed them our letters. One directly replied that he knew my father well, and had heard of my grandfather. We also told them that we had no passport, and that we were going to Konigsburg to an uncle of my mother's, with the expectation that he would get us a passport to England.

After this conversation he left us for a couple of hours, and then returned and told us it was dangerous to travel without a passport; and that if we would go with him to Memel, he would take care of us, and see us safe to Konigsburg. We thanked him, and were very pleased to accept such a benevolent offer. With this he immediately set off to the Burgomaster, and had our names inserted on his passport as his servants. When he returned and told us, our spirits were raised, as we were quite out of danger. Through the kindly aid of this merchant we arrived safe at my uncle's at Konigsburg, leaving, by the advice of my father, my brother at Memel.

A Dreadful Disappointment

Having obtained a passport through the interest of my uncle, Israel and I (this was the young man's name) left Konigsburg on foot for Frankfort-on-the-Oder, in which place we stayed a fortnight. It is the custom for all strangers who enter the town to stay one night, or more, to deliver their passports to the Burgomaster, and when they leave, they are returned to them. When we called for our passports, the Burgomaster addressed himself to me, saying I must return to my native country as I was a runaway, and specified on my passport to that effect; at the same time Israel received his passport to enable him to pursue his journey. This news so terrified me that I could say nothing; but after I left the office, I charged my companion with informing against me, and he confessed that he had done so the day before. Thus we parted, and I told him that his sin would find him out, and that God would punish him, as I was the means of getting him his passport; and in the end it was so. He committed suicide a few years afterwards in London.

The thought of returning home by myself, and the treachery of my companion, filled me with such horror and distress that for a whole day I neither ate nor drank, and did nothing but cry. Having my phylacteries and Hebrew prayer book with me, also remembering the advice of my grandfather, I prayed to the God of Israel to support, strengthen and deliver me, as I was young and in a strange country. This going back reminds me of my spiritual pilgrimage. Sometimes I feel that I am advancing in the divine life, pressing homeward towards the heavenly Canaan; while at other times, alas, I feel I am going backward, and have to go over the same ground step by step, mourning as I go by reason of sin and darkness of soul. The holy apostle had to go to Rome to preach the everlasting gospel; and although his journey was rough, yet he arrived safely. This was my case; I had to preach the everlasting gospel in England, therefore nothing could hinder. Satan is permitted to do many things, but the Lord works all for the good of His people.

But to return. Through the covenant mercy of my God, I again reached my uncle's at Konigsburg, who at the sight of me was greatly surprised. He told me to be easy, as he would get me another passport, which he did. I then stayed with my uncle a month, after which I informed him that I should like to proceed on my journey towards England. He advised me to go to Dantzic by water, kindly paid my fare, and provided me with every necessity for my journey.

IN PERIL BY SEA

There is a certain path we must tread, ordered by the God of Providence. Mine was to be a trying one, therefore I could not escape appointed trouble any more by sea than by land. On crossing the Gulf of Dantzic we encountered a violent storm. The vessel was loaded with wheat, which was all obliged to be cast into the sea. The main mast and rudder were destroyed, and the captain discovered a leak in the vessel, so that sailors and passengers had to pump alternately, day and night, expecting every moment to sink. There were a great number of adult passengers of both sexes, and some children, whose cries and lamentations were heart-rending. They were all strangers to me, and I had to keep my peculiar grief to myself. The captain told us there was no hope of escape; we must perish. The signal of distress was hoisted. One night we were informed that a vessel was approaching us, which afforded no small joy; but, alas, it was but short, it was a mistake. The next morning the captain told us that we were drawing near to a port, where we should most likely meet with vessels; the same day a vessel came to our assistance, and all the passengers were taken on board. When we got on board we began to feel the effects of fright and want of food; many, with myself, were very ill. But at length we arrived safely at Dantzic. The day after we arrived at Dantzic, I heard that the vessel had sunk. Here again I have cause to erect an Ebenezer to my covenant God and Father who once more plucked me like a brand from that abyss where hope never cometh.

My dear reader, since I was quickened by the Spirit of God, my soul has had to encounter many storms. Often I am tossed with tempests, and not comforted; sometimes with the storms of indwelling sin and corruption; sometimes with doubts and fears, almost despairing of life. At other times with darkness, and the hidings of God's countenance, shut up and cannot come forth. Sometimes with presumption and pride, which makes me exclaim, "Save me, O God, for the waters are come into my soul; I sink in deep mire, where there is no standing. I am come into deep waters, where the floods overflow me." How distressing it is to a living soul when he cannot feel his standing upon the Rock of eternal ages, and no promise applied by the Spirit of God to the soul. These things I have to experience; tossed sometimes by the north wind, and at other times by the south. But hitherto hath the Lord helped me, blessed be His name!

I stayed in Dantzic a month. I resolved to see a little of the country, instead of taking a direct course to England. Having heard of Leipsic, I made up my mind to go there, and proceeded thither on foot. My journey to Leipsic made an impression on my mind never to be forgotten. Arriving one Friday afternoon at a small town to spend the Sabbath (Saturday), as it is prohibited to travel on that day, I went in the evening to the synagogue, and met a very kind reception by my brethren Jews. One, a very rich man, the head of the synagogue, invited me to spend the Sabbath with him. The next day, among other conversation, he enquired where I was going. I told him to Leipsic. He then said if I would stay until Monday, which was market day, I could cross a river, as there were vessels plying to and fro which would save me a day's journey. I thanked him, and took his advice.

FURTHER TRIALS

On the Monday evening I proceeded to the water side, and took my place in a vessel. There were only a few very rough fellows in the vessel, and they were intoxicated. The men, seeing by my dress that I was a Jew and a foreigner, began first to tease and then ill use me; they at last resolved to throw me into the river, and they would have done so had it not been for the interference of the manager. When we arrived on the other side, we got out, and they all walked off and left me. I felt too ill to walk, and it being late at night, I remained all that night on the river side. It was the summer season.

Early in the morning a gentleman, taking his walk on the river side, came to me, and seeing me very ill, asked me how I came there. I related to him the circumstances. He was a Jew, and recognised me as one. He took me to his house, and there I remained for a full month under medical treatment, with little hope of my recovery. Here again I was plucked from the jaws of death. Upon the mount of danger the dear Lord appeared; His ways are past finding out. The holy apostle speaks of perils of robbers, and I have experienced somewhat of the same, both literally and spiritually. Sin! O what a robber it is! It robs me daily of my heavenly comforts, it robs me of the manifested presence of my dear Redeemer. Satan is another robber, who also spoils my heavenly peace. The world is another robber, who steals my better joys. I feel that I am in danger of these robbers daily. I am sensible if it were not for the power of God the Holy Ghost keeping me every moment, I should fall a victim, and bring a disgrace upon the dear Redeemer's name and cause.

I will again return to my subject. The gentleman in whose house I stayed found out the manager of the boat, and threatened him that if he did not give up the names of the parties who had behaved so cruelly, he must be responsible. Being afraid of the consequence, he delivered their names; this gentleman wished me to appear against them, but I refused. Being at that time better, I wished to proceed on my journey.

CHAPTER 4

BARON ROTHSCHILD

Having left that memorable spot, where I had realised the goodness of God in restoring my health and providing me with friends, I, like my forefather Abraham, removed my tent, not having a foot of ground my own, not journeying towards the land of promise, but to Leipsic. When I arrived there, it was the great annual fair. This journey was mixed with joy and sorrow; not all pleasure, neither all trouble. Here again I pitched my tent for a month. The sight of this great fair was wonderful to me, as I was informed there were merchants from almost all parts of the world. Here for the first time I met with one of my countrymen who knew me at home. Here also for the first time I saw an Englishman; I thought them very proud and haughty. Nothing particular occurred during my stay here that would interest my reader.

My countryman and I agreed to take a journey to Frankfort-on-the-Maine. One morning, drawing near a town, we saw a large concourse of people. I enquired the cause of this great assembly, and was informed that a man was to be beheaded for drowning a young woman with whom he kept company. I and my companion went to behold this awful execution. So terrific was the sight that I hope never to see the same again, and for some time after I could not enjoy my food.

At length we arrived at Frankfort-on-the-Maine. The journey from Leipsic to this place was more pleasant than any since the loss of my first companion. The wise man says, "Two are better than one," and so I found it. At this place we stayed for a time. Here I had an interview with the late Baron Rothschild, uncle to the present Rothschild of London. Although he was a very great man, and immensely rich, yet he was very unostentatious. His pew in the synagogue, contrary to the usual custom, was among the poor, instead of being in the highest place. My dress, youth and devout manner during the service attracted his attention. On coming out of the synagogue he requested a gentleman who was with him to invite me to him. He enquired from whence I came, and wished me to call on him the day after the Sabbath, which is Sunday; and of course I did not forget my engagement. My companion told me that my fortune was already made, but it did not prove so exactly.

According to appointment I went to his house, and delivered his card which he had given me, with my name, to the porter. After I was admitted, the grandeur of the house made me feel very awkward. Presently the baron and another gentleman made their appearance. This gentleman was a Rabbi whom the baron kept in his house. The baron told me not to be afraid of answering the questions this gentleman would put to me. These words made me tremble, not knowing what was coming. My dear reader, you may depend it was not about the Lord Jesus Christ, neither His blood and righteousness. The questions were these: the cause of my leaving home, and what I had studied at school. The Rabbi brought a large folio of the Talmud, and catechised me from it. I answered to the best of my ability, and they both appeared pleased; the baron told me I was a good boy, and that pleased me. He then enquired where I was bound for. I replied to England. He also asked me where I was staying. Having informed him, he left the room for a few minutes, and brought me a note to give to my host, the purport of which was that he would bear all my expenses during my stay, at the same time wishing me to call again, which I did in the course of a few days. Thus the Lord provided a friend for me here. All hearts are in His hands, and all at His divine disposal.

As I was to come to England, the Lord again interposed in providing a friend at least twelve months before I needed it. Having occasion to call on a gentleman at a place where Jewish merchants resort, while I was talking with the said gentleman, there was another standing by, a friend of the party with whom I was speaking. Hearing our conversation, he afterwards addressed himself to me. The usual questions were put to me – whence I came and where I was going, and my reply was as usual. He gave me his address, and asked me to call upon him in the evening at his apartments, which I accordingly did. Then he asked me whether I had any letters from home; I replied in the affirmative, and gave them to him. When he had read them he returned them to me with his card, and said, "If you come to Rotterdam, call upon me, and I will pay your passage to London." O, how great are the bounties of heaven! Not only are our present needs supplied, but also supplies are provided for the future. Here again, I can recognize the extraordinary interposition of a covenant God in so bountifully bestowing temporal riches for an unseen end upon one who was an enemy and a rebel to Him. "Herein is love, not that we loved God, but that He loved us, and sent His Son to be the propitiation for our sins." "Ye have not chosen Me, but I have chosen you, and ordained you that ye should go and bring forth fruit, and that your fruit should remain."

FURTHER PERILS

My companion and I began to think of leaving Frankfort-on-the-Maine, but not agreeing as to the route we should take, we separated. Here the reader must not expect either minuteness of detail, either as to time or order, as I never kept a diary, neither had any thought that my history would ever appear in print. I will only mention the principal cities that I have seen, as Brunswick, Berlin, Hanover, Brandenburg, Hamburg, in short almost the length and breadth of Germany; from thence to Copenhagen in Denmark, and Stockholm in Sweden, and some parts of Holland. I remember one remarkable interposition of providence during my travels in the above-mentioned places, but the name of the precise spot I do not remember. Once being overtaken by night, I got into a wood, and through confusion and fright could not find my way out, and so remained all night expecting every moment to be destroyed by wild beasts. After longing for the morning, and being spared to welcome its approach, I spied an apple tree; feeling very hungry, I climbed the tree, which was very high. I was just in the act of taking some fruit, when a branch gave way, and down I came, where I remained for a length of time, to my own apprehension, lifeless. On recovering, I scarcely knew where I was. Being never without my phylacteries and prayerbook, I put the former on, and opening the book said my morning prayers, crying bitterly to the Lord to deliver me from this wood.

The dear Lord soon appeared. Between ten and eleven in the forenoon, while walking about almost frightened at my own shadow, I heard a footstep. Pausing for a moment as to what I should do, I resolved to approach in the direction of the sound. I had not walked many paces when I met a tall stout man with an axe on his shoulders. At seeing him I began to cry. I spoke to the man in German, and he in a language that I could only understand here and there a word. He spoke in evident kindness, and told me I had advanced between four and five miles in the wood, and that he would put me in the right way to find the road out. He appeared to understand all I said, and kindly took from a very clean bag a piece of nice bread, and gave it me, and also walked with me a full hour. At length he put me in a path, and told me if I kept in that path it would bring me to a village. Here, again, I can say with the holy apostle, "In perils in the wilderness, in hunger and fastings, often." And at this present moment I feel I am still in the wilderness. O! how often do I feel bewildered in my soul, full of confusion and perplexity; how solitary and lonely do I find the way to eternal bliss! Often do I long for the morning star to dawn upon my soul, and for the Sun of Righteousness to arise with healing in His wings, to scatter the clouds, and dissipate the fogs that have gathered through the long night.

But to return. Through divine protection, I arrived in Holland, pursuing my journey direct to Rotterdam. On my way I was attacked with fever, which laid me aside for a month; part of the time I was very dangerously ill. When only partially recovered I had a relapse, with severe affection of the brain, those about me expecting every moment I should breathe my last. When I was sensible, I used to talk with them about my father and mother and home. My thought of dying, in the absence of my dear parents, was then very painful to me. Here once again, I was plucked from the jaws of temporal and eternal death.

A Friend in Need

Having arrived at Rotterdam, I made enquiry for the gentleman who gave me his card at Frankfort-on-the-Maine. The landlord told me that he did not think I should get admittance as he was one of the richest bankers in that part, and that his residence was about two miles from the town. However, the day following, I went to see this gentleman. When I came to the lodge, I delivered the card and my name; also the same when I came to the house, where I gained admittance. The gentleman instantly recognized me, and shook hands very heartily, saying he was glad to see me arrive safe at his house. His carriage was just waiting at the door to take him out; he observed he was rather in a hurry, having some pressing engagement. He enquired where I was staying – I told him; he then said, "I will send my footman with you to take you to another place," and invited me to dine with him in the evening.

Accordingly, I went at six o'clock, when he introduced me to his lady and three daughters, remarking, "This is the little Pole of whom I was telling you." At the dinner table the lady said, "We shall expect you to dine with us every day during your stay at Rotterdam." Accordingly, on the following day I dined with them again. Of course my reader will understand that this banker was a strict Jew. At the dinner table he asked me whether I should like to remain at Rotterdam. If I would remain, he would see me provided for. I thanked him warmly, but told him my mind was fixed upon proceeding to England. He answered that England was a very wicked place and that, if I took his advice, I should stay there. However, finding that he could not persuade me to remain, he said I might stay as long as I liked, and he would bear all my expenses and, when I wished to go, I might let him know. I stayed about a month, in some partial indecision of purpose, and then told him I should like to leave. He replied that he was very sorry indeed. My refusing to remain at Rotterdam I can now attribute only to the overruling power of God, who had appointed London as my spiritual birthplace. "There are many devices in a man's heart; nevertheless the counsel of the Lord that shall stand."

EDWARD SAMUEL

ENGLAND AT LAST

The day arrived for my leaving Rotterdam. The banker paid my fare to London, in the first-class cabin. When I left him, he told me to write and let him know how I was getting on, and whether I felt inclined to return. But I never wrote, therefore heard no more from him. My voyage from Rotterdam to London I have reason to remember, inasmuch as the vessel was wrecked, and I escaped in a similar manner as on a former occasion. Here, again, through the free grace of God, I was plucked as a brand from eternal burning. I have read many times the 107th Psalm with pleasure, and I trust with profit to my soul. "They mount up to heaven, they go down again to the depths: their soul is melted because of trouble. . . . Then they cry unto the Lord in their trouble, and He bringeth them out of their distresses. He maketh the storm a calm, so that the waves thereof are still. Then are they glad because they be quiet; so He bringeth them unto their desired haven. Oh that men would praise the Lord for His goodness, and for His wonderful works to the children of men!"

Through the goodness of the Lord I was brought safely to London.

CHAPTER 5

ARRIVAL IN ENGLAND

Soon after my arrival in England, my brother that I left at Memel (who remained there by the advice of my father) came also to England, and we met at Bristol, and a happy meeting it was. We commenced business in the jewellery trade, and travelled a great deal round that neighbourhood.

A few months after we had commenced business, I was taken ill at Bristol, and went into the infirmary. It proved to be another attack of fever. It so happened that the physician could speak German; here again the Lord provided me another very kind friend. He told me he would watch over my case, and do all in his power to restore me to health. One Saturday I was very ill indeed. My brother came to see me, and finding me so ill, sat by the bed side and wept. Just at this time the physician entered. He told him I was dangerously ill, but desired him not to weep, assuring him he would do the best to restore me. This kind physician would often sit a quarter of an hour or more talking to me, and comforting me.

One evening I was bled. The next morning I put my phylacteries[1] upon the same arm from which I had been bled, and tying them rather tightly, the blood began to gush out. The nurse, seeing this, came and tried to take them from me; I resisted, and told her I would rather bleed to death than give way. I struggled hard, but she overcame me. Thus much for a superstitious and natural religion. I would rather have died than have given up my phylacteries. What an infinite mercy to be delivered from a natural religion! Nothing short of the power of the Holy Ghost can do it.

---

[1] See Matt. 23. 5. These phylacteries were small cases containing strips of parchment on which were written four passages of Scripture. They were bound on the forehead and the arm according to the Jewish understanding of Exod. 13. 16.

O how rich, free and sovereign is the grace of God! When the physician came I told him how cruelly I had been used by the nurse, and related to him the circumstance, and of course she told her tale. The physician told her that she ought to use kindness, not force, knowing I was a foreigner and a Jew. The Lord was pleased to bless the means to my recovery; therefore I left the infirmary. Thus the watchful eye of the Great Shepherd of Israel was upon me when a blasphemer.

My brother and I leaving Bristol, we travelled in various parts of the country, and so strict were we in our religion that we went for three and four months at a time without tasting animal food, not being within the reach of a Jewish butcher, living chiefly on fish, eggs, bread and butter, as cheese is also prohibited. We had at the different inns where we put up our own saucepans and such like utensils, with our names written in Hebrew in the inside, to prevent their being used by any one beside ourselves. This way of living undermined our constitutions.

My brother and I lived on most affectionate terms; we were as one soul. On one occasion my brother had to go to London, leaving me in Wiltshire. While in London, hearing a great deal about America, he made up his mind to go there, and wrote to me to that effect. I wrote to him saying, I would go with him if he would meet me at Warminster in Wiltshire. I was obliged to leave Warminster on business for a fortnight and left my address with my landlord with a message that if my brother should come, to give him my address that he might write to me, and I would return immediately. Soon after I had left, my brother came to Warminster but the landlord lost or mislaid my address; therefore he could not write to me. He stayed a week and, finding that I did not return, was obliged to leave for Liverpool as the vessel in which he had engaged a passage sailed at a certain time.

On my return to Warminster my landlord told me what had transpired and that my brother was gone. This was the greatest trial that I had ever experienced, even greater than my first leaving home, as I never expected to see him again. The first few days I ate but little, and did not sleep at all; my rebellion was very great under this providence. I made an attempt twice or three times to follow him, but each time something occurred to prevent me. Here, my dear reader, I can see the mysterious ways of God's providence, and can say with the poet Cowper,

> "God moves in a mysterious way,
> His wonders to perform,
> He plants His footsteps in the sea
> And rides upon the storm."

The angel of the everlasting covenant watched over me by land and sea, like the Israelites of old in the wilderness, brought me to England, and then watched over me that I should not leave this country, and the reason we shall see, as we go on in our narrative.

A BITTER TRIAL

My brother had left England about eighteen months when I came to London on business. Calling one morning at a Jewish eating-house, I sat down at a table where two gentlemen were seated at the opposite end. I heard one say to the other that he had just come from New York. Hearing that, and knowing my brother was there, I listened more attentively – when he went on to say that the same week he left New York for England, a very shocking occurrence took place; that a young man whom he knew well was burnt to death, and that he had a brother in England. The other gentleman enquired his name. Hearing my brother's name mentioned, I immediately fell from my seat, and fainted away. When I recovered I told them he was my brother; the American seeing the effect it had on me, tried to withdraw his statement, but finding he could not, he related the whole circumstance.

It appeared that when my brother arrived at New York, he joined in partnership with another Jew in a large business in which they were very prosperous. One evening my brother and his partner had been to the theatre, and had had a little too much to drink; they retired each to their separate sleeping rooms, and it is supposed that my brother forgot to put out his candle, and in consequence the house was set on fire. The rest of the inmates escaped, but he was burnt to death. The gentleman told me that he left a good deal of property, as it was all insured, and that if I went to America I could claim it. But I felt too much oppressed with grief to trouble myself about his property. The death of my dear brother brought me into a low, desponding state for six months, so that I could scarcely attend to business.

There is one circumstance more I will mention that took place before the Lord called me by divine grace. I met with a French Jew at Dover, whom I took into partnership. We kept a small vehicle, and one morning leaving Dover for Folkestone, there being a very steep hill to descend, I got out, and wished my partner to do the same, but he would not. He went at a rapid rate down the hill, was turned out, and broke his arm. I stayed with him about a week after, and went to London on business, of course, leaving with him all my property. During my absence, he collected in all the money he could that was owing to us in the neighbourhood, came to London unknown to me, sold off all the stock, chaise and all, and went off to France, leaving me almost destitute. Thus the Lord did not suffer me to enjoy the world when I tried all that lay in my power to do so. Indeed, I promised myself many great things, but the Lord crossed me in everything. He had something better in store for me, imperishable riches, life eternal and a crown that fadeth not.

When I take a retrospect, I cannot but admire the goodness of the Lord, and can truly say, "He has done all things well." O the long-suffering of God in bearing so long with my ill-manners, and taking so much pains, in order that I might know what was in my heart; also to bring me to Himself! "And thou shalt remember all the way which the Lord thy God led thee these forty years in the wilderness, to humble thee, and to prove thee, to know what was in thine heart, whether thou wouldest keep His commandments or no." Thus, my dear reader, I have given a brief account of my natural state.

THE TRUE MESSIAH

I will now give a very brief account of my new birth, or call by divine grace. Here, also, my reader must not expect order for the reasons before mentioned.

In the year 1836, I came to London for the purpose of keeping the Passover, expecting to meet a countryman of mine, who for years had kept his Passover in London. During my stay, I called at the same eating-house where I heard the melancholy news of the death of my brother. As I was sitting conversing with my brethren Jews, a gentleman came in, seated himself at the same table, and called for a cup of coffee. He proved to be a converted Jew.

He first began to talk about business, and by degrees he introduced religion, and the Messiah. I heard one in the room say, "This is a converted Jew." I said to the party with whom I was talking, "We will have a bit of fun with him." I then addressed myself to him by saying, "You are one who has forsaken the religion of our forefathers, and deny the law of Moses, and believe one to be God, who was condemned by our rabbis and priests, and who was hanged on a tree: Jesus of Nazareth, whom you say was the son of David. Where can you prove it from our Bible?" He replied that he had not forsaken the religion of our forefathers, nor the law of Moses. He said, "I believe that the Messiah is come, and that Jesus of Nazareth is the Messiah, and will prove it from the Word of God." I replied that if he could do that I would believe, but it must not be from the Christian's Bible, but from ours. A Hebrew Bible was placed upon the table, and he took another from his pocket. The principal references on which we discoursed were: Gen. 49. 10, Isa. 53, Zech. 12. 10. But my companion and I considered we had gained the point in argument; therefore, I said, as he could not prove from the Bible that the Messiah is come, much more that Jesus of Nazareth was He, I could not believe. He then replied that if I believed not, I should die in my sins and perish. We then commenced ridiculing him, and he left.

Soon after I also left, and while in the street, these words, "Who can tell but that this Jesus was the Messiah?" came to me very powerfully, so that the thought made me uncomfortable, partly because I believed that the very thought itself was blasphemy. I tried all I could to shake it off, and to get it from my mind but the more I tried to get rid of the thought, the closer it clave to me. The arrow of the Almighty was sent forth into my heart, and there it must remain. Such thoughts followed me for some time, awake or asleep, at home or abroad, so as to make me very restless and miserable. Such feelings I never realised before.

One day at my apartments, I took up a Hebrew Bible and began to examine those portions before referred to. Finding nothing to satisfy me, I shut it up, when the words spoken by the Jew came to me: "If thou believest not, thou shalt die in thy sins and perish." They came with such power that for a short time I knew not what to do with myself – not knowing whence they came or what they meant. The uneasiness of my mind kept increasing until I was much distressed.

I remember one evening, on retiring to rest, saying my prayers. I begged the Lord to remove the blasphemous thoughts, as I then considered them. These words came to me: "If thou diest in thy sins thou shalt surely perish." I then, for the first time, went down on my knees and wept bitterly, calling upon the God of Israel to show me the cause of my misery. Bending the knees is contrary to the Jewish custom, as well as to pray with the head uncovered: but I did both – how it came to pass I could not tell. That night I had no sleep, as the thoughts of death and perishing were dreadful to me. The Jews believe in a place of reward and punishment, but deny any knowledge of where they are going until the dissolution of soul and body. Again, they say that death makes atonement for all their sins. That night I tried to take comfort from this, but alas! it afforded me none. I believe that atonement is made by the death of one Man – the God-man – Christ Jesus.

FURTHER CONVICTION

Having heard that there was a house in New Street, Bishops-gate Street, where Jews might converse about Christianity – the house was occupied by a converted Jew named Saul, who was also clerk in the Episcopal Jews' Chapel, Palestine Place, Cambridge Heath – one day I resolved to go there. I met a gentleman in Bishopsgate Street, and inquired of him for this place; he replied, "I am going that way, and I will take you to it." When we arrived at the house, he walked in with me and asked me to sit down. He enquired my errand and I told him I had heard there were gentlemen there who would converse about the Messiah. He said that he was an Israelite, and was convinced from the Word of God that the Messiah is come, and that Jesus of Nazareth is the One; also, except we believe in Him, whether Jew or Gentile, it is impossible to be saved. After two hours' conversation I left him, without any advantage from his arguments except from the words he mentioned: "If we believe not that Jesus of Nazareth is the Messiah, we cannot be saved." This was like a hammer driving the former conviction deeper into my conscience. "What!" said I within myself, "without believing, impossible to be saved! What! must I perish eternally?" This was an addition to my former troubles.

One day, as I was musing on the state of my mind, the words came to me with great power: "The soul that sinneth it shall die." This was in my conscience like a mighty thunder, which shook me to the centre. My whole frame trembled; I begged the Lord to open my eyes to understand His Word, to teach me things that are right, and not suffer me to be led astray. I thought within myself that I would go again to the before-mentioned place, as the gentleman asked me to call again. When I came there, I saw the same Israelite, whose name was Alexander, who afterwards became Bishop of Jerusalem. It was rather remarkable that I should find him there, as he only visited occasionally, taking his turn with others belonging to the London Society for Promoting Christianity among the Jews. During our conversation, he asked what effect our last interview had had upon me, which I related, with tears running from my eyes. He gave me some tracts and his card, and told me to call upon him at his private residence.

THE FIRST HOPE

I remember the first portion of the Word of God that I received a little comfort from: "For the oppression of the poor, for the sighing of the needy, now will I arise, saith the Lord" (Psalm 12. 5); and at another time, "The needy shall not alway be forgotten, the expectation of the poor shall not perish for ever." These passages afforded me a little comfort, and for the first time, a gleam of hope appeared in my soul; the *comfort left me, but the hope never did.* Calling once upon Mr. Alexander, he asked me how I was getting on. I told him a little of the troubles of my soul. He said that he believed it was a work of God, and if so, all my rebellion and opposition would prove nothing. I then said that I thought that my troubles came on through thinking of the Messiah; he replied "No, that is a temptation from Satan."

I believe Mr. Alexander was a man who knew the plague of his own heart, and that he has since gone to glory. When I left him, he asked me to call again. This visit proved profitable. I felt a little more established; I began to have greater desires for reading and searching the Word of God, feeling, at the same time, a love towards it.

One evening, as I was on my knees praying to the Lord to teach me, thoughts sprang up in my mind so that I trembled. I could not tell whence they came; they were so awful. Here I began to find out that I could not pray just as I liked; also, that I was insufficient to resist them. I recollect hearing about this time a Jew blaspheme the name of the Lord Jesus Christ; this was like a dagger to me. I was compelled to go away; I could no longer indulge in ridicule, nor listen to any one else. Upon one occasion, I was reading Isa. 53, "But He was wounded for our transgressions, He was bruised for our iniquities, the chastisement of our peace was upon Him, and with His stripes we are healed," also verses 8 and 11. I felt a little sweetness. I thought, if this is true of the Messiah, that He was wounded for our transgressions (and I felt myself to be a transgressor), there was a hope that I should not perish eternally.

———————

CHAPTER 6

A Jew's Perplexities

My dear reader, you must know that when a Jew is called by divine grace, the conflict differs in some respects from that of a Gentile. The Jew has to conflict with the fiery darts of Satan about the Messiah: 1st, Suggesting that He is not come; 2nd, With regard to His deity, as the Jews deny the Trinity; besides their conflict as touching a personal interest in the Messiah. Every denomination that passes under the name of Christian believes either that Christ was a true Prophet, as the Unitarians, although they deny His divinity, or that He was God by office, as the Socinian; others acknowledge both His deity and humanity. *But the Jews deny all.* Here consisted a great part of my soul conflict.

One day I called upon Mr. Alexander, who asked how I was getting on. I told him how I was tried about believing that Christ was the true Messiah. He then persuaded me to go into the Institution belonging to the London Society, where I would receive instruction and have time to read and search the Word of God. I replied I could not. But when I left him, I began to think of it; things began to crowd into my mind which distressed me much. Here my mind began to be tossed like a man on a broken board on the ocean. Sometimes my family was presented before my mind. Should it come to their ears that I had forsaken the religion of my forefathers, it might almost prove their death. It also came to my recollection what my dear mother told me when a child, namely, that she would rather die or follow me to the grave than that I should forsake my religion. At other times, the thought of bringing an everlasting disgrace upon them was very distressing. And then again, suppose that the Christian religion should prove false? Thus was I tossed upon a sea of perplexity, first by one wave and then another; but under all these trials, I was enabled to cry to the Lord to teach me and lead me in the right way.

While I was musing upon these things, and grief like a fire burning within me, not knowing what to do nor which way to steer, the dear Lord was pleased to appear and decide the case for me from these words: "Hearken, O daughter, and consider, and incline thine ear: forget also thine own people, and thy father's house," especially the latter part of this verse (Psa. 45. 10). Also: "When my father and my mother forsake me, then the Lord will take me up" (Psa. 27. 10). Here the Lord was pleased to break the snare that the bird might escape the hand of the fowler. O the mercies of a covenant God, to look upon the oppressed poor, and to hear the sighs of the needy! Being comforted by these words, and taking it to be a divine direction, I called upon Mr. Alexander and told him I would follow his advice; I would go to the institution.

THE SABBATH

Here, my dear reader, I pass over many things. I was then received into that Society. Here I had to struggle with other conflicts. The Jewish festivals, especially the Sabbath and Passover, were very great trials for me as I could not pay that regard to them as formerly. In this conflict, the instruction I received from Mr. J. C. Reichardt in the New Testament proved, under the Lord's blessing, a great comfort to me. This gentleman is still living and fills the same office he then did. I could then say, as the eunuch said to Philip, "How can I understand, except some man should guide me?" As the eunuch desired Philip to instruct him, so it was my desire to be instructed in the mysteries of the kingdom. My questions were many and subtle, and Mr. Reichardt patiently and kindly answered them from the Word of God. After a few weeks' instruction from this gentleman, I commenced reading the New Testament with interest, and the Lord sanctified it to my soul, as while reading I felt a little love spring up in my soul towards the Lord Jesus Christ. I was comforted to find that through reading the New Testament, I could understand the Old better. I compared them, and could see the blessed harmony that exists between both.

One Friday evening, which is the commencement of the Jewish Sabbath, I felt much tried in violating that Sabbath by touching fire, as it is prohibited in the law of Moses; also other things beside this. While thinking about the violation of the Sabbath, these words came to me: "And remember that thou wast a servant in the land of Egypt, and that the Lord thy God brought thee out hence, through a mighty hand, and by a stretched out arm: therefore the Lord thy God commanded thee to keep the Sabbath day." I began to consider these words. The cause of keeping the Sabbath in these words was the deliverance from Egypt; but this was done away by the Messiah in delivering us from spiritual Egypt. Although this scripture was not a complete deliverance, yet it afforded me a little comfort. At another time the Lord was pleased to grant me a complete deliverance by these words: "And He said unto them, The Sabbath was made for man, and not man for the Sabbath: therefore the Son of Man is Lord also of the Sabbath" (Mark 2. 27, 28).

THE PASSOVER

When the Passover drew nigh, fresh troubles came, as the eating of leaven is strictly prohibited. This portion distressed me much: "For whosoever eateth leavened bread, from the first day until the seventh day, that soul shall be cut off from Israel." These words were like a worm gnawing me, giving me little rest day or night. I kept it all to myself, although there were other of my brethren Jews with me. These, with other troubles, pressed heavily upon me so that I began to feel the effects on my constitution. Now was the time for Satan to tempt; for first, I was not established in the letter of the truth, second, I was distressed in mind, third, in darkness, and wavering. These things added force to Satan's temptation, who suggested that I was wrong in coming to this place, and was altogether deluded. Rebellion, murmuring and discontent rose like mountains high, and at times I thought I should be crushed beneath them. Indeed, had it not been for a secret support by an almighty arm, I should have sunk. From this distress, the dear Lord condescended to cast His eye of pity, and delivered me by applying a portion of His Word with greater power than ever any other before: "Therefore, behold, the day is come, saith the Lord, that they shall no more say, The Lord liveth which brought up the children of Israel out of the land of Egypt, but the Lord liveth which brought up and which led the seed of the house of Israel out of the north country, and from all countries whither I had driven them, and they shall dwell in their own land." The dear Lord was pleased to open my eyes to see in these words a greater deliverance than that from Egypt; and this deliverance came by the Messiah, the Lord Jesus Christ; therefore the Passover, which was a commemoration of the deliverance from Egypt, is done away, and this was a comfortable time to my soul. Two or three days after, the Lord was pleased to bless me with a complete deliverance about the Passover, so that I was never tried again on that head, from this portion: "Christ our Passover is sacrificed for us: therefore let us keep the feast, not with old leaven, neither with the leaven of malice and wickedness, but with the unleavened bread of sincerity and truth." This blessed deliverance strengthened me for greater trouble yet to come. In this way, the Lord has been pleased by degrees to deliver me from the Jewish ceremonies. I then began to hope that I should not be so troubled as I had been, although, at the same time, not one day passed but I was tried more or less.

BONDAGE AND LIBERTY

I now began to build castles in the air – that I would pray often, think more about God and the things of eternity, and read more the Word of God. But, alas! my castles were soon dashed in pieces. One evening, sitting reading, these words came to me with great power: "Cursed is every one that continueth not in all things which are written in the book of the law to do them"; and another passage soon after: "For whosoever shall keep the whole law, and yet offend in one point, is guilty of all." These portions came with such power, dread and terror that I could scarcely keep my seat; so that I was compelled to cease from reading and close the book. Fear, bondage and condemnation followed so that I was afraid to pray lest it would prove presumption. When I thought upon God, it troubled me. I viewed Him sitting on His throne judging and condemning me. I viewed Him holy, terrible and angry. The sins of my youth were brought to my remembrance – they stood as so many witnesses against me. I viewed God too holy to look upon me, myself too sinful to approach Him, my sins too great and heinous to be forgiven. Hardness of heart – hard thoughts of His dear and precious name – condemnation was stamped upon all my actions. Every page in the Word of God condemned me; the word, "Cursed is he," followed me up so that I began to wish I had never been born. Yet I could not leave off praying, groaning and sighing. I used sometimes to steal away from my companions to go to my room and cry to the Lord that, if it were His sovereign will, He would pardon my sins, for they were many and great. For three successive years I do not remember offering up a prayer without using these words: "If it be Thy sovereign will, and in accordance with Thy honour and glory" – as I could not then see how God could remain just and pardon my sins. Conscience also would rise up in condemning me; it said, "Thou art the man" – "verily thou art guilty." I was afraid to read, pray, hear the gospel preached, or to speak, look, or eat and drink. I felt that I was cursed at home or abroad, awake or asleep.

My dear reader, it is impossible to pen words to express what were my feelings. The law was like a fire in my bones and thunder in my soul. My health began to decline with this weight of trials, I was too miserable to wish to live, and the thought of dying made me more so. I felt enmity rising towards God, and was persuaded that if I were to die in enmity, where He is I could not come. The dear Lord is faithful to His promise; He had told me, "The needy shall not alway be forgotten," and I proved Him here again faithful. In this thraldom, under this iron bondage and in this furnace of affliction, I was helped with a little help ("I was brought low, but the Lord helped me") from this portion: "For Christ is the end of the law for righteousness to every one that believeth." This was not a final deliverance; but it refreshed, revived and strengthened me in this bondage, so that I was encouraged to hope in a dear Redeemer.

CHAPTER 7

Joining the Church of England

For the sake of brevity, I will leave out many things, and pass on to the day I was sprinkled, and received as a member of the Church of England, which took place on Sunday, December 24th, 1837, at the Episcopal Jews Chapel, Cambridge Heath, London, by Mr. J. P. Cartwright. My godfathers were Mr. M. S. Alexander, the gentleman I had the first interview with about Christianity, and Mr. Saul, whose name I before mentioned, and Mrs. Alexander officiated as godmother. On this day I was presented by Mr. J. P. Cartwright with a prayer book of the Church of England in Hebrew, and a hymn book in Hebrew and German, which I still have in my possession. It is customary when a Jew is sprinkled to take another name, which I did in compliance with that custom, doing as the rest of my brethren have done, not knowing why or wherefore. The name I chose was Edward.

This day proved an unhappy day to my soul as Satan came with another temptation. The Jews believe that there is no pardon for those who confess publicly that Jesus of Nazareth is the true Messiah, and the Son of God. With this suggestion the enemy came into my soul like a mighty flood, so that it swept away all my past comforts, yea, even the remembrance of them for a time. So was my soul inundated that I could find no standing; I felt, as it were, my hope perished from the Lord, that I was cut off from the land of the living. I was just kept from black despair.

I remember the first time going with my brethren Jews to receive the Lord's Supper, feeling like a criminal going to be executed. As I was stepping from my pew to go to the "altar," these words came to me, "For he that eateth and drinketh unworthily, eateth and drinketh damnation to himself, not discerning the Lord's body." Each step I took added to my trouble. I received the ordinance, returned home with my brethren, keeping all these things to myself, cursing the day I was born, feeling the arrows of the Almighty within me, the poison whereof drunk up my spirit.

These temptations brought me on the bed of affliction. Mr. Reichardt was very kind, and acted towards me as a Christian. I had a medical man who could not tell the cause of my illness; he examined me, and said my lungs and my heart were sound. It was true there was no disease on my heart, but the disease lay in my heart. And none but the great Physician of souls could cure the disease there. He did so in His own time; ten thousand crowns upon His dear and sacred brow, deliverance came in the right time, fittest and best. My medical attendant advised me not to confine myself too much, and when able to take as much air as possible, which when I got better Mr. Reichardt kindly wished me to do. In this state I wrestled with the Lord for deliverance. Now and then passages from the Word of God came to me, which only afforded me momentary help. I cannot remember them; they were a kind of prelude that the Lord would visit me again.

On my awaking one morning, these words came to my mind with sweet power and comfort: "When the poor and needy seek water and there is none, and their tongue faileth for thirst; I the Lord will hear them, I the God of Israel will not forsake them." This was to me like cold water to a thirsty man who travels the desert of Arabia; it was food to my soul for many days. This brought me on my knees to bless and praise His dear and precious name.

LED MORE DEEPLY

After some time I was confirmed by the Bishop of London in a church in Newgate Street. About this time I became acquainted with a lady, who was a godly person, well taught in the things of eternity, who attended the ministry of an Independent minister, Mr. Hughes, of Hackney.[2] This person was made a very

---

[2]Thomas Hughes (1795-1872). At one time his church consisted of 800 members and his preaching was attended with unusual power and savour. In later years he embraced strange notions on the Millennium and lost his influence among lovers of experimental truth, often preaching to only twenty.

great blessing to my soul. I felt great liberty in opening my mind to her, and as an instrument in the hand of the Lord, she administered to me much comfort. Through her I was more clearly led into the doctrines of free grace. She invited me many times to go and hear her minister, but for a long time I refused. In hearing the gospel preached in the Church, I used to feel there was something wanting, although I could not tell what. One Tuesday evening I went to hear the said Mr. Hughes. I cannot recollect his text, but the effect I well remember. He spoke of things that I had passed through, almost from the beginning up to that time. I can remember the very expression I made use of to my friend the next day when I saw her. She enquired how I heard Mr. Hughes. I answered, "He appeared to have two candles, one in each hand, and was walking about in my heart and telling me all that was going on there. I could say with the woman of Samaria, 'Come, see a man who told me all things that ever I did.'"

I know that empty professors will say that this is enthusiasm. I felt the power of it in my soul, and I bless the dear Redeemer for it. Persons might as well try to persuade me that I am not a living creature as to tell me it was mere fancy. That sermon humbled me, produced love in my heart towards God and towards His people. My dear friend understood me well, and so will every gracious soul. This sermon was the very thing I wanted.

SEPARATION FROM THE CHRISTIAN JEWS SOCIETY

But I soon returned to my sad state. Going to church time after time and receiving no comfort, life nor power, I became dead and barren in my feelings and rebellion rose up and discontentment. After praying to the Lord many times for divine direction, these words came to me: "And behold I am with thee, and will keep thee in all places whither thou goest." Soon after this I resolved to leave the society. My godfather, Mr. Alexander, was the first to whom I named my intention. He tried to persuade me not to take such a step, and told me that I should be doing exceedingly wrong, I being but young in the way and not established in the truth; that if I did so I should expose myself to all kind of temptation, and throw myself on the wide world. I replied that God, who had kept me from my youth and preserved me hitherto, was able to keep me for the future. After this, I mentioned my intention to Mr. Reichardt, and he argued in a similar manner, trying to dissuade me from my intention. I then remained a little longer, but found I could receive no food for my soul. I do not, by saying this, intend to convey to the reader that the gospel was not preached there; such is not my meaning; but I speak of my personal hearing. At length I fully made up my mind to leave, and acquainted Mr. Reichardt with my resolution. As he was the superintendent, he told me if that was my determination, I must come before the committee of the society and give my reasons. I said that if required, I would do so. When the usual time for the sitting of the committee came round, I was called before them. Dr. M'Caul, Mr. Alexander and Mr. Reichardt were present; many questions were put to me, and the reason of my wishing to leave, which I answered accordingly, and soon after left.

Subsequently I attended the ministry of Mr. Hughes, of Hackney, under whose ministry I was much comforted, strengthened and established in the truth. My health began also to improve, but I still felt much bondage, full of doubts and fears with respect to my eternal state. New trials came on. While connected with that society, I was treated with kindness, but when I left I had no means of support. Here again Satan had fresh ground to work upon. When Christ was hungry, Satan tempted Him to turn stones into bread; he saw Him poor, and tempted Him with riches; being obscure, He was tempted with worldly preferments. With these three things I was many times tossed up and down, and often at my wit's end. Sometimes I viewed myself as a man suspended between heaven and earth, and many things crowded into my mind. To the Jews I dare not return, and I knew the society would not receive me again, as I left contrary to their wish. As to a trade, I had none whereby to get an honest livelihood. Unknown and friendless, it seemed as though ultimately I must perish. Thus much has my religion done for me. Sometimes I was tempted to go back to the society. Sometimes Satan tempted me to join the Arminian camp;

I should be sure to do well there. But my covenant God kept me from going back, or turning to the right or to the left; He kept me still looking unto Him.

EMPLOYMENT AND TRIALS

One summer's evening I was walking in the Hackney Road, not having that day broken my fast. These words came to me with very great power: "Bread shall be given, and your water shall be sure." When these words came, I thought it a strange portion of Scripture, being just then in want, and without any prospect for the future; but the words were repeated again with still greater power. After this the Lord soon appeared. Soon after I obtained employment at Bermondsey. My employer was a good and gracious man; he acted towards me as a father and brother. Here my cup was mixed with mercies, with sorrow and with comfort. Sometimes my temptations were great; at other times the Lord granted me His presence. As is generally the case, before the day dawns the night is at its darkest, so was the case with my soul. Before I was brought into the liberty of the gospel my state got darker and darker. We read that the disciples feared as they entered into the cloud, but in this cloud they heard a voice, "This is My beloved Son."

As I was one day busily engaged in my employ, blasphemous thoughts came crowding into my mind. Fearing lest I should speak out, I put my hands to my mouth, at the same time groaning to the Lord that He might not suffer me to blaspheme His name. This brought a great cloud of darkness upon my soul. These thoughts followed me for several days.

One day Mr. David Denham,[3] a godly minister, now in glory, came to see me. I now and then attended his ministry, being near to where I lived. Seeing me so cast down, he said, "Brother Samuel, why are you so cast down? Why is your countenance so

---

[3] 1791-1848, Particular Baptist minister; compiler of the well-known Denham's Selection of Hymns.

sad?" I replied, "A heavy heart makes a sad countenance." As he was a kind and humble man, I generally felt liberty in opening my mind to him. He told me that "he was as sure that I should enjoy glory as that the Apostle Paul is now in glory," and spoke many things to comfort me. I told him I believed in the promises of God, but that they did not belong to me as they were only for regenerated characters. Except these promises were applied by the Holy Ghost, I dare not lay hold of them. I said, "A wounded spirit who can bear?" and that nothing less than an application of the blood of atonement could heal my wounded spirit; that the Lord had sorely wounded me, and He only could heal me. Thus Mr. Denham left me, saying that he believed the Lord would soon reveal Himself to my soul, as the night was very dark.

CHAPTER 8

TEMPTED TO DESPAIR

One Tuesday evening, soon after this conversation with Mr. Denham, I went to hear Mr. Hughes. As I went along I begged the Lord to give the minister a message that should comfort my soul. I then hungered and thirsted for the bread and water of life. I used the means, and embraced every opportunity. Neither rain, snow, darkness nor distance (at least three miles from Bermondsey) kept me away, and I was generally there before the service commenced, the Lord strengthening me so to do. My reason for being early was because I knew that the Lord is a Sovereign, and that He could bless as much in singing the hymn or in reading the chapter as in the sermon. But to return. The minister read and prayed, then gave out his text. The text I cannot remember; the substance I do. He entered into the inquiry how far it was possible to go in a profession, and yet to be lost at last; and went on to expose hypocrites in a variety of forms and ways. It appeared to me that he fixed his eyes upon me, and as he was speaking I feared that I was most assuredly the character he described. The distress of my soul was indescribably great. On coming from the chapel, I met with the friend before mentioned, who was the first cause of my going to this place. Asking me how I got on that evening, I replied, "I am lost! I am lost to all eternity!" She said, "No, no, no; not as long as Christ can save. You are one of His sheep, and they shall never perish." With these words I wished her goodnight, and left her.

As I was going home a new temptation came; that was to destroy myself, thinking the longer I lived I only added sin to sin, and that my condemnation would be greater. This appeared blacker than anything before; it disabled me for a time from attending to my employment. The people with whom I lived were professors; they considered I was in a melancholy state, and that I should soon go out of my mind. Under all these temptations I was still enabled to wrestle with the Lord for His divine appearance, and at times felt much liberty in so doing. Then these temptations would come in again.

One day, being confined to my room, it was suggested to my mind that I had been guilty of the unpardonable sin; here I seemed quite to sink. In this case I was afraid to pray; I thought my prayer would only sink me deeper in the gulf. I attempted to walk the room but could not, feeling so weak and distressed. Sometimes I "roared like a bear," and sometimes "mourned like a dove." My language was, "O Lord, I am oppressed; undertake for me." I was afraid to pray, yet could not help crying to the Lord. In the evening, while reading the Word of God, these words came to me very forcibly, "Thou fool, this night thy soul shall be required of thee." After reading this portion of the divine Word, I was afraid to shut my eyes, fearing that if I went to sleep I should open them in hell. This passage remained on my mind during the whole week, day and night.

About this time, one evening between eleven and twelve o'clock, having a candle burning in my bedroom and my Bible open before me, musing upon my miserable state, thinking upon a solemn eternity, and upon the Judge of all, and the great day of judgment, feeling as standing before Him a condemned criminal, I told the Lord that if He sent me to hell, He would be just and righteous in doing so; but that if He *could* bestow mercy in accordance with His divine justice, for Christ Jesus' sake I begged He would have mercy upon my soul. "O Lord, have mercy upon me! Son of David, have mercy upon me!" Then these words came to me, "But Thou hast utterly rejected us; Thou art very wroth against us" (Lam. 5. 22). I cried out, "I am damned; my damnation is sealed." In this horror of soul I remained until the night following, when the Lord spoke pardon. The promise is that "at the evening time it shall be light" (Zech. 14. 7). The Lord is faithful to His promise, and I blessedly experienced His faithfulness to the joy and rejoicing of my heart.

COMPLETE DELIVERANCE

The night following was very dark. Having a candle burning in my room, and my Bible before me as usual, deploring my unhappy state, these words came with very great power: "I am the God of Abraham, and the God of Isaac, and the God of Jacob. God is not the God of the dead, but of the living." I exclaimed, "Lord, is it me? Art Thou *my* God?" The clouds immediately began to disperse; the horror of my soul fled; I burst into a flood of tears, and said, "Lord, can it be me?" when the same portion was repeated thrice with as much power as before. Glorious light broke into my soul; the light appeared greater than the former darkness; I went down on my knees, blessing and praising the Lord for this infinite deliverance. "What," said I to myself, "instead of hell, have I heaven? instead of damnation, have I salvation? instead of the wrath of God, have I His love? instead of His frowns, have I His smiles? O my soul, bless, bless the Lord, and forget not all His benefits; who forgiveth all thine iniquities, who healeth all thy diseases." Tears continued flowing, when another portion came, "I have blotted out as a thick cloud thy transgressions, and as a cloud thy sins. Return unto Me for *I have redeemed thee.*" The words, "I have redeemed thee," were very precious to my soul. "What," said I, "me! Redeemed ME from eternal destruction! Blessed be Thy dear and precious name." Another portion followed: "Yea, I have loved thee with an *everlasting* love; therefore with loving kindness have I drawn thee." And another, "Son, be of good cheer; thy sins be *forgiven* thee." Also many others which I cannot now recollect.

O what a happy change! to be brought out from the power of darkness and to be translated into the kingdom of His dear Son. A deliverance from eternal darkness into eternal light, from eternal death to eternal life! Instead of being eternally separated from the fountain of living water, to have a divine assurance of being with the Father, Son and Holy Ghost to all eternity; to be with Christ, see Him as He is, and be like Him. This was my case; I was *sure* that my sins were forgiven; I could feel or find none; I could say, "My Lord, and my God; My Beloved is mine, and I am His." He was and is the altogether lovely, and the chiefest among ten thousand. I felt heaven in my soul; all, all was calm, serene, and tranquil. It was joy unspeakable, and full of glory. I by precious faith then sat at the feet of Jesus, clothed and in my right mind and, with Mary of old, washing His precious feet with tears. I could sing with the poet,

> "Here would I sit and gaze away,
> A long, an everlasting day."

And with the apostles, "It is good for me to be here." The suretyship of Christ was gloriously opened to me, and also the sovereignty and electing love of God. I felt and was assured that I had not chosen Christ, but that He had chosen me and loved me first, and that from all eternity; that His holy love and divine choice was the cause of mine, His the root, mine the fruit from that root.

WALKING IN LIBERTY

This happy deliverance took place between eleven and twelve at night, being precisely the same time that on the preceding evening that portion came: Lam. 5. 22. It was a jubilee to my soul, all liberty and freedom, walking my room, singing for joy. The old gentleman and lady with whom I lived told me the next morning that the nature of my madness had changed, for instead of being a melancholy madness, I now sang and rejoiced. So, according to their opinion, I was out of my mind both then and previously. I told them it was soul sorrow before, but now it was soul joy. That day I went happily to my employ, the great Physician healing the disease in my heart by sealing my pardon with the broad seal of God the Holy Ghost, which came streaming down through the crimson sea of the atoning blood of the Son of God. I felt better in my body, but being so overjoyed, I could scarcely tell what I was about, taking one thing for another. Some of the men, observing this, exclaimed I was mad. Just at that time my employer came in and, calling me aside, said, "I know where you are. You had better have a holiday today." I thanked him, and left, making up my mind to go and see a friend, who lived in Bethnal Green.

On leaving Bermondsey, instead of turning to the right, I turned to the left, and walked some time before I gave a thought as to where I was going. At length I found myself quite lost. After wandering about for some time, I got into an omnibus which brought me to the city, and from thence I found my way. This joy lasted about a week, although nothing like that of the first day – praying, praising and reading the Word was then my delight. These holy privileges were precious to my soul. The Lord sweetly opened His Word to me. "The entrance of His Word giveth light; it giveth understanding to the simple." How precious are the Scriptures when the Holy Ghost opens them! Otherwise the Bible is a sealed Book. Since the Lord was pleased to speak pardon to my soul, I have not been brought into that state, neither have my darkness or trials been of the same nature. Since then, I have had to mourn the absence of Christ, walking days without the sun, feeling a daily, yea, hourly conflict within, sin and corruption bubbling up, some new monster making its appearance. Pride, the world and Satan are the enemies I have to combat with. Often have I to cry, "O wretched man that I am! Who shall deliver me from the body of this death?" Many changes do I meet with. Doubts and fears try to get the ascendancy, and I have been brought to question the very existence of divine grace in my heart. But, blessed be God, this has lasted but a short time. The Lord has entirely removed from me the terrors of hell and the fear of death.

O the free grace of God, how rich, how sovereign! It is "higher than the heavens," and "deeper than hell." Its height, depth, length and breadth, who can find out?

CHAPTER 9

SPEAKING IN GOD'S NAME

The Lord enabling me, I will now give a short account of my call to the ministry.

When I was under the law, I often told the Lord that if it were His sovereign will to bestow mercy upon me and deliver my soul, I would spread His fame abroad and tell sinners what He had done for my soul. When delivered I felt a great love towards immortal souls; and as before said, the Lord was pleased to open His Word very sweetly to me. The first time I opened my mouth publicly was at Mr. Denham's prayer meeting. Mr. D. called upon me to engage in prayer, and continued to do so occasionally. He also held prayer meetings at various private houses occupied by his members. These meetings I attended when opportunity afforded me as I often enjoyed the presence of the Lord on such occasions.

About the same time I became acquainted with a godly man, who one evening invited me to go to another prayer meeting, which I did. The minister being absent, I was asked to read and expound a chapter. At first I refused, but being pressed I complied with the request. I felt liberty in speaking, and the Lord was pleased to bless it to the comfort and edification of the souls of those present. Often afterwards this good man invited me to the prayer meeting, but I refused going. However, one Friday evening he prevailed upon me.

Coming from the meeting (it was a dark, wet night), my friend said, "There is a little chapel in this neighbourhood where a good man preaches. I should like you to hear him." I replied that I did not know where it was. He said, "I will go with you now, and point you out the place." He did so; but it being so dark a night, and I knowing very little of the neighbourhood, I could not find it when I next attempted to do so.

It was my general custom, on Lord's day mornings, to rise earlier than usual, having to walk to Hackney, as I still continued to attend Mr. Hughes's ministry. The Lord's day after the Friday alluded to I overslept myself. It being nearly ten o'clock, the people with whom I lived began to be alarmed and came and knocked at my door, and that awoke me. By the time I had dressed, I found it impossible to go to Hackney; I then thought of going to hear Mr. Denham. When I got out, finding it so late, and being well known there, I did not like to go in. I then thought of this little chapel which my friend had shown me only the Friday evening previous. I tried to find it, but could not. It was now a little past eleven so I gave up the idea of going anywhere that morning. I had just purposed to go back, and had gone a few paces, when it seemed someone said to me, "Return." I looked round, thinking someone had spoken. I made another attempt to find out, and could not succeed, when the same word was repeated. I then saw an old lady, who appeared to be going to a place of worship. I followed her, and it proved to be the very place I had been seeking.

The minister of the said chapel was from home, and he had engaged a supply for that day, who had disappointed them. When I entered the place, the deacon saw me and came to me, asking whether I was the supply. At first I could not understand what he meant by it. When he repeated the question, I replied, "I am no preacher." He left me, and returned to his pew, and then came to me again, putting the same question, I answering as before. When he left, these words came to me: "But when He saw the multitudes, He was moved with compassion on them, because they fainted, and were scattered abroad as sheep having no shepherd," especially the latter part of this text: "as sheep having no shepherd." These words melted me down. The deacon came the third time, begging me to go into the pulpit, if it were only to read a chapter. After this I could not resist. I went into the pulpit, read and engaged in prayer. When I concluded prayer, these words came into my mind: "There was no room for them in the inn." I first showed that there is no room for Christ in a graceless heart, and how the Holy Ghost empties a sinner before He fills him, strips him before He clothes him, and brings him to feel his lost state before salvation is revealed to the soul. These were some of the things I spoke about.

A Strange Dream

After service, I asked the deacon how it was that he pressed me so much to speak. He then called a lady and said, "This lady will give you the reason." She said she dreamed the night before that she saw a stranger preaching in their pulpit, and that the moment she saw me enter the chapel, she recognised me as the individual she saw in her dream. Sitting near the deacon, she told him that I was the man who would preach for them. Although he twice met with a refusal, she insisted upon his asking me again. That morning the Lord was pleased to bless the message to many poor souls. I heard of that morning years afterwards.

I was then solicited to speak in the evening; I told them I could not promise as I had never before spoken in a chapel. The deacon said, "Will you come as a hearer?" I replied I had no objection, as it was near my home, if they would get a supply. Just at that time I did not see his aim; on leaving him, I began to ponder in my mind what might be his motive. For my word's sake I went in the evening at the same time, making it half an hour later than the usual service. On entering the place I took a seat. The deacon came to me and said, "Mr. Samuel, we are depending upon you (or rather upon your Master) to speak for us this evening." I refused, but he would hear nothing of the kind. I went into the pulpit. After the singing of the hymn, I read and engaged in prayer. While they were singing the second hymn, I thought it was pride and presumption in me to attempt to speak in the name of the Lord. I began to tremble and shook life a leaf; I thought what an awful thing it was to speak in the name of the Lord if He had not brought me there. Other thoughts also crowded into my mind: "You have nothing to say – you told the people all you knew in the morning." While thus tossed in my mind, these words came to me: "Awake, thou that sleepest, and arise from the dead, and Christ shall give thee light." The Lord was pleased to own the message in liberating a female who had been in bondage about eighteen years; I visited her several times afterwards. Thus, the Lord's ways are past finding out. He chooses "the foolish things of this world, to confound the wise; and the weak things of the world, to confound the things which are mighty; and base things of the world and things which are despised, hath God chosen, yea, and things which are not, to bring to nought things that are, that no flesh should glory in His presence."

A HUMBLING EXPERIENCE

When their minister returned, they informed him what had occurred on the past day, and that, if he should go out again, they would like me for a supply. One day he called upon me, told me who he was and what his errand was, asking whether I would supply his place one week evening as he was going from home. I replied I had no objection to speak to his people, if it were the will of the Lord. Having a sense of the great things God had done for me in secret, I was willing to proclaim it publicly. The night previous to the evening I expected to preach, I sat up the whole night reading, in order to prepare my sermon. Now Satan began to work upon my pride. On the appointed evening, I went to the chapel filled with pride, as full as any poor wretch could be; none were allowed to approach me. The thought of speaking to people was quite out of the question, but it was how to preach a great sermon. However, the Lord in His sovereign mercy prevented me giving vent to my pride. God knows how to humble His people. When I arrived at the chapel, I saw many persons standing at the chapel door. A person came up to me and said, "There is no admittance." I answered, "How is that?" He said, "The pew opener has gone out, and taken the key with her in mistake." I waited a short time. The Lord began to work on my mind; I thought of my pride, and that it was from the Lord that the door was not opened. Thus the loftiness of man shall be bowed down, and haughtiness of man shall be made low; and the Lord alone shall be exalted in that day, and the idols He shall utterly abolish.

As I returned, I felt what a mercy it was that the dear Lord had broken the snare; also the neck of my pride. When I came home I shut myself up and wept as a child, blessing and praising the name of the Lord for not suffering me to speak that night. Oh! thought I, is this a right spirit to speak about the lowly Lamb of

God? I prayed that the Lord might preserve me for the future from such pride. Whenever I think of it, it fills me with shame and confusion. I would advise every preacher of the gospel to think before he goes into the pulpit.

About half an hour after came a message to inform me that the chapel was open and requesting me to come, but I refused. The Lord overruled this circumstance for my good; none but He could do it. This impressed my mind with the holiness of the office, the responsibility attending it, the greatness of God's name, and the value of immortal souls. The impression of these things has not left me, and I hope never will until the hour of my death.

CHAPTER 10

Trials of the Ministry

After I commenced speaking, my employer frequently threw out hints that he who preaches the gospel should live by the gospel. I well understood him. One day he plainly told me that I must either leave my employment, or leave off preaching. These words were as a dagger in my heart. For a moment or two I stood speechless. I told him that I would consider the matter. Here I was much tossed in my mind as to what I should do, which I should let go. If I gave up my employment, I had nothing to maintain myself; and if I gave up preaching, I feared that would be wrong. That night I prayed earnestly to the Lord to direct me. Next morning, going with a heavy heart to my employment, these words came with sweetness and power to my soul: "And Jesus said unto him, No man having put his hand to the plough, and looking back, is fit for the kingdom of God." This decided the case for me. I therefore told my employer my decision, and shortly after I left.

From this time new trials commenced with respect to the ministry, as to whether I really was called to preach the everlasting gospel or not, besides other trials in providence. I begged the Lord that if He had sent me to preach the gospel, He would make it manifest in a conspicuous manner. The dear Lord condescended to answer me, but it was by terrible things in righteousness. I was engaged one Sunday afternoon to preach an anniversary sermon at a chapel in London. That morning I was much tried, darkness of soul was very great, temptation very vehement, indwelling sin rising very high. I was almost distracted in my mind, and came to the conclusion I had no call to the ministry. Instead of going to preach, I made up my mind to go by steam-packet to Gravesend. As I was going towards the wharf, these words came to me: "Elijah, what doest thou here?" and another portion followed: "Go, and preach the gospel to every creature." These portions broke the temptation, and scattered the cloud.

A Poor Woman Delivered

As I was going to the chapel, being a little late I walked very fast. While walking, the following thoughts were suggested to my mind: "Who is Christ? What ado about Him? Who was He? He was but man." I made a dead stop for a moment or two, when I asked myself the question: "Who is Christ?" "He is the Son of God, the great Redeemer of sinners; and Satan, in spite of you, by the help of Christ, I will go and proclaim His name." After service a poor woman came into the vestry, weeping for joy, and began to tell me that she had been for many years tried about her state as regarding the things of eternity, and that morning it came to her powerfully that she was guilty of the unpardonable sin. She that afternoon had put her house to rights, kissed her children, and left her house with the determination of drowning herself. But passing by the chapel, and seeing a bill on the wall stating that a converted Jew would preach, she said within herself, "I will hear one sermon more before I go to hell." She also said that under that sermon the Lord had spoken pardon to her soul; instead of hell, she was assured of heaven; and she added, "Now I am going home rejoicing in the God of my salvation." She attended my ministry for a short time after. Thus I saw the cause of the pangs of my soul, that I, as an instrument in the hands of the Lord, should bring out a soul from the horrible pit and the miry clay.

The Lord did not suffer my mouth to be closed, but kept opening doors, unsought for, round the neighbourhood of London, within twenty or thirty miles. Also, the Lord blessed and owned the message to the comfort and edification of His family. Disliking an unsettled life, I begged the Lord to open an effectual door. I was once supplying at Hartley Row, Hants, staying at a gentleman's house, Mr. Goodchild's, who is now in glory. I was asked to preach one week evening in Farnham, in Surrey. I spoke in a large loft.

Concern about Believers' Baptism

I will here digress a little, and give a brief account of the manner I was brought to see the ordinance of believers' baptism by immersion. During my stay in the late Mr. Goodchild's house (this gentleman being a lover of the ordinances of the house of God, as well as the experimental truth of the everlasting gospel, and who in truth adorned it by his walk and conversation), he would occasionally bring forth the ordinance of baptism. He had been accustomed to speak on this and other subjects in a very kind, affectionate manner, at the same time with much fervour and reverence. One evening when we were conversing on the subject, Mr. G. mildly said to me, "Mr. Samuel, have you ever prayed to the Lord that He might open your eyes on this subject as He has done on the other parts of the gospel?" I replied, "No." He then said, "It behoveth you, as a minister of the Lord Jesus Christ, so to do."

This impressed my mind, and I asked the Lord to teach me the whole truth and lead me in the right way, and if this was the right way, to remove my prejudice and enable me to obey His divine command; and thus, prayerfully, I was enabled to search those portions of the Word of God that refer to it. I was acquainted at the same time with a gentleman who was a very great friend to me in temporal matters, but a great opponent to the ordinance of believers' baptism. I was quite sensible that, should I be led to embrace this ordinance, I would lose his friendship, as the event proved. This was a mighty barrier in my way, as I very highly esteemed him as a friend. As I was one day meditating on it, these words came to my mind: "Whosoever he be of you that forsaketh not all that he hath, he cannot be My disciple."

I then began to contemplate these words, which appeared to signify that I must leave all for Christ, and follow Him in this ordinance which I was then meditating on. Here a new struggle commenced between the flesh and the spirit. The flesh and the devil said, "Follow me"; and the Word of God tells us to follow Christ; and when that Word comes with divine power to the soul, it breaks down all opposition and the living soul is enabled to tread on flesh and blood, and follow the Lord, not only through water, but through fire. As the conflict kept increasing, so earnest supplications at a throne of grace also increased. I trembled lest I should embrace an error; especially as a preacher of the gospel, I might be the means of leading others astray. These things caused me many groans, cries and sighs.

One morning as I was going from Hartley Row to the railway station, just as I was stepping into the carriage, these words came to me, I believe, in the power of God the Holy Ghost: "The baptism of John, whence was it, from heaven or of men? And they reasoned with themselves, saying, If we say from heaven, He will say unto us, Why did ye not then believe him?" This was a blessed season to me; it produced great humility of soul and contrition of spirit. The sufferings of Christ in the Garden of Gethsemane were opened to me in such a glorious way that I never had before nor since in like manner. Being quite alone in the railway carriage, I took out my Bible, and as I read I wept for joy all the way to London. I told the Lord that by the power of His grace enabling me, I would obey His divine command. I then no more conferred with flesh and blood. All future consequences, friends or foes, I was enabled to leave in His hands.

BAPTIZED BY IMMERSION

I was baptized at Hartley Row [we understand, by David Denham] and preached the same evening previously to being baptized. The chapel being very crowded, I was extremely hot. While in the vestry a medical gentleman, who attended that place, came in and told me that as I was so overheated, if I were to go into the cold water, it might prove instant death. I replied, "I will leave this with the Lord." The joy of my soul was very great at that time. I, like the eunuch, went away rejoicing in the ways of God, having the approbation of heaven in this ordinance.

Thus I have given a brief account of how I came to embrace the ordinance of believers' baptism. Since that time I have met with many persecutions on account of this ordinance from friends and from foes, sinners and saints. But "none of these things move me." With God's help I will preach and defend it as well as any other part of the gospel. I am not ignorant of man's reasoning on this subject. Some say it is not essential to salvation. I would ask, Is the ordinance of the Lord's supper essential to salvation? I believe the ordinance of believers' baptism is essential to the obedience of the divine command of the great King of Zion.

CHAPTER 11

SETTLED AT FARNHAM, SURREY

The Word being received at Farnham on my first visit, I was invited again and preached in the same place, as there was no place of truth in Farnham. After that I preached there a whole month, the people gathering from different parts in that neighbourhood, and the Lord owned and blessed the message from time to time. One Lord's day morning there were four souls brought into the liberty of the gospel under that sermon. Three out of the four adorned their profession when alive, and have died in peace of the Lord. The last of the three died a few months since in a most triumphant manner; the account of her death I have in my possession, and is worth publication.

The Farnham friends, seeing the Word blessed, invited me to settle there, and I accepted their invitation [c. 1845], believing it was a call from the Lord. This was my first stated place. During my ministry there the Lord blessed me with many seals, and honoured me as an humble instrument in constituting the first Baptist church ever known in that place. I have preached there twice, if not three times since I left. The reason of my leaving Farnham I will forbear mentioning, having no wish to bring up past grievances.

A REMARKABLE CASE

Before I go any further I will mention one instance in reference to Farnham, which will show forth the honour and glory of God. There was a young woman, who lived, and is still living, about a mile and a half from Farnham, and had been afflicted about twelve years, and part of that time confined to her room. All the medical men who visited her gave no hope of her recovery. In her affliction the Lord was pleased to call her by divine grace; she is well taught in the things of eternity, and very spiritual in her conversation. Her mother, who was a member of our little church and has since gone to glory, asked me to visit her daughter. She was so weak and reduced that, seeing me pass the window, she was taken in a kind of fit. I waited outside until she recovered.

When I came into the room there were two or three friends. After a little conversation with her, she requested me to read and engage in prayer, which I did. I felt great power in prayer while pleading with God for her recovery, and was assured that the Lord would answer. Before I left the room, I told her in the presence of those present that I should live to see her come to Farnham and hear me preach, which she had not been able to do for twelve years previously. When I left her, I began to be very tried in my mind, thinking it was presumption in me to make such an assertion, especially in the presence of others. Supposing I should be disappointed, how foolish I should look.

It was my usual custom to visit her once a week. At my second visit, I felt the same power in prayer as before, and again told her I believed I should live to see her come to Farnham. I had a holy persuasion in my mind that the Lord would answer my prayers on her behalf; and on leaving was equally tried as before. This conflict continued for some time, assurance in prayer and diffidence afterwards. On one occasion I asked her whether she had faith in the Lord that He would raise her. She replied, "I cannot tell you." This answer made me think I was deceived. I thought if the Lord intended to restore her, He would give her faith as well as me. On my return home I begged the Lord, if it were His will, not to suffer me to be deceived or to deceive her; when these words came, "This sickness is not unto death, but for the glory of God." The week following I put the same question as before. She said, "I believe the Lord will hear and answer your prayers." This confirmed my faith, together with that portion of the Word before mentioned. After this I was no more tried; my faith remained firm.

Soon after she began very gradually to get better, and before I left Farnham I had the happiness to see her not only come to Farnham, but to my house, which was a half-mile further. Herein was the glory of God manifested. O for a heart to praise Him, and to love His dear and precious name! Here is encouragement for sensible sinners to call upon His name. Although He tarry, wait for Him. I have corresponded with her from the time of my leaving, and have many letters in my possession well worth publishing. In the last letter I received from her, dated January 15th, 1857, she alludes to this very circumstance, without having the slightest idea that I intended publishing anything. I will here insert a part of it. Speaking of her dear mother, and in reference to her own affliction, she thus writes:

"I have been constrained to look back at the dear Lord's goodness towards me in bygone days. When many times to all outward appearances I lay as it were on the very threshold of heaven, there truly appeared but one step between me and eternity. What my soul was then favoured with! How sweetly did I then commune with my precious Lord! What a precious peep I had within the veil! O the foretastes of heaven that were let down into my soul no tongue can fully tell! How I longed to snap the cords asunder that bound me to earth, that I might flee to the bosom of my precious Jesus who had done so much for me, and how I watched from hour to hour longing to hear His blessed voice, saying, 'Soul, come up higher'! I thought what a grief it would have been to me at that season if my dear friends, that sat watching at my bedside, had grieved because the dear Lord had granted my desire in taking me from this world of sin and woe, to be for ever with Himself, where sin can never enter.

"O, when I look back on the many years I have been spared since then, how much have I to be thankful to the dear Lord for, who has preserved and kept me thus far! I well remember what a dread I had to come back into the world again, and many a cry was put forth from my heart that sooner than I should get well and fall into sin, and bring a disgrace upon His name, that I might rather be afflicted until the day of my death. Ah, when you used to pray so earnestly for the dear Lord to bring me out to unite with the people of God here on earth, you little knew the working of my soul, and what fear I had to come forth. But as you still continued the same petitions at a throne of grace, I became more reconciled, and I believe to this day I was brought forth in answer to your many prayers. I was laid on your heart, which caused you to plead and wrestle with the Lord. He has ever been known as a prayer-hearing and answering God, and He was pleased to answer yours, and bring me forth. May you and I have grace to praise Him here below, and in His own good time may He bring us, with all the blood-washed throng, to join in that one song of never-ending praise: 'Unto Him who has loved us, and washed us from our sins in His own most precious blood.' We may well say, 'None but Jesus can do helpless sinners good.'"

_____

CHAPTER 12

Edward Samuel's own account of his life ends fifty years before his death. The last chapter saw him settled as a pastor at Farnham (c. 1845). Here he did not remain long. From Farnham he moved to Hitchin and thence, about six years later, to St. Peter's Lane Chapel, Leicester. In the late 1850s we find him pastor at a Strict Baptist chapel at Salford, Manchester, and eventually in 1862 he removed to Sleaford, Lincolnshire. What was the reason for all these moves we have not been able to determine. At Sleaford he remained for the last thirty-five years of his life, first at Providence Chapel, and then at a chapel built for him and named The Temple.

LATER YEARS

We regret that we have been able to find out very little about the latter part of Edward Samuel's life, though there are persons living who well remember their parents speaking of hearing him preach. At Gower Street Chapel, London, he was a most acceptable visiting preacher, and was one who took part there at the 1893 Jubilee, along with Charles Hemington and Robert Moxon. Mr. Samuel preached in the evening from Galatians 5. 1, and John Gadsby commented in the *Christian's Monthly Record* that he was specially profitable on that occasion.

HIS DEATH

There is a short notice of his death in the 1897 *Gospel Standard*. He died on December 10th, 1896, aged 84. His wife wrote: "My dear husband was taken away suddenly at last. A week before he died he was taken with severe pains about the region of the heart. The doctor gave him medicine to relieve the pain. He did not keep his bed one day, but did everything as usual, so I had no idea of death being so near, neither do I think he had, though he always prayed for the Lord to prepare him for the 'sudden change.' The following are a few words which occasionally dropped from the lips of my dear husband during the last week:

"On one occasion, after an attack of pain, he said, 'It is all by weight and measure.' He would often say, 'I know in whom I believe.' Another time, 'Why should I be cast down, when I have such a glorious prospect?' He would often say, 'I have a good home to go to.'

"On the Monday before he died, he said, 'I have been reading the 27th Psalm, and I have found it so sweet'; and he read it the following morning at family worship. He often repeated the verse:

'O that in Jordan's swelling
I may be helped to sing,
And pass the river, telling
The triumphs of my King!'

"Wednesday he was unusually cheerful; indeed, he had been so the last month of his life. He said, 'I have had several visits lately from the Lord Jesus Christ, and He assured me that where He is I shall be.'

"For this last two months he had an impression he would not be here long; the words, 'The end is come,' were often on his mind. The evening before his death, he conducted family worship as usual, and read the hymn which ends,

'As to man's merit, 'tis hateful to me!
The gospel – I love it; 'tis perfectly free.'

He said, with much emphasis, 'So say I!' He retired to bed, and had several attacks of pain during the night. At 3 o'clock he changed suddenly for death. In about ten minutes, with a sweet smile, his ransomed spirit quitted the clay tenement.

"He preached the last Lord's day of his life. The evening text was 'He hath done all things well.'"

I remain in Gospel Bonds
G. Mockford

GEORGE MOCKFORD: 1826-1899

The Sussex shepherd boy.
George Mockford was so poor at times in his life that eating a few rats was a delicacy! His introduction to the truth of the gospel was through a stranger handing him a tract on the Sussex downs as he minded his sheep.

Being much blessed by God, he was compelled to leave the formality of the established Church. So clearly was he led into the truth that he was able to confound all the vicar's attempts to overthrow his beliefs.

Raised up by God to preach, for nearly forty years he was pastor of the church at Broad Oak, Heathfield, Sussex.

CHAPTER 1

EARLY DAYS

I was brought forth into this world of sin and sorrow at a place called Southerham, in the parish of South Malling, Lewes, Sussex, on December 27th, 1826. My parents were poor, the occupation of my father being a shepherd. I was the eldest surviving member of a large family of twelve children, the firstborn having died in infancy; and this being the case, I had, as soon as I was old enough, to be mother's help to nurse the baby, clean the house, and do sewing like a girl, so that I was not only prevented from playing with other boys, but also from going to school. I did go for a short time to a dame's school, and thence for a little while to the British School at Lewes. My parents were what is called church people, who did not like dissenters; but they only went to church to have their children christened, or to attend a funeral. We were taught the church catechism on a Sunday afternoon, were also instructed to use the Lord's prayer, and for a time I was sent to the church Sunday school.

I was soon noticed as one paying great attention to my instructors, who I remember excited my wonder as to how they knew so much, and I had a great wish to be as wise as they. Therefore I drank in very eagerly all they told me; and by their instruction, the church and her ministers, ordinances and ceremonies were soon looked upon by me as having something mysteriously angelic or heavenly about them. Being naturally very credulous, particularly of anything that had some mystery about it, I could easily be made to believe the statements of the mysterious, learned men, the clergy or church ministers.

I can remember, when quite young, having very serious thoughts about the great God that made the heavens and the earth, of the judgment day, and of hell. I remember what an effect some conversation between my father and mother had upon me when very young. I heard father tell mother that some person (mentioning the name), who lived in my mother's native place, was dead, and that in his lifetime he had sold himself to the devil for so much money. On the bearers attempting to lift the coffin in which the body lay, they could not do so because of its great weight. This could not be accounted for until they opened the coffin and found the body covered with brimstone, the smell of which was unbearable, and this they said was a proof that the devil was going to take him into hell for ever.

When about eight years of age, I was employed during the summer to scare the birds from the corn, etc., for which I had a shilling a week, seven days to the week; for though the master went to church, the rooks would go on stealing the corn if they could.

When I was ten years old, I was taken entirely from school to help my father in the capacity of shepherd boy, for which I had two shillings per week, which I thought was a great deal, though I never had the money, as of course my father took it.

I was always rather delicate in health, and had no stamina about me for outdoor exposure, the food for us young ones consisting of little else than potatoes with a little bacon fat on them. Having commenced my new occupation in the winter, I felt it much; my feet and hands became covered with chilblains which soon broke out into open sores, yet for a time I had to work getting the turnips out of the "pie," as we used to call this heap of turnips, covered over with straw and earth. I had some old leather gloves on, but the dry earth used to get into my gloves and fill my sores, and so bad did they become that the doctor was called in, who ordered me to be kept at home for a week at least, and gave directions to my mother how to treat my hands and feet. I got better in a fortnight and went to work again, but caught a severe cold; indeed it must have been a bad attack of bronchitis, as I can remember how I had to labour for breath, and the wheezing noise in my chest could be heard all over the house. For this again I had the doctor, but my father, who was naturally strong and healthy, had no sympathy with his whitefaced son; he said I must be hardened to it or I should never be any use. So one of the means employed was to send me on frosty mornings to pull up the turnips in the field, laying hold of their frosty tops without gloves on; but as my father was remonstrated with by some of the workmen on the farm about it, I did not go many mornings. The great ambition of my father being to save money, his study was that his children's little strength and time should be all put to such an account as would be conducive to this end. This kind of treatment had no tendency to foster love to him; I began to have a great dread of him, and all I did for him was done under fear of the lash.

I remember about this time, some young gentleman from Lewes often walked in the evening to Southerham, and seeing me in the garden at work would talk to me and give me tracts, etc. that produced sometimes solemn thoughts about death and eternity. Finding I was willing to listen, his visits were more frequent than was agreeable to my father, who said he was most likely someone learning to be a parson, so he busied himself with talking to others; but as for boys who had their living to get, he could not see the good of their reading or being religious.

But as I grew older in years, so I did in sin. I was encouraged to keep rabbits, and my profit I made by them was to be used in buying my own clothes. My father would have been pleased for us to buy all our clothes, though he would not have encouraged me to do what I did to get profit, as I used to steal my master's turnips and hay to feed my rabbits. At first I was much scared in doing it, but soon grew bolder by seeing some of the workmen who kept rabbits do the same.

In a little while, I could go into my master's garden and orchard and fill my pockets with fruit; but I had at times such guilt on my conscience on account of it that when I have been out on a dark night, I have felt as if Satan was upon me and would surely carry me off. I vowed and promised to do so no more, but as soon as the light of day returned and I got into the company of those who could curse and swear and take the name of God in vain, my resolution melted away like ice before the fire, and I began to join with those who went to the ale-house and hear them sing songs. All I heard and saw there was quite congenial to my natural heart; I was delighted while in it, but O, the guilt and fear I felt in walking home alone on a dark night after leaving my companions! I kept repeating part of the Lord's prayer or some such language to keep the devil (as I thought) from grasping me; and on reaching my home, I have opened the door, and getting inside, have suddenly closed it to shut out the devil. There was no hatred to sin, no sorrow for it; but the dread of hell and punishment of my sin often made me cry out, "Do save me; do pardon me, and I will lead a new life." I do believe that persons from the effects of natural conviction may have great sorrow and long much for mercy, and yet there be nothing in it but the workings of nature.

REMARKABLE ESCAPES

I remember about this time being much alarmed. I attempted to take a jackdaw's nest that was built near the top of a high chalk pit. I tried to reach it from the top by lying down and reaching over, when a portion of the earth underneath me gave way, and but for the presence of mind I had to work myself gradually back by my feet, I must have been dashed in pieces.

At another time I was passing through a field in which was a vicious ox. I did not see him until I heard him close upon me; I cried out, "Lord, help me," and ran towards a fence, which I just reached and leaped over as the ox overtook me, but the fence being on a bank stopped him. I had also a second deliverance with respect to this same ox, when I was trying to detach him and another from a cart. The men would go in front of them to take the locker out that fastens the cart to the yoke, but as I was afraid to do this, I went in between them and the neb of the cart, and they started with me in that position, the ox pressing his body tightly against mine. I was so jammed against the neb that I could scarcely breathe; but suddenly the wheel of the cart came in contact with a wall, which stopped the animals, and the pressure being removed, I dropped on the ground, and the master coming along at that instant pulled me out from under the feet of the oxen. It was of course thought that I must be fearfully crushed. I was taken indoors and restoratives given me; but wonder of wonders, no harm had come to me beyond the shock to the system. How plainly we see the truth of the Word of God, "Preserved in Christ Jesus, and called"; and with the poet I can say:

> "Preserved in Jesus when
> My feet made haste to hell;
> And there should I have gone,
> But Thou dost all things well;
> Thy love was great, Thy mercy free,
> Which from the pit delivered me."

CALLED BY GRACE

But at length the set time came, "not to propose, but call by grace," and "to change the heart, renew the will, and turn the feet to Zion's hill." O how I love those words of the poet:

> "There is a period known to God,
> When all His sheep, redeemed by blood,
> Shall leave the hateful ways of sin,
> Turn to the fold, and enter in"!

When I was between sixteen and seventeen years of age, some unknown person came upon the Downs, and addressing me said, "Well, my lad, do you like reading?" I replied, "Yes." "Then," said he, "I will leave this tract with you and when I come again, I shall know how you like it." I put it into my pocket, and thought, "I am not going to read that religious book"; he might keep his book for aught I cared, but this thought came, "Well, you had better look at it, or you won't know what reply to give him when he comes again." So I took it from my pocket to look it over, but never did look it over in that sense, as all at once it looked straight into me.

It was in this way. As I took the book from my pocket, these two scriptures met my eye and went to my heart: "The soul that sinneth, it shall die"; "He that offendeth in one point is guilty of all." I was struck as with a flash of lightning; the book dropped from my hand, and I fell to the earth. How long I lay there, I cannot tell, but presently I began to crawl into a hedge nearby. I was afraid to look up as I felt sure if I did, I should see the eye of God upon me from above; and while lying in the hedge, I cried for the first time in my life, in the language of the publican, "God be merciful to me a sinner." O what a solemn sight I had of the majesty, holiness and justice of God! and I proved His Word to be as a sharp sword piercing my heart. I felt there was no hiding myself from God. I wished that I could find some place to hide myself from the presence of my angry Judge. How I got home that night I cannot tell, but such was the effect upon my body that I could scarcely walk. My parents were terrified at my appearance, and kept wanting to know the cause of my illness, but I could not tell them.

Being able to eat but little, and sleep less, I soon became so ill that I was sent to a doctor who examined me and shook his head, but said, "I will try if I can do anything for you." Everyone supposed that I was in a rapid consumption. The church clergyman visited me, to whom I told my trouble. He laboured hard to comfort me, telling me God was very merciful, and only required us to do what we could, and He would do the rest. I puzzled him much because I was so anxious to know what my part was, and how much I was required to do. This he could not satisfy me about; but by reading the books he lent me and attending to his instructions, I began to feel more quiet in my mind. As I was in real earnest to be right, I gave the greatest attention to my adviser, whom I held in much reverence. I felt sure all his instructions must be right, so I worked hard to do all he told me, and I soon could leave the rest, believing what he said, that God was a merciful God.

FALSE PEACE

I soon became quite religious and was looked upon as such in the parish where I lived. I began to take tracts to people's houses, and visited the sick, exhorting them to turn to God, repent and believe, and they would soon be as safe as I was. My case excited much interest, as the clergyman set me up as a Christian young man. I was still very weak and feeble in body, and I could not get after the sheep, as I was not able to walk fast enough to keep pace with them as they passed from one part of the Downs to the other.

I remember one of the workmen on the farm saying to me one day, "Do you know what the doctor thinks of your case?" I said, "No, what is it?" "Well," he said, "your father and mother do not want you to know, but the doctor says you cannot live long." "O," said I, "I am quite ready to die; my peace is made with God." It is true I felt as I said, so wrapped up was I in a false peace, and so incased in a false confidence; and had I then died, every one would have said what a good end I had made. I knew not my need of Jesus Christ, nor had I any faith in Him or desire after Him. My ground of hope of going to heaven was the peace I felt – a peace that I had made with God, as I thought. O what a delusion of the devil! But so he deceives thousands. Of such it is said that they "have no bands in their death; their strength is firm." "Like sheep they are laid in the grave, and death shall feed on them." But my God had thoughts of peace towards me of a very different nature, blessed be His dear name!

———

CHAPTER 2

RELIGIOUS ATTAINMENTS

The reader will observe that the sense of guilt that I had felt was on account of actual or outward sins; I knew nothing of heart sins. I was a hearty devotee of my (falsely so-called) spiritual adviser, and at his earnest desire I was confirmed by the bishop. Being honest as far as I knew, I wanted to attend to all things in a way that would not break my peace; but I felt adverse to confirmation, and told my instructor that I shrank from it. When he asked the reason, I answered that I understood I was to relieve my sponsors of their obligation made at my baptism, and take it upon myself; but I would rather not take it upon myself, as I considered they had promised so much, and now if I failed, all the blame would rest upon me. His reply to this was that as I had arrived at the age to which these vows extended, even if I were not confirmed, my sponsors would be free of their responsibility, and it must rest with me. So I was confirmed, and then, of course, I was entitled to attend the Lord's supper.

This for some time I resisted, as that scripture so stood in my way, "He that eateth and drinketh unworthily, eateth and drinketh damnation to himself." This word "damnation" was very solemn to me, for I often feared I was not quite right; so the church minister and I had several talks on the subject, and I was told that it ought not to read "damnation," but "condemnation," the difference being explained in this way: that it simply meant that persons who lived in drunkenness, adultery, or open sin, in partaking of the Lord's supper did so unworthily, and thus their sinful acts condemned them. So I was persuaded to attend, and I remember it was a very solemn act in my estimation; but I was greatly put out by seeing some at the table who I knew frequented the public house, were often intoxicated, and cursed and swore.

However, by these means I was engrafted into the church, bound by her bands, and safely folded, and it was suggested to me that I was now safe, and safe I thought myself, not knowing that destruction was close at hand. "Thou turnest man to destruction;

and sayest, Return, ye children of men." I was filled with pride on account of what I had attained unto, and through the praise of others I was lifted up and built my nest in the stars, but, saith the Lord, "From thence will I bring thee down."

SOUL DISTRESS

I had built my house upon the sand, and when God put into practice His own word, "I will overturn, overturn, overturn," my house fell, and great was the fall of it. I fell into open sin again, and I had made a vow to God that if I did so any more, He might damn me. I would not ask forgiveness again; and now I felt as if God would take me at my word and at once hurl me into hell for ever. His divine law that I thought to be unto life, I now found to be unto death; it required perfection in thought, word and deed. The fountain of the deep was broken up within, I saw the thought of foolishness is sin, and I stood before God a condemned criminal, all hope of salvation being gone. I had besides such a discovery of the holy majesty of God in all His divine attributes – a God who could by no means clear the guilty – that I felt I was only allowed to live that I might prove a spectacle of His just judgments by carrying, like Cain, the mark of His curse upon me. This produced hard thoughts of God for ever permitting our first parents to fall; and now His Word, as I read it, was like a candle searching into the inmost recesses of my heart. I began to discover the doctrine of predestination and election as revealed in the Scriptures, but O the enmity I felt against it, and against God on account of it! "Where was the justice of God in it," I asked, "as the doom of all was fixed, and that nothing man could do, would or could turn the mind of God?" This was what I absolutely refused to believe. How hard I tried to make the Word of God speak a different language! But the more I read it, the more I found the sovereignty of Jehovah set forth in its pages. The passage I particularly disliked was, "Jacob have I loved, and Esau have I hated"; so I tried to persuade myself that it was wrongly translated.

For months this deep distress continued, and my teacher, the clergyman, and other church people who visited me, pointed out how wrongly I was acting in trying to look, as they said, into those secrets that belonged to God; I was putting a very wrong construction upon these doctrines. They tried hard to persuade me that Jesus Christ died for all mankind, quoting many passages to prove what they said, and I brought forward those parts of God's Word I had felt the power of in my heart, which were quite against the doctrine of universal redemption. Sometimes they pitied me, and sometimes spoke very harshly to me. My parents were advised to take any books away that I might have, as they feared my mind was already greatly impaired by much reading.

The weakness of my body increasing, I was taken from the sheep, and removed to the farmhouse to act as groom, and do anything the servants might require of me. This was supposed to be the only means of prolonging my life, as I should now be sheltered from the weather, and it was hoped that the good farmhouse ale, of which I was permitted to take as much as I liked, would strengthen me, and the company of the servants bring me out of my melancholy state. It *did* make a difference, for these servants were full of tricks and jokes, in which I was soon induced to join, and the trouble of soul began to be less. But not as before. It could not be stifled. And as to my not asking God for mercy, I could no more help doing that than I could help breathing. I did indeed feel in a strange state; there was inward enmity to God on the one hand, and a crying unto Him for mercy on the other, confessing the sin of my enmity and hard thoughts of Him.

Now I felt sure that Jesus Christ was the only channel through which mercy could flow to a poor sinner. I was led to see that He was set up from everlasting as the Saviour of the church; He was the God-Man Mediator between God and His elect people. O if my name had but been in His book of life! O if He had died for me, then I should have some ground of hope! O that I could persuade God to add my name, to take me in! But no; the election obtained it, and the rest (of whom I feared I was one) were blinded. I had many talks with the clergyman upon different parts of Scripture, and he would sometimes reprove me by saying I ought not to say this portion of the Word of God meant so and so; *he* was my instructor, and I ought to know nothing but what he taught me.

I remember on one occasion he said, "You talk like a dissenter." I told him I knew not what he meant. "What is a dissenter?" I enquired. His answer was that dissenters were a people who broke away from the church as sheep sometimes did from the fold. I understood him to mean people who went to chapel, and those I hated, as I had always been taught to look upon them as canting hypocrites, and what he said made me feel more bitter against them. And yet strange to say, there were two of them who walked past our house every Sunday on their way to Lewes, and they both spoke so kindly to me – one of them giving me a shilling on two or three occasions – and their manner seemed so different from that of the people who went to church, that I sometimes did wish I was like them. And when I have seen them pass, I have felt at times such a love to them that I was quite vexed with myself for being so silly as to have any regard for such deluded people, as they were represented to be.

DIVINE TEACHING

As time went on, God deepened His work in my heart so that I was brought to see and feel that it was not of him that willeth, nor of him that runneth, but of God that sheweth mercy; and what an increased fulness I saw in the word *mercy!* It was welcome news indeed unto me. Also the work of the blessed Spirit in the grand and great economy of the salvation of the church was more and more unfolded to me. I felt that all the actings of the new life in the heart of a poor sinner were the work of the Spirit alone, that all my professed prayers, if not indited by the Spirit, were only natural, and that faith, hope and love, repentance and obedience could not be spiritual unless they were the work of the blessed Spirit in the heart, and that this was in the new heart that God gives His people, which is a pure heart. These passages were sweetly applied: "A new heart also will I give you, and a new spirit will I put within you." "After those days, saith the Lord, I will put My law in their inward parts, and write it in their hearts." "And I will make an everlasting covenant with them, that I will not turn away from them, to do them good; but I will put My fear in their hearts, that they shall not depart from Me." And this scripture stood forth: "That which is born of the flesh is flesh; and that which is born of the Spirit is spirit."

A SORE DISAPPOINTMENT

About this time my mother died of consumption, but before her death she manifested much concern about her soul. The church clergyman visited her, but her request was for me to read and talk to her, which I was enabled to do in the way God had taught me, and I have every reason to believe that the conversation was blessed to her, and that she died in the Lord.

So marked was this that the clergyman said, "Mockford, I believe God intends you to fill some prominent place in the church. He has done such things for you as He does not do for young men in general." And soon after this he spoke to my employer about it, also to his mother and others, and it was agreed amongst them to send me to Chichester Training School to prepare me for a missionary. This subject now occupied my mind much, as I had a secret desire that the Lord would pardon my sins and make me a minister. But the Lord frustrated their schemes and plans by laying me aside again by affliction, so that my life was despaired of. O what a blow it was to me when I was told the thought of sending me to Chichester was given up, the clergyman saying it would only be a waste of money as I should live but a short time!

BACKSLIDING AND FURTHER TRIALS

About this time I made the acquaintance of the person who became my wife; she attended the same church that I did, her father being the organist. My natural affections were ardently set upon her, though not a partaker of grace. Some of my friends remonstrated with me, but I argued that I believed she would be made a real Christian. *O what a vain argument without a divine warrant! And how contrary to the revealed mind of God in His Word!* I soon left my situation, and went to live at Brighton, where I generally attended St. Peter's Church. The people with whom I lodged were dissenters, but not, I am persuaded, partakers of grace. They often jeered and sneered at my religion, though God knows I had but little of any value.

I soon got married without any legitimate prospect of obtaining a living; and as to my soul's concerns, they were very much in the background. I took to selling milk retail, buying it from an uncle who sold wholesale, and through this occupation I became acquainted with a Scotch lady, to whom I shall have occasion to refer hereafter. This milk business did not bring us in a living, so I tried to get a little work to do as well. I worked a little for a plumber sometimes. I remember the before-mentioned lady asking if I knew anyone who could clean the windows of the house in which she lived. I replied that *I* could as I had done some for the man whom I have just mentioned.

I accordingly went; but while cleaning the outside of a drawing-room window, I nearly fell, and in attempting to save myself, broke the window, which frightened me much. The lady was out. I measured correctly (as I thought) the size of a piece of glass required to mend it, and went to the man I had worked for and told him my trouble. He cut me a piece of glass and gave me some putty. I returned quickly to replace the pane I had broken, but to my consternation I found I had not measured correctly one way, so that the glass I had was almost one inch too narrow. I ran back to the man telling him of the dilemma I was in. He said, "I can cut you a piece more if you pay the extra price." I told him I had not one halfpenny more than what I had paid him for the other. He replied, "I shall not cut you another piece, but will give you a slip to put down beside the other, and that will do."

Well, I went back and put in the pane with the slip at the side, as he advised; but, of course, it did not look nice, and I feared the result when the lady returned, which she soon did, and at once called the servant to know how the window was broken. I was summoned into her presence to give an explanation, which I did honestly, at the same time pointing out to her that I would have put in a proper-sized pane most willingly, but as I had not the money, the man would not let me have it. She said, "I am of course sorry that the window is broken, but I will get a man to put a proper pane in, and I will pay you for the glass you have bought." Then she began to enquire after my welfare, asking if I had a wife, and I felt a freedom to tell her all. She wanted to see my wife, as she said she could find her something to do, which she did, and the Lord raised up in her a great friend to us, as will be hereafter seen.

I obtained another situation, and things went on better for a time; but I had not much felt concern about my soul. I attended for a time the Presbyterian Church at Brighton, and felt more satisfied with some of their forms than I did with the Church of England. Most of the men I worked with were openly profane characters, and I had much to endure from their taunts and jeers, though I said nothing to them with my tongue about religion, but I could not do as they did. My bodily strength being small, I do not think I was able at all times to do my master justice. But the foreman took a dislike to me and got me discharged. Now I was brought into great straits, having no means of obtaining the bread that perisheth, and things not being right between God and my soul. I cried unto Him, but felt He would not hear me on account of my marriage being contrary to my own convictions, and the Word of God. O how true we shall prove that word to be: "If ye walk contrary unto Me, then will I also walk contrary unto you"!

———————

CHAPTER 3

SAVED FROM TAKING HIS OWN LIFE

About this time, the before-mentioned lady left Brighton and sent for my wife, and gave her the coals she had left and the remaining food, which was indeed a Godsend to us. She also wished me to write and send my address if I left Brighton. But into such a state of distress, both with regard to my circumstances and my soul, did I now sink, that I was sorely tempted to take my life. Every time I shaved I was continually tempted to use the razor on my throat; so that I dreaded shaving myself, or allowing any one else to do it for me.

Having been very short of food for some time, and all one day without any, I went to a shop in the London Road, kept by a Mr. Trangman, where I dealt when I had money, and telling him I was out of work, asked him if he would let me have a loaf of bread and a quarter of a pound of butter. He replied, "No, not without the money." O! this cut me to the quick on account of my wife. I did not mind so much about my own sufferings, but she had done nothing wrong; the wrong was on my side. She had had no food the day before, and had no prospect of any this day. I felt almost in despair, and without letting her know, I purposed going to Hove to cast myself into the sea; and such was the state of my mind that I walked through the streets without noticing anyone until I was nearly at Hove, when I heard a voice behind me calling, but I did not look back for some time.

However, as the voice continued calling, I looked round at last and saw a man hold up his hand, but thinking he did not mean me, I went on; but he called out again, so I turned back and walked up to him, saying, "Did you call me?" "Yes," he replied, "what a deal of calling you want!" I said I did not think he was calling me. "Do you want work?" he enquired; and on my answering that I did, "I have," said he, "a garden I want dug and put in order." I gladly agreed to do it (he was butler to some lady), so he said, "Come into the house," bidding me follow him. I told him nothing of my hunger and want, but he said, "Before you go to the garden you must have some refreshment," and set before me the remains of a leg of mutton, several pieces of bread, and a jug of beer. I was so overcome that I felt as if I could not begin to eat. I suppose he saw my embarrassment, for he said, "You can take it away if you like as it is all yours." I thanked him, and said that as I must go home for my spade to dig with, I would take it with me. "Come in here to dinner," he said.

My heart was full. I hastened home to my wife to take the food to her, poor thing, as I knew she was suffering from hunger. I ate but little of it myself as I had the promise of a dinner, so I hastened back and worked until dinner time, then went to the house and sat down to some nice food with almost a broken heart under a felt sense of the goodness and mercy of God to me. I did try to thank and praise Him for preserving me from self-destruction, and so strong was the persuasion that the Lord had thus mercifully interposed on my behalf that it produced deep, godly contrition in my heart. O how I confessed my sins to Him and entreated Him to pardon me! I felt enabled to commit my way to Him and trust my all in His blessed hands. The temptation to self-destruction was entirely gone, and I felt a persuasion that the Lord would provide; and so He did.

I finished the garden, and just then the lady before referred to sent for me to do some work for her. But the time came for her to return to London, and again she gave us all the food that was in the house with the coals and several other things. On bidding me goodbye, she said, "I should like to hear from you sometimes. Let me know if you remove from your present address."

REMOVAL TO LEWES

Soon after this I felt led to go back to Lewes to see if I could obtain anything to do; so I went and saw my old master, but he said just at present he did not think he could employ me. I asked him to lend me a horse and light cart to bring my goods and chattels from Brighton to Lewes; so my readers will be sure I had not great possessions if a light cart could carry them, and indeed I had not. He said, "Yes, you may have it"; so I returned to Brighton with the horse and cart to fetch my wife and goods, having hired one little room at Lewes to live in. Of course, I did not get to Brighton very early in the day, but I must if possible return before night as I had only borrowed the horse and cart for the day and I had not money to pay for stabling for the night, only just enough to get the horse some food. Before I got to Brighton it began to snow, but we filled the cart with our few things and hoped to start; but we found the snow was so deep that it would be impossible to get to Lewes that night, so we were obliged to wait until the next day. Well, we left the things on the cart, and I went and found somewhere to put the horse up, and we sat in the house all night. It was not empty, as my wife's sister lived in the same house, so we had a fire.

The next morning I went for my horse, and the man who had charge of it said there was two shillings and sixpence to pay, I told him one shilling was all I possessed, and that I had not intended staying the night but the snow prevented my leaving. So he kindly let me have the horse, and I paid him the one shilling. Then we took our departure for Lewes; but on the journey, my wife, who was riding, was taken ill. The cold, with an insufficient supply of food, had such an effect on her that I thought she would have died. I had nothing with me to give her to relieve her; so we hastened on, and before we got to Lewes she felt a little better. I did cry unto the Lord to spare her life.

We unloaded our few things in the room we had hired, and a woman living next door, as well as the people in the house from whom we rented the room, knowing my wife and seeing how very unwell she looked, soon got her something to do her good, and I went to Southerham with the horse and cart. My old master wanted, of course, to know why I had kept the horse two days, so I told him the reason, and he said, "It is trying for you, and I am sure if the poor horse could speak, he would say it was trying indeed not to have more food than he had during his absence from home."

HARD TIMES
But it was some time before I got work; so my wife went to her parents and I to my father's for a while. My wife's parents

were exceedingly kind people and would have taken us both, but they were poor. My father did not manifest such a spirit, though I did what work for him I could. I used to make a pudding of ground oats and boil it with potatoes; and once I helped to clean out the barn and caught a great number of rats, several of which I cooked and enjoyed. During this time I was favoured with a spirit of prayer to the Lord, and was kept from murmuring against Him and still had the feeling that He would appear for me.

I heard that more hands were wanted on the railway then being made between Lewes and Keymer; so another young man and I went to enquire, and found we could have night work – one party working by day and another by night. So we engaged to go by night and worked one week, at the end of which time we went to what is called the pay-table for our money, and were told our gauger had it and we must find him. This we could not do, though we tried, so we never got a penny. Then I said we would work no more by night; we must try to get on by day, which we did, getting beach [sand; shingle?] from the sea-shore near Hastings to finish the line. Here I worked for a season,[1] sometimes at one part of the line and sometimes at another. I met with much opposition as I could not join with the others in drinking, etc. Though they knew me not, nor did I say anything about religion, they taunted me with being a Methodist;[2] and one principal cause of this was because I would not work on the Sunday as many did, receiving more money in consequence.

My life with them became a burden. I cried unto the Lord in my trouble, and He delivered me out of my distresses by providing a situation for me at my old employment as a shepherd, my old master wishing me to take a flock belonging to a friend of his for a time, which I did, and remained with him as long as he needed me. He had two farms, but after a while he gave one up, so my

---

[1] [G.M.] How often have I thought of it since when riding to Hastings, sometimes with a broken heart under a feeling sense of the goodness of the Lord!

[2] This word formerly meant anyone whose life was strict and separate, irrespective of denomination.

services were no longer required. Then my old master sent me to another friend of his to help pick his hops, where I remained for a month and slept in an ox-stall with many other hop-pickers. After I returned home, I worked at digging up potatoes for my old master at one penny per bushel, my wife picking them up and measuring them.

CONTACT WITH ROMANISM

After this I worked with another man in the marshes cleaning out the ditches, at one shilling per rood, nearly all the winter. This man being a Roman Catholic by profession, we had many talks about religion. He told me of the many miracles he had known the priest to perform and of his strong faith in the power invested by God and the holy Virgin in the priest, that their curse was God's curse and their blessing God's blessing. His conversation was made profitable to me in this way: it was the means of leading me to search the Word of God that I might be able to reply to him therefrom. I was also led to cry to the Lord to keep me from being carried away by his errors, and that I might know the Holy Scriptures which were able, by the power of the Spirit of God, to make me wise unto salvation. In fact, my soul was first brought to feel its need of experiencing the power of the truth of God in my own heart. I could see so clearly by the conversation of this man that his faith was in the priest, not in the Lord Jesus Christ. O what a mercy not to be left to such devilish delusions and lying dogmas!

One thing I was greatly struck with, and that was the close resemblance between much of the conversation and arguments of the ministers in the Church of England and these Romish priests. And I believe, were the country brought under Romish rule, the clergy – with but very few exceptions – are ready to serve, and would manifest as great a spirit of persecution as ever against those who did not obey them.

But to return to my narrative. I worked for my old master that winter and the next summer; both I and my wife went hay-making, and then harvesting, etc. I still attended the parish church and liked the clergyman very much. I believe he preached a great deal of truth, but he was not generally liked as he was by far too truthful and honest; so he was dismissed and another chosen who was more agreeable to the majority of the congregation. But I could not get on with his preaching, and as I was in the Sunday school belonging to the church, I felt it the more difficult to separate from them. I had many talks with the clergyman, and the Lord so enabled me to answer his questions that he was confounded, and would exclaim, "You are right, Mockford, you are right!"

CHAPTER 4

SOUL TROUBLE

About this time the Lord laid me aside by afflicting my body again, and I was reduced to such an extreme state of weakness and prostration that my life was despaired of, both by myself and others; and worse still, I was brought almost to despair in my soul. I felt near death, without a grain of real religion. Night and day did I cry for mercy, for some token for good. Never had I found such language as this to fit me before: "O Lord, I am oppressed; undertake for me." "O save me for Thy mercies' sake, O Lord." "O bring my soul out of trouble, that I may praise Thy name." "From the ends of the earth will I cry unto Thee," etc. But not a ray of hope did I seem to have, as I felt so sure that, though so much of the language of the dear saints of God in their trouble suited me, yet they had a ground to plead that I had not. The psalmist could say in his trouble, "O my God, my soul is cast down within me: therefore will I remember Thee from the land of Jordan, and of the Hermonites, from the hill Mizar. Thou hast been my help; leave me not, neither forsake me, O God of my salvation." Much of the fifty-first Psalm expressed my soul's feelings, yet I could not use all the words of the man of God in the Psalm. Poor Jonah also cried out of the belly of hell, but he could say, "Yet I will look again." I felt I dare not say that as I feared I had never looked rightly unto the Lord.

"GO AND HEAR MR. VINALL"

The clergyman called on me and said, "Now is the time to prove if you have any real religion." "O!" I said, "I fear I have not." But as I began to recover a little strength of body, I wanted to get to the church, hoping the Lord would meet with me; but a voice seemed to speak to me, "Go and hear Mr. Vinall."[3] "No,"

---

[3]John Vinall, minister at the Independent Chapel, Lewes, from 1815 to 1860.

I replied, "I have heard such strange things of that man, I could not go to hear him." But still the voice said, "Go and hear Mr. Vinall"; and it was repeated many times as I lay on my bed. So I argued thus: "The church is too far for me to walk to yet. I will go once. I shall feel a little stronger by another week." So to the surprise of my wife, I said on the Sunday morning, "I am going to chapel," and I went.

Never shall I forget the feelings under which I entered the chapel, afraid someone that knew me would see me go in. I sat down on the first seat I came to. Mr. Vinall was in the pulpit, as he was afflicted and was taken there before the service commenced. He was a very different man in appearance from what I had pictured him to be, so solemn and grave. I had never heard a man pray like him before; he took my heart with him in his prayer to God, and when he gave out his text, in what a solemn way he did it. I felt a peculiar awe come over my spirit as the words fell on my ear: "I will take you one of a city, and two of a family, and I will bring you to Zion." I was astonished indeed to hear all about myself in a way I had never heard before. I felt it was really too bad to expose me so before all the congregation. I could not look up as I thought the people all knew whom he was pointing at. Who could have told him, and why did he not send to speak to me in private? I had a peculiar feeling of love and hatred working in my breast; I loved the dear man of God and the truth he preached, yet it so exposed me and the power of it was so great upon me that it produced a fierce opposition within to it, and I felt, "I will never come to hear you again; I will not be so exposed." Then such solemn questioning as this arose: "Is it not the truth?" "It is, it is," I replied. "I will go to hear again. I want to be right; I do, Lord, Thou knowest."

So on the following Lord's day I went again, and Mr. Vinall's text was: "And we know that the Son of God is come, and hath given us an understanding, that we may know Him that is true, and we are in Him that is true, even in His Son Jesus Christ. This is the true God, and eternal life. Little children, keep yourselves from idols. Amen" (1 John 5. 20, 21). The dear man of God spoke of the knowledge God gave to His people by putting

His fear in their hearts and writing it upon their minds; and this fear being joined to saving faith in the Son of God, by the teaching of the blessed Spirit, He was revealed to the soul by the Word of God. Thus God's people were brought to know that Jesus Christ His Son was come, and this knowledge produced a longing desire to be assured that they were in Him that was true, and in the Lord's time they were brought to know that also. O how he described my soul's exercises all through the first part of his discourse! But when he went on to speak of those who were brought to know that they were in Him, he went past me, and I cried within myself, "O thou man of God, I do want to follow thee." I felt such a reaching out after it: "O Lord, do bless me with that knowledge; do, I beseech Thee."

Such was the effect of the preaching of the gospel by this man of God that I was spoiled for attending the church. But as my bodily strength was increasing and I stood so connected with the church as a principal teacher in the Sunday school, I went there again for a time in the day with the Sunday scholars and to chapel in the evening. *But I could not mix it.* I only got confusion in hearing in the church so that I was led to cry earnestly unto the Lord in the matter as I well knew what a fire of persecution I should have to face if I left the church. But my soul was more than my body, and the things of eternity more to me than the things of time.

I so well remember standing in the middle of the road one Sunday morning and crying unto the Lord to direct my way. O how I could appeal to Him that He knew my heart's desire was to be made right, and also to be enabled to do right in His sight! I felt, too, such a strong love produced in my heart toward the saints of God that met at Providence Chapel and to the truth preached there, and the words - with, I believe, the feelings also of Ruth - came into my mind: "This people shall be my people, and O that their God may be my God!" All desire to go to church was taken away, nor did I think of the trouble I might bring upon myself in taking the step; I walked to the chapel in such sweet meditation that when I found myself inside the building, I almost wondered how I got there, and I never returned to the church again. I am persuaded that had not the Lord brought me out of the Church of England to which I was so closely wedded, I should not have come out. It cost me something to do so, but I was enabled to commit my way unto the Lord, to trust also in Him, and I have indeed found it better to trust in the Lord than to put confidence in man, or in princes. They that trust in the Lord shall not want any good thing. I am a witness that He is that God, and that His words are true.

THE AFFLICTIONS OF THE GOSPEL

As I had expected, my leaving the church began to make a stir, and I was requested to meet the clergyman to give an account of my conduct. We had many talks, and the Lord so favoured me with words to speak to him that he was not able to gainsay what I brought forward, and on one occasion he said, "You are right, Mockford, you are right"; but so unwilling was he to yield the point that he wrote me a long letter, and spoke to my old master about the matter and other folks in the parish, so that I began to be talked about by nearly everyone in it. And though this clergyman never persecuted me, nor that I know of showed a bad spirit towards me, yet it was taken up by others and their bitter spirit made apparent in different ways; one being that when in the winter a blanket, a little flannel, or coals, etc. were given to the poor in the parish, I was no longer a recipient, and when I was ill (as I often was) their opposition was shown also.

On one occasion an old retired clergyman called at my house and asked my wife how I was (I was then upstairs in bed so I heard all he said), and was told I was rather better. "Ah! he's a dissenter," he said, "and doesn't want to see me." "I do not think," my wife replied, "that he would mind seeing you." "He's a dissenter," he repeated, and my wife said, "You had better go upstairs and see him yourself." So up he came with, "Well, how are you?" "Thank you," I answered, "I am better." "You are a dissenter," said he. "That," I replied, "is what you call me, but I do not call myself so, as I do not dissent from the articles and doctrines of the Reformation, but it is you clergymen who are dissenters from those articles." "I have been to college," he answered, "and been trained on purpose to teach you, and you are taking the place of a teacher to me. You are an antinomian." "I do not know, sir, what you mean," I said. "Then from your own mouth I prove your ignorance," he replied, and began to explain to me the meaning of the word antinomian by giving its Greek origin. I told him I did not understand Greek or Hebrew, but should think it meant those who said, "Let us do evil that good may come." "Ah!" he said, "you are an all-faith man." "Sir," I replied, "I am at times much tried to know if I have any of the right kind"; and he said, "Now which do you think the most important, faith or works?" "Well, sir," I returned, "I find in my Bible that James saith 'faith without works is dead'; therefore one is as important as the other. But now, sir, to prove that I am not against the church, I will say that had I been able to get the food my soul requires in her, if you" – handing him one of Toplady's books – "and the rest of the clergy preached like that man, I should not have left the church." To that he made no reply, but said, "If you had stayed in the church, we would have taken care of you and your family. We had agreed that you should have the clerkship, but as it is you have brought misery upon yourself and family by turning your back upon your friends"; and in a great rage he asked, "What may you take?" "The doctor orders anything that is nourishing," I answered. " Well," he said, "I am commanded to look after your body; your religion I hate. I will send you a bottle of wine"; and downstairs he stamped as though he would break every step, and I never saw him again as he was soon cut off by death.

Gospel Liberty

Now a little while before I quite left the church, I had obtained, by the kindness of the Lord, a situation at a soap factory. My old master said to me one day, "A hand is wanted for a fort-night at the factory. I have spoken to Mr. Evershed about you, so you are to go at once." The work there was entirely new to me; but without seeing the master, I went as I supposed for the two weeks. The master and I never had any agreement, but the two weeks passed and nothing was said to me about leaving, so I continued going. I afterwards heard that if I had not suited, I should have been obliged to leave at the end of the fortnight. But the dear Lord instructed me and much favoured me after I had finally left the church.

I remember after being laid aside by affliction for about a month, I was favoured with much importunity with the Lord in prayer that He would seal my pardon to my heart, and give me a full assurance that I was His and that He was my God, according to His own Word: "I will say, It is My people; and they shall say, The Lord is my God." Well, the first day I walked out of the house by the riverside, O the blessed peace I was favoured with – peace with God through our Lord Jesus Christ! Everything in nature looked new; all spoke of the goodness and praise of God: the birds of the air, the water in the river, the grass on the hill-side. I had never seen them look so before. That scripture came into my mind: "If any man be in Christ, he is a new creature: old things are passed away; behold, all things are become new." I felt a new creature. I blessed and praised the God of my life, and called upon everything to help me to praise Him who had done such great things for my soul, redeemed my life from destruction, and crowned me with lovingkindness and tender mercies. "He is my God, and I will praise Him." I cannot in words describe the blessed state I was in; I felt all my sins were pardoned and cast into the sea. How long I stayed out I do not know, but when I returned home, I took up the Bible and read a little, and to my great joy it was also new. There was no condemnation anywhere and the peace and love I felt increased. I kissed the Book and blessed the God of it. "Yes," I said, "bless the Lord, O my soul: and all that is within me, bless His holy name."

A measure of this happiness lasted several months, but not to the same extent; and sometimes I was tried because it was suggested to me: "How do you know that your sins are pardoned as you did not see Jesus Christ, nor had you any scripture applied, neither did you find that your guilt was removed by the application of the blood of Jesus Christ?" This tried me as my guilt was not removed suddenly but by degrees I lost all the guilt and fear, and a sweet peace followed without any word. So I begged of the Lord to give me a word, if His dear will; and bless His holy name, He granted me my request and said, "I have blotted out, as a thick cloud, thy transgressions, and, as a cloud, thy sins"; also this: "I have cast all thy sins into the depths of the sea." O what joy and peace were again produced in my heart! It was well, and I felt sure it would be for ever well.

———————————

CHAPTER 5

I had for a long time been much exercised about the ministry, sometimes feeling it was right, and then again fearing that I was altogether deceived about it. But now it was laid upon my mind with much weight and I had liberty before God on the matter, with a deep feeling of love to the Lord's people and a sincere desire to honour and glorify the Lord in whatever way He was pleased to use me. I said nothing, however, to my fellow-creatures on the subject, as I was so afraid of being left to follow man's advice, which, as I told the Lord, He knew I did not want to do, unless I were sure such advice was in accordance with His blessed mind and will. I therefore begged of Him that He would Himself lay it upon the minds of His people if it were His will to send me unto them.

One Sunday afternoon, a few friends called upon me, and as we were talking together, one said, "How I do love to walk behind the Lord's people and hear them talk." I replied, "So do I." An elderly man said, "You do?" I answered, "Yes," and began to think, I fear that he can see I am destitute of grace; so I again said, "I hope I do." "Well," returned the good man, "we believe that the Lord intends you should go *before* His people; in other words, we feel sure that the Lord is preparing you for the ministry." "O!" I said, "you don't know what you are talking about." I felt as if I should have dropped from my seat with the little child I had on my knee. My friend saw my agitation and said no more. But like Mary I pondered his words in my heart, for I knew what I had asked the Lord.

PAST OFFENCES CONFESSED

When I was a shepherd boy, I and another lad on one occasion played a poor old man a trick. He was a flint-digger, and was in the habit of bringing a bottle of beer [the staple drink at that time among farm-workers] to the Downs containing enough to last him the week. This bottle we got hold of, carried it to the top of the hill, and started it down the steep into the valley below, and, of course, when it reached the valley, it was dashed in pieces. This was done after the poor man had left work. Well, after the Lord had called me by His grace, I heard that this was a godly man and that he was ill. I did so want to see him to confess my fault and ask his forgiveness.

Accordingly, I went to the dear man's house and found him ill in bed, in a most blessed place in his soul, calm in the enjoyment of solid peace, and only waiting to be called up higher. He had been told I was coming to see him, so as soon as I got there, he said, "Now, my lad, sit thee down in this chair" (pointing to one by his bedside) "and tell me what the Lord hath done for thy soul." "But I have come to confess my sin against you," I said, "and ask your forgiveness." "Sin against me!" he exclaimed. "What do you mean?" I then told him what the shepherd boy and I did with his bottle. "Ah!" said he, "I thought it was you two young trimmers; but where is the other?" "O!" I cried with tears flowing from my eyes, "he is transported beyond the sea." "Ah!" said he, "one is taken, and the other left." I burst into a flood of tears at this as I felt so broken down with the goodness of God to me. Why me, blessed God, why me, and leave the other to reap the just reward of his sin, of which I had been a large partaker?

As soon as I had recovered some composure, the good old man said, "I most heartily forgive you, my dear friend. Now do tell me a little of the goodness of our covenant God to thee." So I told him a little, and we both wept together to His praise for the mercy we had found. I spoke a few words in prayer at his request. "And now," he said, "you must come and see me as often as you can as long as I live." This I did, and before he died he said, "I have one request to make, which is that you will continue to visit my dame after my removal home." I readily promised and went once a week to see her, and after a little time she asked one friend to come in the same evening and then another until there were several. I used to read one of dear Mr. Philpot's sermons and speak a few words in prayer.

FIRST ATTEMPTS TO SPEAK IN THE LORD'S NAME

On one occasion when I took my sermon out of my pocket to read as usual, one of the company took it up to see, as I thought, by whom it was preached, but as it was not returned to me, I said, "With your permission I will read the sermon," when to my utter surprise the person said, "We are persuaded you have no right to read other people's sermons as we believe the Lord hath anointed you to preach His truth. There is the Bible; tell us what the Lord hath done for your soul." I begged and entreated him not to press it as they were quite mistaken about that matter. "Do give me the sermon to read," I cried. They did so; but I cannot describe the confusion I was in as I had denied that I was exercised about the ministry, not in word, but in spirit.

I went home that night with a very guilty conscience and I stayed away a fortnight this time, and it was a fortnight of trouble as I had asked the Lord to lay it upon the minds of others and then had denied it. O! if the Lord would pardon my sin and I should be asked again, I would not deny it.

Well, when I went again, I carried a sermon as before, but as soon as I laid it on the table it was taken, and when I asked for it, the reply was, "We are more convinced than ever that the Lord has designed you for the ministry, and this time we will not allow you to read the sermon." My fortnight's trouble was before me as well as my promise to the Lord. I therefore with fear and trembling took the Bible and opened on Psalm 107, and read until I came to this verse: "They fell down, and there was none to help"; and I spoke on that verse for about half an hour feelingly, and so in future I made a few remarks upon some portion of the Word of God. But this was only privately. I was still much tried as to whether the Lord had called me to the work, for I felt that this gift to speak in private might have been given me, but that was no proof I was called to speak publicly.

THE TRIAL OF FAITH

One day a friend who lived at Newhaven said to me, "I feel sure the Lord has anointed you to preach the gospel to the poor, and I give you an invitation to Newhaven to speak in my house." I replied, "No, I cannot come; you will find some day you are mistaken." But on the next Good Friday (so called) a friend from Brighton came to Lewes in the morning, and said, "We must go to

Newhaven today, and either you or I must preach; it is so laid upon my mind." It had been much upon my mind also as we did not work that day. I therefore answered, "Well, William, I feel we must go as I have had the same strong impression."

So we went; and when we arrived at my friend's house, he was delighted and said to me, "You will speak to us this evening." I replied, "I do not know; we are come to see what the will of the Lord is in the matter." "O!" he said, "I will go to Mr. Young's and some others, and we shall have a nice number of folks this evening." We thought the service had better begin at half-past six as we had to get back to Lewes that night, so my friend went out to invite the friends to come but all had some excuse and not one came so, of course, we had no service. Now what could I say about a divine call to the ministry? Now both Satan and my unbelief had plenty of scope to work, and my friend and I had almost a seven miles' silent walk, and yet a great deal of talk within. Indeed, I concluded this was a proof that I was not called to the work of the ministry.

O what wonderment many that are determined to preach would have made of the fact that both myself and my friend from Brighton were impressed with the same thing! Well, now I felt a secret relief that I would think no more about preaching, and months passed away until one morning, when going home to my breakfast or dinner, I met a minister I knew but to whom I had never said a word about my exercise. He had a friend with him whom I did not know. He came up to me, and putting his hand on my shoulder said to his friend, "Don't you be surprised if you see this man in the box at Heathfield some day" (meaning the pulpit). I said to him, "What are you talking about?" "Good morning," said he to his friend, "I am going home with this man."

When alone, "Now," said he, "can you look me in the face and say that you are not exercised about the ministry?" "I cannot, but I feel that of late it has not been so much on my mind, so that I think it will never be." "Well," he replied, "whatever *you* may think about it, I am convinced that God intends it *shall* be. Moreover, I feel it so laid upon my mind that you will hear from me soon respecting preaching to a few people next Good Friday."

He then left me, but his words did not leave me: " I am convinced that God intends it shall be." This brought on a deeper concern than ever about it, so that it was a day and night burden. I sighed and cried to the Lord in this my trouble that He would not suffer me to run unsent by Him. Well, the Good Friday came and passed, and I heard nothing from this friend. At first I was much tried at not hearing, but afterwards felt a secret relief that it was not the Lord's mind to send me, and that He had shown His servant that he was mistaken in the matter.

INVITATION TO PREACH

Well, after I had got settled down under the feeling that I should not have to speak in public, one morning, when just sitting down to breakfast, the postman brought a letter which, upon my opening, I found contained an invitation to go next Lord's day to Barcombe, a village a few miles from Lewes, to speak to a few people there – wishing an answer per return, and it must not be nay. This almost took the breath out of me, nor could I take my food; and as I was musing on it, a knock came at the door. On opening it, who should it be but the aforementioned friend, who said, "Well, my boy, have you had a letter from Brighton this morning?" I replied, "Yes, and I believe it is through you." "Yes," he said, "it is; and what answer are you going to give?" I said, "I cannot go." "Well," he cried, "I have no time to stop parleying with you as I have to catch a train; but mark you, if you refuse, you will bring yourself into such a state of bondage and distress as you have not had lately. I leave you to settle the matter with God"; and so left me.

O this settling the matter with God! Well, I do hope it *was* settled by God. The whole of the day God and my soul were together upon it, and I felt enabled to fall into His hands in this way – that I would write and tell the person who wrote that if health and strength permitted, I would venture to go; but at the same time told him I was not a preacher and had never spoken in public but was much tried upon the matter, and that I had been enabled to leave it all in the Lord's hands in this way: that if He had not sent me, that I might not be able to speak; but if He had, that He would open my mouth and give me and the people to feel His witnessing within to the same. After I had posted the letter, I fell into such distress about it that I went to the post office and asked the postmaster (who was a friend of mine) if he would kindly open the box and give me a letter out with such an address upon it as I did not want it to go now. I did not say anything to him of its purport. He replied, "My friend, I dare not, it being contrary to my instructions." So it had to go, and O what a week of trial I had! Sometimes I would venture, and then again I would not.

———————

CHAPTER 6

VISIT TO BARCOMBE

Now I had not said a word to my wife about what was on my mind, nor this engagement, but on the Sunday morning I got up early, having had but little sleep all night. My wife enquired why I was getting up so early. "O! I am going a little way into the country." "What for?" I tried to evade the question, and said I should be home again in the afternoon. So I set out, it being about four miles through the fields from where I lived. I knew nothing of the place nor the people, excepting one man living there, a grocer, whom we supplied with soap. It being the first day of June, 1856, it was nice walking through the cornfields. On my journey I met a man I knew as a hearer of dear Mr. Vinall's, of Lewes, on his way there, and I was so afraid he would ask me what I was going that way for, that had it not been in a cornfield where we met, I should, when I saw him coming, have turned aside. However, I was very glad that he only said, "Good morning," and went on.

When I got into the village, I did not know where the chapel was, or if there were more than one in the place, so was passing through the village and met the afore-mentioned grocer who called out, "Where are you travelling to this way?" "Well," I said, "I scarcely know." Not know! That's strange; I suppose you are an Englishman? "Yes," said I; but I did so want to get away from him as I knew nothing of his profession. I suspected he was a churchman, but I ventured to say this to him, "Have you any chapels in this place?" "Yes," he replied, "there is one," pointing to it. "What time does the service begin?" I enquired. "About half past ten," was his cool reply, and I walked away and hid myself among some trees where I could see the chapel; and soon I saw a woman come and unlock the door, and go away again. Now, I thought, is my time to slip in. I did so, and into the pulpit I went, and sat there wrestling with God that if He had sent me, He would be with me and help me.

Presently I heard footsteps coming into the chapel, and now it darted into my mind, You cannot run away as you are in the pulpit and the people are coming in. I hid myself as much as I could, and did not venture to look up until the clerk gave out the hymn (if I mistake not, one of Hart's), and as they were singing, I ventured to look up, and the first man I saw was the grocer before mentioned. O! I thought I must sink through the floor, but the Lord strengthened me, and after they had sung, I read and prayed, yes, *and unto the Lord,* with so much heart-feeling of nearness and humble boldness that I felt to be permitted to draw very near to Him, and some words were on my mind to speak from, if the Lord would enable me.

When they had done singing, I told the people that I had been requested to come to speak to them in the name of the Lord, but I was not a preacher and had never spoken in public; in fact, I told them I was there on a trial between God and myself respecting the matter. I then read Romans 1. 16 as a text ("For I am not ashamed of the gospel of Christ"), and all fear of man was removed. I felt instead a sweet liberty and opening of the words concerning which I myself had *proved* the truth; so that if it might be called a sermon, it was an experimental one. I spoke both morning and afternoon from the same words. After the morning service, the grocer I mentioned stood at the bottom of the pulpit stairs with tears in his eyes, and said, "O my friend, do forgive me for speaking to you as I did this morning. I had no idea that you had come here to preach, and now you must come home with me to take dinner, and never you come to Barcombe again without coming to my house"; and I found him the same friend ever after. At the close of the afternoon service, many friends came to shake hands and said what a good day it had been to their souls, and that they were sure I should come again. Well, I feel I may truthfully say that my four miles walk there was in prayer, and my four miles walk home was in praise. Now I could tell the Lord that I knew He had sent me and that I was willing to go wherever He should open a door for me.

One thing I must mention. After the service, the friend who paid the ministers gave me four shillings. I said, "No, my friend,

I have not come by rail so you have not to pay me" (as I really did not know that those who went out as supplies were paid anything beyond their expenses). "Yes," he said, "it is yours; it is what we pay all." So I took it; but though I was in debt at the time, I did not feel I could spend the money in helping me to get out of it, so I begged the Lord to direct me respecting the matter. Well, I had not an umbrella, so I bought one with the money for the Lord's service, and that umbrella accompanied me many miles in the service of my God.

SHUT UP – A BITTER TRIAL

The following week I had another letter asking me to go again to the same place the next Lord's day as the Word had been so blessed to the people. I replied, "Yes," at once, saying I would go, God willing; and felt a longing for the time to come to

> ". . . tell to sinners round,
> What a dear Saviour I had found;
> And point to His redeeming blood,
> And say, 'Behold the way to God.'"

I did not journey the four miles in prayer as on the former occasion; I felt the Lord had called me to preach and He would be with me. I read and spoke in prayer, in which I felt some sweet nearness to the Lord, and gave out these words as a text: "Go out into the highways and hedges, and compel them to come in, that My house may be filled." Well, I spoke for about fifteen or twenty minutes, and then I felt just as if a black sheet was let down between me and the subject; I stammered about for a short time, and sat down. The friends tried to encourage me, saying they were sure I was sent to preach. Well, I tried in the afternoon, but felt so shut up and confused that I told the friends I felt I had run unsent of God and that I should never go into a pulpit again; and I *felt* I should not. "O Lord," I cried, "do pardon me in this great sin in running unsent by Thee," for I *did* feel it was a great sin. I sank almost as low as when I feared that I had committed the unpardonable sin. Yes, and to this day I feel it to be a very solemn and weighty matter to stand up professedly as God's mouth to deliver

His message. How few that are called and call themselves preachers appear to know what the *"burden* of the word of the Lord" is!

THE GOSPEL MINISTRY

I feel persuaded that those whom the Lord sends into His vineyard to labour have a *special* and a *distinct* call to the work and are expressly fitted and qualified for it by the teaching of the Holy Ghost in the school of affliction and temptation and trials, where they are brought to *prove* both God and His Word to be true, in hearing and answering their prayers; so that they have a "Thus saith the Lord" to go with. It is not with them, I *think* so and so, but they, having tasted, handled and felt the Word of life, speak with authority and not as the scribes. O what a little looking after *the divine anointing* to the work in the men who go out to preach by the churches! I feel this to be one of the principal causes of the deathly, barren, carnal state of the church in the present day. It is for the want of power attending the ministry. That power will attend in a greater or less degree the ministry of those whom God has taught, prepared, anointed and endued with power from on high for that work. The gift to speak in public alone will not really benefit the church of God, and yet how often we hear it said, "He has a gift for speaking," or "He speaks the truth"! Yes, thousands may do that in whom you have no proof that God hath anointed them for the work of the ministry. Many go forth in that work because (as they say) it is such an *honour* to be a minister, but before godly honour is humility; that part by them is left out.

Then again, many, I feel sure, take it upon them in order to get a living: "Put me into the priest's office for a morsel of bread." I know some in these parts who, I feel sure, have gone forth into the ministry from these motives in the background, and I say this without prejudice against them as *good men.* One good man with whom I was in communion until he became a preacher will not even ride with me in a railway carriage because I cannot encourage him in his false position and recommend him to the churches.

And, again, I do feel it so sad that there are those called pastors, who encourage such men and recommend them to the destitute churches and feel very sore if their recommendation is not acted upon. I am persuaded such men will only bring destitute churches into greater destitution spiritually. It is true they will have their admirers and those who cry them up, but what kind of hearers are they, even if gracious people? Are they living near the Lord? and from a felt want of right and living things themselves, are they trying the spirit of those they hear? I am sure those who are good hearers do so as nothing short of realities will do for them, that which hath the seal of heaven upon it in their own souls.

It will be a mercy for the church when the Lord thoroughly purges His floor from such would-be parsons, who have far more their own ends in view than the welfare of the souls of the Lord's people. As dear Philpot says, "The first distinctive feature of the ministry of the gospel is that it is the ministration of the *Spirit*, and not merely of the letter of truth." The Lord says, "O My people, they which lead thee cause thee to err, and destroy the way of thy path" (Isa. 3. 12). And James Bourne remarks, very truly, "The minister of the letter, though preaching every truth, tender in his walk, and approved of men, yet, not being sent of God, cannot minister the Spirit to the afflicted, but will always bring them into bondage, and leave them there."

A DOOR OPENED AT HEATHFIELD

But to return to myself relative to the ministry. I came home from Barcombe that afternoon very sad indeed, begging the Lord to pardon me; and on meeting with a dear friend the next day, he asked me how I got on on the past day. "O!" said I, "it is all over. I shall never attempt to preach again." He laughed, but I said, "Ah! it is not a laughing matter with me." He replied, "I am more than ever convinced that God has appointed you to preach the gospel, and I am sure you will go again, and that soon." This I did not believe, but my thoughts and the Lord's were very different in the matter. He saw good to lay His servant aside by affliction, who was one of the supplies at Heathfield, the person before mentioned, and he wrote to me saying that he had heard of my casting down on account of being shut up at Barcombe, and that I had said I should not attempt to enter a pulpit again. But he entreated me, as a friend, to go to Heathfield for him as there were a few of the Lord's poor there who would be without anyone to speak to them, and he said, "If you cannot speak to them, you can read and conduct the service that way." The result was that I consented to go.

I had fifteen miles to walk on the Sunday morning and knew not the place nor the people, except the one I saw with my friend from there, as I before named. On my way to the place these words came with power on my heart: "Stand still, and see the salvation of the Lord" (Exod. 14. 13). They abode on my spirit with such weight, and the Lord the Spirit conversed with me upon them until I arrived at the place, so that I felt I must tell the people of the Lord's dealings with me in bringing me to prove the truth of them in my own soul (though I afterwards found that there was much more couched in the words for me to know and prove in connection with the ministry and Heathfield than I had then any idea of). An aged man, a member of the little church, was labouring under a heavy trial; the Lord so blessed the word spoken to that dear man that he was completely delivered from the trial, though the circumstances of the trial still remained. And I afterwards heard that the Lord put His seal to the word spoken that day.

The Lord removed to his eternal rest His servant for whom I had supplied; the result was that the church requested me to supply the pulpit twice a month. This I did, riding up by the mail-cart on a Saturday night, and walking back to Lewes after the afternoon service. Sometimes a friend would take me part of the way. But the more I went among the people, the more I felt that there were a few that feared the Lord. The good man who was the deacon was a well-taught, staid, sober man, a man who said but little, but that little was at the right time and in the right spirit. I soon found my very soul knit unto him.

Through my returning home on the Sunday evening to be in my place of work on the Monday morning, I heard but little of what was going on in the minds of the people or the effect that my youthful testimony had among them, but each time I went I found there were more people. I found that some of them were hearers of Mr. Crouch of Wadhurst; Mr. Russell of Rotherfield; Mr. Cowper of the Dicker; Mr. Pitcher of Horsebridge; and Mr. Hallett of Hadlow Down. When I heard of this, it made me tremble, and my knees often smote together as I entered the pulpit, but through mercy I was kept from saying much to man of my solemn exercises and heart-sinkings but was enabled to cry unto my God for direction and strength to follow it: and I will say of the Lord that He was then, and still is, "My rock, and my fortress; in Him will I trust." I trusted in Him, and was helped!

CHAPTER 7

TRIALS AND DELIVERANCES AT WORK

But I must now return to relate a little more of the Lord's wonderful works to me in providence. The staff of the soap factory soon conceived a great dislike to me. It began to shew itself in this way. The master was often out from home, and the men were in the habit of spending much of the time in his absence in gambling and drinking beer. My place was on the ground floor of the building, to prepare lees and do the bidding of the foreman. Well, he said to me one day, "If the master asks you what quantity of lees has gone upstairs, say, so many." I replied, "That quantity has not gone up." He tartly replied, "What has that to do with you? You do as I tell you." I answered, "I shall not say any more has gone up than has done so." At this they were much offended, and said they were sure that I was a canting Methodist, and began to make it as unpleasant as they possibly could to get me to leave the situation of my own accord. But I was enabled to make my prayer unto my God, and set a watch day by day.

Finding they could not succeed in getting me to leave of my own accord, they sought means to accuse me to my employer for they were determined to get rid of me. Things went on in a very trying manner for some time until one morning, on my being called upstairs by the foreman, he falsely accused me, and I not only denied it but told him he might do what he wanted me to help him to do himself, and I went downstairs again. This was as he would have it; I had refused to obey him in that which was plainly my duty. He therefore left all the work in a stand-still state until the master came. On seeing things as they were, he asked how it was. The foreman told him that I had refused to help, and that I was useless, in fact, he could not put up with me.

I was, of course, called by my master into his office, and he began very sharply to speak to me. "How is it that you allow all my work to be on the stand-still like this?" Now, I had laid my case before the Lord and asked Him to judge between me and these men, and that He would enable me to reply properly. So I said,

"Sir, I hope they have told you the truth about the matter. I own I refused to help take the pump out of the copper, but I was provoked to act as I did by their conduct towards me." On my thus speaking, my master shut the office door and said, "Now tell me the whole truth," which I unreservedly did, relating the whole affair. "Now," he said, "I have for some time past been sure that there was something wrong in this factory, but I could not tell in what way. Now you go out, and take no notice to others of what has passed between you and me, but as long as you prove faithful and look after my interests, I will stand by you."

Well, of course, they all thought that I should be discharged on the Saturday night following, but on the Monday morning I again entered the factory, when the foreman said, "What do you do here this morning? Were you not discharged on Saturday night?" I replied that I had not heard anything about it. He said, "Then you *shall* hear about it, for if you do not go, I will." So when the master came down, he said to him, "How is it, sir, that Charles is not gone?" (They called me Charles as the foreman's name was George). "If he does not go, I will." The master very coolly observed, "Well, you can go as soon as you like"; but before the week's end, he said to the master, "I will alter my mind and stay." "No," said the master, "You will leave next Saturday night week." This was a blow; they could not make it out.

Before this man left (who was the maker of the soap as well as the foreman), the master said to me, "Would you take his place?" I replied that I could not, as I knew not the art of soap-making. He answered, "If you are willing to take it, I will employ a traveller, and stay at home myself and teach you." I thanked him, and told him I would do my best to learn, which I did sufficiently to be left alone in a good measure in a month, the master taking great pains to teach, and I was very willing to be taught. After this the clerk (who had been one with the foreman) left, and another was engaged for a time, who soon sickened and died of consumption. After that I acted as clerk, and maker, and foreman, and I must say I very much liked my employer and we got on well together.

It was about this time that the Lord called me to go with His message to the people, and it was not long before my master heard of it. As it required some one to attend to the weighting of mottled soap during its cooling, it was my duty to see to it as I had the keys of the place and was not supposed to give them to anyone else. He said to me, "I hear you go out to preach." "Well," I replied, "I do." "But how do you manage when your services are required here on the Sunday?" I said, "I have instructed my wife how to adjust the weights, as I do not think it right to give the keys to anyone else." "O," he said, "don't get your wife to come; when it requires looking after and you are going out, tell me; I will do it for you." And this he did as long as I was with him.

DELIVERANCE FROM DEATH

One circumstance I must mention. My calls to go out to speak were for every Lord's day somewhere, and I had an invitation to speak at Bodle Street, where I had a desire to go, having heard much of them through their pastor. In the week before I was to go there, I was doing something on a plank over some portion of the hot soap and the plank slipped and I fell in, standing upright in the hot liquid. I screamed; the master ran to my assistance, and got me out. Had the copper been full, this would have been sudden death, as it would have covered the whole body though standing upright; or had it been boiling hot, with only the quantity that was there (up to my waist), of course I must have died as the caustic nature of the lees was such as quickly to eat through the skin into the flesh, so that my sufferings were great for a time. They stripped me in the factory, and in taking my stockings off, the skin of my legs came away with them. They carried me home, and soon two doctors were attending me. This was not needed, but the first one sent for being from home, another was brought; and when the first one came home and was told he had been asked to attend a person who had fallen into the soap copper, he thought perhaps it was full, so came immediately.

After a time the pain abated and I fell into a sleep. But so low did I sink in my mind under this affliction that I felt sure I should not get over it, and I neither felt ready nor willing to die; and I felt tried respecting my call to the ministry as I argued if the engagement to go to Bodle Street was of the Lord, I should not be thus laid aside. A Christian friend, who often came to see me, said, "I am persuaded you will be raised up again as when I was pleading for you this morning these words came with power:

"It is the Lord, whose matchless skill,
Can from affliction raise
Matter eternity to fill
With ever-growing praise."

And further he said, "I am persuaded that the Lord will make you His witness to many people, and you will have to suffer many things for the truth's sake." The means used were blessed, and I was able in a fortnight to walk out on crutches, and soon was at the factory again. My master was very kind to me, and paid me all the time I was laid aside; and many of the friends who worshipped at Jireh Chapel, Lewes, were kind and sympathising, and sent me nourishment, and old linen to dress my wounds, etc.

Further Engagements

As soon as I could, I went to Heathfield again and found more people, and the deacon paid me six shillings instead of five. I must remind my readers that the people were very poor, most of them labourers. After a time, the friends at Heathfield wished me to come among them *three* times a month when I could, so at times I did. I often used to go also to Bodle Street, and to a little chapel at W., near Willingdon, and to Horeham, and other places.

Having been brought, I trust by the Lord Himself, to see that baptism by immersion was right, and that only believers in the Lord Jesus Christ were the right subjects for that ordinance, and though I had not been brought to that place in my experience, "See here is water, what doth hinder me from being baptized?" it had not been laid on my mind to do as the eunuch did, yet I *was* a Baptist.

Changes

After a time a fresh trial came upon me. My master, having lost money in betting on horses at the races, suddenly left his home and went abroad; we had no thought of his being involved as he was. He came down to the factory as usual in the evening, looked into the copper, and said to me, "Are you going to do so and so?" I answered, "Yes," and he left. The next morning I learned that he had not been home all night; they enquired when I last saw him, and on going to the railway station they found he had gone overnight to London; from thence he had gone to Liverpool, and when they reached that place they found he had left for Australia. His wife hearing from him, afterwards went out to him.

There was a sale at the factory of what belonged to my master, and the owners of the building wished me to stay, saying they should soon let it again. I consented, and did stay for some time; but a godly man said to me, "It will never be let as a soap factory again. This is the Lord's way of bringing you out to give yourself to the work He has called you to do." I replied, "I feel sure that it will soon be let, and if I can agree with the parties, I shall stay." "Ah!" he said, "You never will." I could not believe him, but so it turned out; it was never let again for a soap factory. The whole plant was sold, and the building converted into corn stores, so that I was now entirely thrown out of this calling. I obtained a little employment for a time, haymaking and harvesting, gardening, etc.; and when hop-picking time came, I went to Heathfield for a month's hop-picking, and spoke to them on the Sunday.

During the time I was hop-picking, a person broke into the house of the friends with whom I was staying and stole a watch and other things belonging to them, an overcoat, shoes and other things belonging to me; my shoes, if I remember rightly, I had again as they were found pledged at a pawn-shop in Tunbridge Wells. The thief was caught. I with my friend had to appear at court, and when I saw the person, and noticed that he was a delicate-looking young man, how I wished I could speak to him and tell him I forgave him! I wished that I had not to give evidence against the poor young man, he looked so sad. I dreaded the trial at the Quarter Sessions at Lewes, but there the poor young man pleaded guilty, so I had not a word to say. Some few of my friends made a subscription and collected £2 4s 6d so that my lost coat was replaced by a new one, as well as the other things stolen from me, and I had some money left.

Removal to Heathfield

Seeing that every door was closed at Lewes for me to labour with my hands to obtain the bread that perisheth and support my family, it brought me into a great strait. I cried day and night to the Lord to open a door for me so that I might not be a burden to the dear people of God. I did so dread being a burden to them, and what made me fear it more was the friends at Heathfield were now giving me ten shillings each time I supplied for them, and I did not see how they could continue this. Indeed I knew they could not except the Lord provided.

After much exercise and prayer on both sides, the friends at Heathfield advised me to come among them to live. There was a cottage with a little land to let at a moderate rent, and they thought if I could keep a cow and get what work I could, that we should be able to live. Ultimately I consented, and the friends sent a wagon from Heathfield to take us there. So I, with my wife and family, left my native town, not knowing what bonds and afflictions awaited me. But I felt enabled to commit myself and family and way into the hands of my God, with an inward persuasion that I was taking a step agreeable to His mind and will. I felt the inward voice: "Go, and I will be with thee."

CHAPTER 8

HEATHFIELD

We safely arrived at Heathfield and entered our new abode on the 9th day of October, 1858. My dear wife had never been much away from her parents, had for a long time lived next door to her mother and father, and therefore greatly felt the parting. The house we left was much warmer and more convenient than the one we were now in; we had only green wood to burn (my wife had been used to coal) and the place was filled with smoke every time we lit the fire. In addition to this, I had praised my Heathfield friends so much in her hearing. The day being Saturday when we unloaded our furniture, she had enough to do to get a little straight. She asked me what she was to carry to chapel for her dinner on Sunday as it was too far to come home between the services. I told her they always found me a dinner, and for once I felt sure they would be glad to do the same for her, which might have been the case had I explained the cause of the dinner not being brought by my wife. Well, at dinner time my wife sat with me, and I handed her a part of mine, saying to the person who provided it, "I thought she could have part of mine today." "O," he replied, "I am not going to provide for so many," and appeared very unpleasant, so that it was but little either I or my wife could eat. All this put together made her very uncomfortable, and she said if these were my wonderful friends, I might have them; she would rather go back to Lewes to live. But she found that there were some who desired our welfare, and sent us such things as we needed.

At that time persons were permitted to go into the park belonging to Sir C. W. Blunt, and get up the roots of trees that had been thrown down. Some of these trees were very large, and there was a great deal of wood in the roots, so I went and dug some out, and got a friend to take them home for me; but of course, they were (like me with my country life) *green*, and required a great deal of other wood to make them burn.

HARD TIMES

I borrowed £20 at five per cent interest and bought a cow and some pigs to fatten, and worked when I could get it, gardening for the friends; and in the summer I helped a friend to cut his grass and make hay of it and get it up, and he helped me cut mine and get it up. I took a piece of peas to cut, but could earn but little at this; and when the time came, we all went hop-picking. This we did for over twenty years, with between two and three miles to walk morning and night with our little ones, and when we arrived home we have been dreadfully tired. The children, having fallen asleep, generally had to be carried to bed without supper, and on account of the distance had to be roused up again early in the morning. Of course, the cow and pigs etc. must be looked after when we returned home at night, as well as before we left in the morning, and my wife did her washing, baking, etc. at night, so that she had but little rest.

Well, when the pigs were fattened, I sold them to a man who promised to pay for them when *he* sold them, but failed to do as he had promised. There was another man in partnership with him; and after a time the Lord called one of them by grace, and though it was years after, he paid me all I would take. As my wife could not milk the cow when I was from home, I had to get some one to do it for me, which was not always convenient. This made it trying, as I had to return after speaking at places some miles from home, but we struggled on in this way for some time, much tried in providence, but with marked proof of the Lord's goodness in providing for us. In addition to this, I was favoured with evidences of the Lord's being with me in enabling me to declare His truth in simplicity and, I trust, godly sincerity, according as He had given me to taste, handle and feel its power in my own soul, so that the little place we met to worship our God in was not large enough to accommodate us and hold all who wished to get in.

A CHAPEL BUILT

One day, when in Lewes, I met a gentleman who knew me. After shaking hands and asking after my health, he said, "I find the Lord blesses your testimony among the people at Heathfield; you must have a chapel built." I replied that I had not been among them very long, and most likely there would soon be plenty of room for those who came to hear. He replied, "I do not think so. I have land up near your present meeting-place, and I will give you a piece to build a chapel upon. Go home and talk it over with your friends, and let me know the result."

I accordingly called the friends together to talk the matter over, and we came to the conclusion that we must accept the good man's offer with the hope that the thing was of the Lord. The church members and others met in the field named by our friend, who had also said, "Take as much ground as you like," and we marked out a piece which we thought would be quite sufficient. This piece of land was conveyed from the said gentleman (Mr. Richard Barrett, of Lewes) into the hands of trustees for the express purpose of a chapel being erected upon it, which we at once set about. O the many sighs and cries unto the Lord that we might not be left to take a wrong step, and that if built, it might be for the Lord's own honour and glory, and the good of those that were His! We began with great fear and trembling, as we were but a few feeble and much-despised folk.

The building was to be quite plain, 26 feet by 40, with two small vestries, the cost of which, without the legal expenses, was about £360. It was opened for the service of God the 28th day of July, 1859, by Mr. John Warburton, of Southill, and Mr. Tatham, of Eastbourne. The collections that day amounted to about £20, and we borrowed £100 on loan to be paid back by instalments, and many promised to give 1d per week towards paying off expenses. I went about begging, so we got the debt considerably lowered. Our legal expenses came to over £20, which we felt was very heavy.

I used to fear we should not be able to pay for it, and how many almost sleepless nights I had about it! I also feared that it would prove to be larger than we required. But Gideon's God was our God, and He made His Word quick and powerful, so that there was crying from the sick and wounded among us for mercy from the God of salvation to be manifested unto their poor souls. Some were healed by having God's Word sent to them, while others, who had been brought to feel the galling yoke of bondage, were brought out into liberty.

The church now gave me a call to become their pastor. I felt enabled to lay the solemn matter before the Lord, as I felt that it was a very different thing from being a supply. What should I do to speak continually to the same people? But I trust the Lord brought me to know and feel that I was quite dependent upon His divine teaching to preach one sermon to them, and that God who helped me at one time could help me at all times; yea, and I felt He would.

A CHURCH FORMED

I had for some years been persuaded that believers' baptism by immersion was the only scriptural mode of obeying a divine command, and had begged of the Lord in His own time and place to enable me to follow Him. I was accordingly baptized in the new chapel on December 4th, 1859. I was favoured with the sweet presence and powerful love of the Lord Jesus Christ shed abroad in my heart, so that I felt buried with my dear Lord, and raised again in Him, who I felt was my Resurrection and Life. My poor soul was ready to burst with holy joy and sacred peace. When I returned into the vestry, the minister that baptized me said, "Well, how is it now?" "O bless the Lord!" I replied. "I would willingly go down into the water again if the Lord required it." He said, "Well, I have not encouraged you." "No," I replied, "but I am sure it is a right step, and I have the answer of a good conscience."

I afterwards accepted the church's call to become their pastor on condition that from henceforth it be a Strict Baptist church, as before it was open communion. This was consented to. Therefore from June 3rd, 1860, I became the pastor of the little church, consisting of eleven members and myself, and I trust that we entered into the covenant bond as a marriage bond of the Lord's own appointing. Yes, and I am persuaded it is as long as we both live, unless in the providence of God removed, for I can truly say I felt it was an unbreakable covenant. Some profess so clearly to see the hand of the Lord in bringing together the pastor and people, but in many cases it soon comes to an end, especially if a minister has an offer of more salary.

ENLARGEMENT

Well, soon after we built the chapel, it became evident that we must have more room, but this we feared very much to enter into as we had still a debt; but it was at length decided to build a gallery, which was done in the year 1862, at a cost of £49 10s. We did not add this cost to the chapel debt, but the friends raised the money and paid it the same year. At that time I was often favoured with the spirit of prayer and the grace of supplication, as well as a watchful spirit; and, like Manoah and his wife, I have looked on with wonder and astonishment to see the Lord work so wondrously. In order that the expenses might be kept down, I swept and cleaned the chapel, did the painting, etc.; and this I did for some years.[4]

In the year 1872 a new schoolroom to seat about 100 children was built over the vestries at a cost of £135 18s. 11d. I again took my begging book, first asking the Lord to incline the hearts of the people to give, and it resulted in my obtaining £61 11s. 6½d. The remainder was in time all paid. In 1875 a new porch was built at the entrance of the front door at a cost of £20; and in the year 1881 the chapel was all new seated (as what we had before were only old seats which were given us) and the inside walls cemented at a cost of £93 9s. 11d. and in a short time this was all paid off.

The dear old pilgrims who were advanced in years when I first came among them were one after another taken home. I felt their loss very much, especially that of the oldest deacon, William Errey. Not only was he a well-taught man of God, but blessed also with an excellent spirit. Not a man to say much, but what he did say had remarkable weight and authority with it, being tempered with great tenderness and the fear of God, so his memory is blessed

---

[4][G.M.] Eventually Mr. John Warburton put a stop to this by saying, "If you allow your minister to sweep the chapel, I won't come."

and dear unto me. In cases of trial, wherein he saw I was wrong in spirit or judgment (and I was, and often am), how affectionately and scripturally he would speak to me! Really I felt my soul knit to him as Jonathan's to David. The other deacon was such a very different spirited man and caused me so much trouble and sorrow that at last the church interfered, and he withdrew from membership with us altogether some years before the death of my friend William Errey.

THE PASTOR'S HOUSE

During the time I swept the chapel, one Saturday after doing my work, I went out into a field adjoining the chapel, and while there I had such a spirit of prayer and supplication poured out upon me, and such an impression to ask the Lord to give me a house to live in on that spot, that I felt a persuasion the Lord would grant my request, though I could see no way whereby it could be done. Well, I could not get away from the feeling, but said nothing to any man; it was between the Lord and myself.

Some months after this, one of the deacons said to me, "We as a church have been desirous of showing our thankfulness to you for your endeavours to keep down the expenses and to get the chapel out of debt by doing something for you to be of permanent use, and the conclusion we have come to is this: that if a piece of ground can be obtained near the chapel where a house could be built, we will do what we can to raise some money towards the building of it." I then told him what I had felt respecting the matter, but he said that piece of land was not for sale. "Well," I replied, "If the thing is from the Lord, that is where the house will be." "Ah! well," he said, "this I must leave."

After a time I heard that the person who owned the land was going to build two cottages on it, so I asked a friend to enquire if it was true, and whether he would sell it. On my friend naming it to him, he said, "Yes, I do think of building unless I could sell it. Do you chapel people want it, as it joins yours?" My friend said, "I am not prepared to answer your question today, but will see you again," which he did, and told him he did want it for the minister to build upon; what did he ask for it? He named the sum, and my friend said he was sure that price would not be given, as it was (at that time for land here) an exorbitant price, and far too much. "Ah! well," said the man, "I don't care to sell, as I can build upon it myself." So my friend was rather put out, and thought he should not get it.

But I felt it was the will of the Lord that I should have it, so I asked Him to direct me what price to offer for it; and so I went with my friend the next time, and made the offer I felt the Lord had instructed me to make. He replied, "Indeed you are not going to get it for that sum." "Well," I said, "that is *all* I shall give; I will pay the conveyance." Again he answered, "No." "Goodnight," we said, and left; but we had not gone far before he called us back, and said, "You shall have it at the price you offer." So the bargain was struck, and the building of the house was soon begun. Some gave small sums of money, some gave bricks, others the carriage of materials, and others labour, so that I think on its being finished there was a debt on it of about £150. I took up the £100 at five per cent, and the other £50 was paid off, and only the £100 remained.

After the removal of dear Mr. Covell, of Croydon, to the church triumphant, I was brought into an intimate connection with the Misses Summers, who after a time visited my house, and during their stay with us they asked my wife particulars about the house, and found that I had £100 mortgage on it. I remember on my return home from where I had been to speak, Miss Summers said, "We have found out all about the building of this house, and the debt you have on it." I replied, "This you would not have done had you not ploughed with my heifer." "Never mind," said they, "*how* we have found it out. We will pay the £100 off at once, and make it free to you."

I was so overcome that I could not speak for some time. I thanked them as heartily as I could, and as soon as I was able I went into my bedroom and there thanked and blessed my dear and gracious Lord for His great goodness unto me. I had at times been much weighed down respecting the £100. I could see no way of getting out of the trouble as my family and expenses were continually increasing. O how sure I am that

"When the Lord's people have need,
His goodness will find out a way"!

And the Misses Summers were the instruments in the Lord's hand for my temporal good as long as they lived. "They that observe these things, even they shall understand the lovingkindness of the Lord."

CHAPTER 9

DEATH OF A SON

It was not long after we went to live in our new house before fresh trouble came. The Lord saw fit to lay affliction upon my children, and one was taken away by the icy hand of death at the age of fourteen. O the sighs and cries of my soul, night and day, for the salvation of the lad's soul! But I did not feel that I could talk to him about it until one morning when he said, "Father, do you think that I shall get better?" I said, "What do you feel about it?" He replied, "I shall not get better." "No," I said, "I fear you won't." Then he said, "O father, do pray for me." I replied, "This I continually try to do; I hope you pray for yourself." He said, "I feel I don't know how to pray." The Lord had mercy on me by giving me a sweet hope that He had mercy on him, and took his spirit unto Himself, but this I did not get until after his body was buried. Before his departure, he asked for all his brothers and sisters to be called, spoke to each one separately, giving to each something belonging to himself, and bade them goodbye.

BLESSING AT BRIGHTON

After this, we had the scarlet fever among the children, and all the members of the household were prohibited from going to chapel except myself. I caught it, but had it only slightly, though for a time I was very low both in body and mind. Indeed, I sank very low, and going down to Brighton for a change, I called on some dear friends, Mr. and Mrs. Combridge, and they asked me to stay with them. I did so, and their kindness was great to me so that in a short time I felt better in body, and the dear Lord made that blessed promise good in my poor soul, "I will see you again, and your heart shall rejoice, and your joy no man taketh from you."

It was brought about in the following way. As I sat in my friend's room, feeling almost in despair, Mr. Combridge brought me the late Mr. James Wells's book called *Achor's Gloomy Vale*.

I opened the book and began to read where I opened, and while reading the dear man's bitter complaint and confession of sin, and also of the Lord's great goodness in bearing with his ill ways and crooked manners and not cutting him off, my heart began to soften and melt, and I felt the goodness of God so flow into my poor soul that it brought me to repentance and confession of my sins, and produced such brokenness of spirit that I wept like a child. Indeed, I was so overcome that I believe I felt like the Queen of Sheba, of whom it is said, "There was no more spirit left in her." I felt almost to swoon away with bliss. Mrs. Combridge coming into the room and seeing me in the state I was, exclaimed, "O Mr. Mockford, you are not so well!" I replied, "I am much better." She said, "I will not disturb you," and retired, but soon came back and said, "Do tell me about the change." I answered, "I cannot; I will when I can."

I walked out by the sea with my heart overflowing with love unto my blessed Lord Jesus Christ for the great things He had done for me. The place was crowded with people (it being a gala day in Brighton) but it seemed as if I saw no one but Jesus only. I heard music passing; I felt in my heart, and said with my tongue,

> "No music's like Thy charming name,
> Nor half so sweet can be."

Once or twice the cab-drivers called out, "Get out of the way, you fool; do you want to get run over?" I turned into a by-street, went back to my friends, and was enabled to relate a *little* of the goodness and mercy and lovingkindness of the Lord to me, and we rejoiced together.

I returned home like a giant refreshed with new wine, to relate to my dear people the great things the Lord had done for me. And O what a blessed heart-felt uniting we had! My trials much increased; I lived to prove that the Word of God is true: "Folly is bound up in the heart of a child, but the rod of correction shall drive it far from him." The Word being much blessed, my heart was lifted up and the Lord brought me down. This plunged me into trouble; I was also brought to see and feel the great goodness and mercy of my God in permitting trial as a preservative. O where might I not have stumbled and fell but for trial?

CLOSE PREACHING

There is much, however, I wish to pass over; the cruel spite of Satan through men has nearly crushed me into the grave, but, "Bless the Lord, O my soul," I proved Him to be my Shield and Buckler, and my Strong Tower. By this teaching I was led in the ministry to draw the line more clearly between the flesh and the spirit, between life and death; and as my late dear friend Pert [pastor at Flimwell from 1852-1880] once said to me, "Your arms are too long; when they have done crying 'Hosanna,' they will say 'Crucify him.' Then your arms will be shorter" – so I found it. I began to be called a man of a bad spirit, but doors were continually being opened for this bad-spirited man to preach, and I found more than ever that by the power of the Spirit the Word spoken had a twofold effect: to some it was "the savour of life unto life," to others "the savour of death unto death." And as I was led to shew that all religious fruits that did not spring from Jesus Christ, the only true Vine – which could only be where there was a living union unto Him – were not the fruits of the Spirit, therefore all sprang from the flesh. Some said I should by such preaching discourage the young in the ways of God, but I contended nothing would discourage them more than trying to build them up with untempered mortar. These young real seekers dreaded being deceived; they prized faithful dealing.

PROVIDENCE

With regard to the Lord's dealings with me in providence, we have been brought into great straits, and often knew not what to do. My being called to preach at West Street Chapel, Croydon, has (in the hands of the Lord) been a wonderful help to me; in fact, it looks the only way by which I have been kept from getting greatly in debt, without any means of paying. As my family grew up, I found that increasing years brought increasing trials and heavier expenses that caused me sleepless nights, and at times much wrestling with cries and tears to God on their behalf, as well as my own. I also had many blessed proofs of the lovingkindness of my covenant God and Father in my own soul, as well as in providence, and found as the man of God Hezekiah did, that "by these things men live, and in all these things is the life of my spirit."

DEATH OF HIS WIFE

In the year 1891 my dear wife was taken ill, and died in a few days, but the Lord favoured me with support by giving me to hope that He had taken her unto Himself. Under this keen trial I found great sympathy and kindness, both among my own dear people and many others; and dear Jesus drew me very near to Himself, and favoured me to lean upon Him as my Beloved, and thus brought me up out of the wilderness that I felt this death had brought me into. My dear people, with others, paid all the expenses of the funeral. *These* were great mercies, but O the kisses of the mouth of my Beloved out-topped *all*. It was indeed "better than wine"!

Here Mr. Mockford's account ends.

HIS LAST DAYS

In his last days he was much affected by faintness caused by a heart disease, and was very delicate. At the beginning of 1892 he suffered a severe illness, during which he had a striking dream. He described it thus:

"I dreamed that a most august person took me by the hand and led me down a very long flight of steps. At the bottom was a door, and taking a key from his girdle he said to me, 'This is the gate of death. Shall I open it?' I replied, 'As thou wilt, Lord.' He turned and smiled upon me and said, 'Not yet,' and led me up to the top again. I told those about me I should not die then but should get better."

On February 10th, 1893, he was again married, and his wife was able to care for him to the end.

In the early part of 1898 he had another severe illness and had to give up many engagements. All fear of death was removed and he was kept in a very peaceful frame of mind. On one occasion it seemed as if he saw death standing at the foot of his bed, and he said, "Yes death, if my Master has bid thee strike, I am ready."

On his birthday, December 27th, he had such a sweet visit from the Lord that his soul was filled with holy joy and peace. The opening verses of Psalm 103 were the language of his heart. Before another birthday had come round, he had entered into the full enjoyment of this blessing.

In the early part of 1899, cataracts on his eyes caused his sight to fail, and he found it difficult to read, especially in the pulpit. The last time he preached at Heathfield was on Wednesday, November 1st, when he spoke from Psalm 106. 44, 45, dwelling very sweetly on the word *Nevertheless*. Two days later he was seized with a stroke which affected his left arm. However, at the weekend he ventured to Croydon, preaching ably and clearly, and with much power, from John 17. 3.

After a most trying night, he was advised by the doctor to return home immediately. On reaching home he went to bed, never to get up again. He lingered about a fortnight, often speaking of the goodness of his God over the years, and referred to a promise given: "My God shall supply all your need," adding, "He has *done* it. How many mercies I have! God is very gently taking down my tabernacle."

The night of the 15th was most distressing. He spoke of it in this way. Satan seemed to straddle over him like Apollyon, and said to him, "This is the valley of the shadow of death, and it is only a shadow to God's people but to you it is a reality, and you shall not go through this valley alive. You have often told the people you were not afraid of death, but now *you* will be lost, so the best thing you can do is to take your life and know the worst; it will only be a little beforehand." Then it was suggested, "Curse God! curse God!" "No," he said, "He has been a good God to me." Then these lines came with power and sweetness:

> "When through the deep waters I call thee to go,
> The rivers of woe shall not thee overflow."

He said he saw so much in the words, "I call thee to go" – that it was God who led him through those deep waters. Then followed:

"And passing through a thousand woes,
They get securely home."

Thus faith gained the victory. After this he never sank so low again but for the most part enjoyed a settled peace within though his bodily sufferings were great.

The Lord's day previous to his death, when very ill, he said with much feeling;

"His grace shall to the end,
Stronger and brighter shine;
Nor present things, nor things to come,
Shall quench the spark divine."

Among his last words were: "All is peace within; not a dog moves his tongue"; "Not one thing hath failed of all the Lord spake"; "My God has been kind to me"; "Wonderful, wonderful!" raising his right hand and waving it. Though his speech was almost gone, he seemed to be saying, "Crown Him! crown Him!" right to the end. He died on the morning of November 22nd, 1899, aged 72.

The funeral service was taken by Mr. J. Newton and Mr. W. Smith, both of Tunbridge Wells, a very large number of people being present. He had been minister at Heathfield for forty years. His sorrowing church and congregation erected a tablet in the chapel on which is recorded:

"He laboured abundantly in word and deed for the benefit of this cause. His ministry was eminently useful, and greatly blessed of God, both here and in many other places. Having proved the faithfulness of God to all His promises, he entered into rest."

Yours in tribulation

Robt Ingram

ROBERT MOXON: 1840-1906

A former Arminian preacher who became a champion of free and sovereign grace.

As a young man, Robert Moxon was so wicked that he narrowly escaped committing murder. Wrought upon by the Spirit of God, he at first preached among the Wesleyan Methodists. Amazingly, it was in a Methodist pulpit, where he had gone as a "free will" preacher, that in reading the chapter the doctrine of God's sovereign election was clearly revealed to him.

For twenty-five years he was pastor at Bury in Lancashire.

Dearly loved, the following incident is typical. A young man once visited him, complaining of the cruel and harsh way he had been treated by his brethren, and seeking his advice. Mr. Moxon replied that he too had once been harshly treated; but whilst he meditated how to revenge himself, the Lord showed him, dropping into his heart the words: "Father, forgive them; for they know not what they do."

CHAPTER 1

CHILDHOOD AND EARLY YEARS

One reason for writing a few scraps of my experience is that some poor souls may be encouraged to trust in the Lord. God says by His prophet, "Speak ye comfortably to Jerusalem." The introduction most befitting this little treatise is a prayer to God.

I was born at Clayton West, near Huddersfield, on December 19th, 1840, the year in which Sir Rowland Hill introduced the penny postage stamp – a far greater boon to this nation than I have ever been to my parents, or am ever likely to be. I have often heard my mother tell how busy she was in binding boot uppers, and how unprepared just then for such a permanent visitor, though I have every reason to believe that I received all possible attention and care.

The first recollection that I have is the funeral of a little sister, Emma, who died on 4th December, 1843. I was not quite three years old. I distinctly remember my mother lifting me up in her arms to kiss the baby before it was made up in the coffin.

I have not the least remembrance of learning the ABC, but I well recollect beginning to write, and the master saying to me, "In which hand will you hold the pen?" I held up my right hand and said, "This." He said, "Well, you can begin." He knew that I was left-handed, a true Benjamite.

I used to be very fond of sliding, and one snowy day, when sliding on a pond, the ice gave way and into the water I went; but, my arms being on the top, I soon extricated myself.

Two things were very distasteful to me at school: one was the Church catechism and the other was grammar. My youthful mind was particularly perplexed about the sacraments being "outward signs of invisible and spiritual grace"; and the different parts of speech in grammar were things that I thought absolute nonsense. A game at marbles or spinning tops would have been a pleasure; but this incomprehensible drudgery made me loathe the school altogether.

My parents, being poor, could not afford to give me much education, nor was my inclination in that direction had my opportunities been ever so advantageous. I was allowed to go to the factory for half-time when eight and a half years old, and I left the school altogether before I was ten years of age. Young as I was when on half-time, foolishness was bound up in my heart, and many times did it manifest itself in both word and deed; but an unseen hand guided me and prevented me during those boyish years. When about nine years old, I remember a motto placed against the wall of the school deeply impressed my mind for a time. The words were, "Thou God seest me." I could then see, as well as I can now, that I was under the constant inspection and all-seeing gaze of the great I AM. This was for a time the means of causing me to act more carefully; but all these impressions passed away, and for several years I went on worse than ever I had been before.

One day, as I was going along the road towards Bilham Grange Farm, thoughts and feelings entered into me which I had never known before. I felt sure not only that God could see me, but that I stood accountable to Him for my actions, and that one day He would surely bring me into judgment. I was at that time (1851) nearly eleven years old. But still all was vanity. The veil of ignorance was upon my heart, and I do not believe for one moment that the convictions referred to were of a spiritual nature, or that I was at that time a partaker of God's grace. There is a natural conscience in every man; and it accuses or excuses, condemns or justifies, according to the light and knowledge a man possesses. But in regeneration there is a new nature bestowed, a new life implanted, and it is manifested in two very distinct ways. First, it discovers the exceeding sinfulness of our sins. We then see infinite purity in God, and, though we may know nothing of the letter of the law, we feel ourselves to be exceeding great sinners. Secondly, we are made to long for our wants to be supplied. With the knowledge of sinfulness come misery and condemnation; and, where these things are felt, there will be a longing for mercy and deliverance. Peter says: "As newborn babes, desire the sincere milk of the word, that ye may grow thereby"; and thus there is a longing for the blessings of pardon and justification.

THE WAY OF SIN

At the age of about fourteen years (1854), I was sent as an apprentice to Lockwood, near Huddersfield, to learn moulding. There I continued for twelve months, at the expiration of which time my father had changed his mind in reference to my trade. By this time I had become almost a Master of Arts in every species of wickedness. (Let me urge upon parents to keep their children as much as possible under their own roof and at their own table; and, if they cannot do this, let them use every means to secure for them as good guardians as possible). I could now break the Sabbath with impunity, seldom if ever going to school or chapel except on very wet Sundays, and then playing with other boys at dominoes during the service at the chapel. I could also take the name of God in vain; nothing was too foul or base for me to utter; every kind of oath and curse was as familiar as my name. I could also go to the alehouse and play at all kinds of sinful games, such as brasses, quoits, major, puff and dart, billiards, draughts; and join in obscene songs and recitations. I was also addicted to betting and gambling of almost every kind, frequenting the racecourse, and as full of mischief as I could possibly be. Many times have I gone through the village at night with others for no other purpose but to destroy people's property. This continued for upwards of two years (1856), during which time I was often in jeopardy.

On one occasion, another young man had been with me to Huddersfield, and we were returning home late in the evening when we met with an old man who had been a soldier. He foolishly told us that he had in his pocket a number of gold coins. This was a temptation too strong for us, and when he left us we agreed that we would wait until he had got on the canal side; then we would follow him, take his money and push him into the canal. O how dreadful the thought now appears to me! But I was then prepared to do anything. Well, how was it prevented? By the special interference of a divine providence, the old man suddenly stopped and turned back, and we could by no means prevail with him to go home at all. I am sure the hand of the Lord was manifested in causing him to return and thus to disappoint us in our diabolical design of robbery and murder.

> "Determined to save, He watched o'er my path,
> When, Satan's blind slave, I sported with death.
> And can He have taught me to trust in His name,
> And thus far have brought me to put me to shame?"

REVIVAL MEETINGS

It was about this time that a great revival of religion took place at Clayton West (not God's religion, but man's, as the sequel proved), and almost all my companions were "converted" and joined in church fellowship. I could, however, afford to laugh at them and tell them how foolish they were; but they all seemed seriously impressed and were as happy as possible. Prayer meetings, fellowship meetings, class meetings and love feasts were the constant employment; it seemed as if heaven were begun on earth. This was in the beginning of the year 1858. During the early part of the summer of the same year, I had an only brother taken away by death; and these new converts took the opportunity of this bereavement to remind me of the solemnity of death, and urged upon me the importance of giving my heart to the Lord. But all their entreaties and persuasions were of no avail: I went on as before, making a mock of their profession. And I would just say that nearly all those converts made shipwreck of their faith and profession, went again into the world, became withered branches and died away. Some few remained, but not one that I have reason to think ever knew his ruin by sin or his redemption by Christ. Many times have I had to ask myself, "Who maketh thee to differ from another? and what hast thou that thou didst not receive?" (1 Cor. 4. 7). I have not a stone to throw at any of the above, nor any room for boasting, but need of great humiliation before the Lord and heartfelt gratitude to Him. I believe that I have been baser than them all, the vilest of them all; but the Lord never suffered me either to break off my profession or to cease calling upon His name. I have often feared that such would be the case, but "hitherto hath the Lord helped me." Truly I may say that

> "'Twas grace that kept me to this day,
> And will not let me go."

SPIRITUAL BEGINNINGS

The way in which it pleased God to begin a work of grace upon my soul was as follows: first, by setting my sins in deadly array against me, exhibiting the justice of God against sin, and causing me to reflect upon my state and case. My eyes were now opened to see sin in all its ugly deformity, and my heart was made to feel sin in all its bitterness. There was, in fact, a resurrection of all my past iniquities, which now appeared as heinous, as aggravated, and as insulting to the Most High God as crimes could possibly be. Hymn 238 (Gadsby's) was now my experience:

> "With melting heart and weeping eyes,
> My guilty soul for mercy cries;
> What shall I do, or whither flee,
> To escape the vengeance due to me ?

> "Till late, I saw no danger nigh;
> I lived at ease, nor feared to die
> Wrapped up in self-conceit and pride,
> 'I shall have peace at last,' I cried.

"But when, great God, Thy light divine
Had shone on this dark soul of mine,
Then I beheld, with trembling awe,
The terrors of Thy holy law.

"How dreadful now my guilt appears,
In childhood, youth, and growing years;
Before Thy pure discerning eye,
Lord, what a filthy wretch am I!"

Let the reader observe that during the whole of this period of deep conviction and soul trouble, I was as ignorant as a heathen concerning the Bible and the plan of salvation of a poor ruined sinner by the Lord Jesus Christ.

There was now, I felt, no infidelity in my heart; I was made a real believer that there was a God. I felt sure that He was watching all my conduct, marking every action and every word and every thought. I was convinced that He was perfectly holy and righteous, and that my conduct, all my life long, must have been highly offensive in His eyes. I knew that I deserved His hottest displeasure, and that He would be just in consigning me to hell. I now began to pray, and my constant and almost only petition was, "O Lord, take care of me this day, and I will live free from sin and not do anything to displease Thee; I will amend my ways and walk uprightly before Thee." But when night came I felt that I had not done according to my promise, but that all my endeavours were stained and dyed with sin. And O what bitter reflections did my conduct cause! The times I have sat beside my bed in that little kitchen bedroom at Clayton West, hardly daring to get into bed lest I should wake up in hell! My nightly cry was, "O Lord, spare me throughout this night, and I will do better." I vainly thought I could by perseverance and hard toiling break off all sinful workings and make myself acceptable before the Lord. I was now in my feelings in Job 9. I did not at that time know anything about the Book of Job, but I can see it now as plainly as noonday. God was now dealing with me in judgment and answering me by terrible things in righteousness. I was trying to please God with the filthy rags of my own performances; but alas! how can man by these things "be just with God"? When the Lord searches His people with His candle (Prov. 20. 27) and sweeps with His besom (Isa. 14. 23), what dust and filth does He meet with! When He lays judgment to the line and righteousness to the plummet in the poor sinner's conscience, He sweeps away the refuge of lies and the waters of His wrath overflow the sinner's hiding place. He then finds that his bed is too short and his covering too narrow, and he is driven out of house and out of harbour, and there he stands before the Lord, a poor, perishing, condemned criminal. He has not a plea that he can make, nor an argument that he can use in his own defence. When God contends, we cannot answer Him one of a thousand; we cannot choose out words to reason with Him; if we try to justify ourselves, He makes our own mouth to condemn us; if we wash ourselves with snow water, and make our hands never so clean, yet when the Lord appears, He plunges us into the ditch and makes our own clothes to abhor us. Well might Malachi ask: "But who may abide the day of His coming? and who shall stand when He appeareth? for He is like a refiner's fire, and like fullers' soap."

Solemn Thoughts in a Thunderstorm

During the time that I was under the schoolmaster of Moses' law, learning a little, and only a little (for who can know the whole?), of the ministration of death and condemnation, I was sent on a journey of about five miles to a place called Silkstone; and, while I was on my way, I both saw and felt all that Israel saw and felt when they came to the mount that burned with fire and blackness and darkness and tempest (Heb. 12. 18). I had a load on my back and a heavier load within my poor soul and as Solomon says, "Heaviness in the heart of man maketh it stoop." I was a companion of David: "O Lord, rebuke me not in Thy wrath: neither chasten me in Thy hot displeasure. For Thine arrows stick fast in me, and Thy hand presseth me sore. There is no soundness in my flesh because of Thine anger; neither is there any rest in my bones because of my sin. For mine iniquities are gone over mine head: as an heavy burden they are too heavy for me." This is a dreadful state to be in. This is where the sinner feels at the pit's mouth, and it makes him cry out, "Let not the pit shut her mouth upon me." While I was walking towards the place above mentioned, there came on a fearful thunderstorm. The big black clouds gathered thicker and thicker; the lurid flashes curled and quivered, first in the dense clouds and then at my very feet. The stones in the road were hurled past where I stood. I was terrified and durst not take another step, feeling as if the Day of Judgment was drawing near and that this awful storm was but the precursor of the more terrible day of God's everlasting wrath, which I knew I justly deserved. After halting and hiding myself on the roadside, I returned home, praying, resolving, promising, and vowing unto the Lord what I would do, and what I would be, if He would only spare my life a little longer.

That night, I went to the Independent Chapel. Mr. Axford, the newly appointed minister, gave an address upon "Dreams and Visions." I do not remember anything he said upon that subject; but I well remember that, when his address was over, he alluded to the terrible storm which had taken place that afternoon, and related a circumstance which occurred while he was a student in London. This suited me very much. It was as follows: "One evening, while I was at college, a fearful thunderstorm raged: the vivid flashes of lightning lit up the room, the peals of thunder shook the very bed on which I lay. I was filled with terror. I got out of bed and looked out of the window. While doing so, these words came sweetly to my mind:

> 'The God that rules on high,
> And thunders when He please;
> That rides upon the stormy sky,
> And manages the seas.
>
> 'This awful God is ours,
> Our Father and our love
> He shall send down His heavenly powers,
> To carry us above.'

This so calmed my mind that I fell asleep, feeling that all was in my Father's hand."

WEIGHTY EXERCISES OF SOUL

This seemed to do me good for a season, but it was not the balm my soul was longing for. Shortly after this time, I was singing while at my work, which was shoemaking, in the cellar of the house where I lived. The words I little understood, but had learned them by hearing others sing; and, being in that sad condition of soul feeling above described, I thought I would drive away my sadness. The words I sang were:

> "There is a fountain filled with blood,
>   Drawn from Immanuel's veins,
> And sinners plunged beneath that flood
>   Lose all their guilty stains."

Then there followed a chorus, which I also tried to sing:

> "I do believe, I can believe,
>   That Jesus died for me."

What precious words indeed they are! And thrice happy is that soul that can feelingly adopt them. But at this time they were not my experience; and I had no sooner finished the words than the door at the top of the stairs was opened, and my mother called out: "Robert, dost thou know what thou art singing about?" Her words went like a dart to my heart, and I was filled with more bitter grief than before. I could make no answer. I spoke not a word in reply. What a mercy to have an observing mother, a caring mother, a praying mother! And what influence does a mother exert!

I was now a most miserable sinner, almost distracted all day long. My thoughts were solemnly directed to death and eternal judgment, and I felt I was prepared for neither. I resorted to reading, meditation and prayer; but what I read I little understood. I was like the poor eunuch when he was reading that scripture: "He was led as a sheep to the slaughter; and like a lamb dumb before his shearer, so opened He not His mouth"; he could not tell what it meant. So I remember reading these words: "All that the Father giveth Me shall come to Me; and him that cometh to Me I will in no wise cast out." I thought about them day after day, but I could not make out what they meant. I did not understand what this coming could be, nor did I know anything of the Person a poor sinner comes to. Yet a hope sprang up in my heart, and I felt persuaded that there was a way of escape from my deserved and dreadful punishment if I only *knew* the way ; but there I was held in awful suspense. Sometimes I had a little hope that good would come if I could but get at the right way; and at other times I was almost in despair lest God should seal up my doom and appoint me my portion with hypocrites and unbelievers. I could at this time have endorsed the words of Ezra had I known that such words were in the Bible: "O my God, I am ashamed and blush to lift up my face to Thee, my God: for *my* iniquities are increased over *my* head, and *my* trespass is grown up unto the heavens."

I went to chapel to hear, but, although the minister seemed very sincere and very earnest, his message was not for me; my case was between the Lord and my own soul. I do not remember any individual that the Lord made use of to me either in begetting divine life in my soul or in bringing to the birth my spiritual deliverance. Isaiah 54. 6 seems to describe my case at this time: *"The Lord"* – and He only – *"hath called thee* as a woman forsaken and grieved in spirit, and a wife of youth, when thou wast refused, saith thy God." But, although I was thus forsaken and refused, it was but for a few brief months. Thus I proved what the prophet further says: "In a little wrath I hid My face from thee for a moment; but with everlasting kindness will I have mercy on thee" (Isa. 54. 8).

Just consider, dear reader, whoever thou art, that if what my poor distracted soul went through, as stated in the past few pages, be but a little wrath, a drop, a spark, what must be the cup of the fierceness of God's wrath; what must be the terror of that storm of hail every stone of which is the weight of a talent, which some compute at 60 lb. and others at 114 lb.? Well might John say, "The plague thereof was exceeding great" (Rev. 16. 21)! What, O what must be that fire, the smoke of which "ascendeth up for ever and ever"? May God deliver thee and me from so bitter a death!

CHAPTER 2

JOYFUL DELIVERANCE

I now come to the time of my deliverance and the way in which it was brought about. I had prayed until I could pray no longer; I had cried until I could cry no longer; my face was foul with weeping but, as the prophet puts it, "When the poor and needy seek water, and there is none, and their tongue faileth for thirst, I the Lord will hear them"; and so it was, and so it ever will be. He brings down with hard labour, they fall to the ground and no man can help, neither can they help themselves; at least it was so with me. Tell me not that it is for believing; I did not know what believing was. I can describe it fully and clearly in one word: REVELATION! Christ said, "All things are delivered unto Me of My Father: and no man knoweth the Son, but the Father; neither knoweth any man the Father save the Son, and he to whomsoever the Son will reveal Him." And where that revelation takes place, the soul is at once encouraged. Hence Christ immediately adds, "Come unto Me, all ye that labour and are heavy laden, and I will give you rest"; and I am sure He will. Peter speaks of the grace brought "at revelation of Jesus Christ." I do like that scripture. What sort of grace is it that is brought at this blessed revelation? I say it is believing grace, it is receiving grace, it is liberating grace, it is justifying grace, it is praising grace, it is God-glorifying grace and it is enduring grace, sufficient for every time of need. Paul says, "When it pleased God, who separated me from my mother's womb, and called me by His grace, to reveal His Son in me." And it is said concerning Simeon that "it was revealed unto him by the Holy Ghost, that he should not see death before he had seen the Lord's Christ." And I think it is the same now; not one of the Lord's people is suffered to see death until he has seen the Lord Jesus Christ as his only hope of eternal glory.

It was this divine revelation that was made known to my soul. I could then both see and feel what I had never seen or felt before, namely, that God loved me and had saved me. I was on my bended knees with my head bowed to the ground, when suddenly there appeared an assemblage of bright and glorious persons such as I have since thought would be the case when Christ was transfigured before His disciples on the mount. They saw literally, but I saw only spiritually; and a voice – not an audible voice, but "a still small voice," an inward whisper, an unmistakable persuasion seemed to say to me, "Notwithstanding all that thou hast done, I have loved thee." I felt that such was the case: my burden of sin was gone, and all the feelings of guilt and condemnation were removed as clean from me as if I had never sinned. I was perfectly justified in my soul and before the Lord. I was like Joshua the high priest, a brand plucked out of the fire, my filthy garments all taken from me, and all my iniquity made to pass from me. I stood clothed with a change of raiment and a fair mitre on my head. I felt such a pleasing sensation of liberty and love as I cannot well describe. Bunyan says concerning Christian after he had lost his burden:

"Then was Christian glad and lightsome and said, with a merry heart, He hath given me rest by His sorrow, and life by His death. Then he stood still a while, to look and wonder. . . He looked and looked again even till the springs that were in his head sent the waters down his cheeks. Now, as he stood looking and weeping, behold, three Shining Ones came to him and saluted him with, 'Peace be to thee; thy sins be forgiven thee.'. . . Then Christian gave three leaps for joy and went on singing,

> 'Must here the burden fall from off my back?
> Must here the strings that bound it to me crack?
> Blest Cross! blest Sepulchre! blest rather be
> The Man that there was put to shame for me.'"

I knew a little of this experience of Christian. My days had been "consumed like smoke" and my bones "burned as an hearth," my heart "smitten and withered like grass." I had "eaten ashes like bread and mingled my drink with weeping." But now my language and feelings were, "Bless the Lord, O my soul, and all that is within me, bless His holy name. Bless the Lord, O my soul, and forget not all His benefits: who forgiveth all thine iniquities; who healeth all thy diseases; who redeemeth thy life from destruction, who crowneth thee with lovingkindness and tender mercies; who satisfieth thy mouth with good things; so that thy youth is renewed like the eagle's." "He hath not dealt with us after our sins, nor rewarded us according to our iniquities. For as the heaven is high above the earth, so great is His mercy toward them that fear Him. As far as the east is from the west, so far hath He removed our transgressions from us." I felt that I was delivered out of the mire and the clay, and that the Lord had put a new song into my mouth, even praise unto my God.

For several months I went on mostly in a comfortable frame of mind, though not entirely so. I remember one sudden flash of temptation which, for a moment or two, staggered me. It seemed as if someone stood before me and whispered, "Thy joys and thy deliverance may, after all, be only a deception and a cheat." I felt horrified for a moment or two, but I was soon delivered out of the temptation.

THE TIME OF LOVE

My time was now spent in reading the Bible and any religious book that I could lay my hands upon. I used to put the open Bible in front of me at my work, read a few lines, and then try to commit them to memory. O what precious things did I see in God's holy law! It was the joy and rejoicing of my heart, and I verily believe that the Holy Ghost directed my mind to portions of sacred truth suitable to my state and case and encouraged me to a further perusal as much as ever Boaz encouraged Ruth when gleaning in the field. He "said unto her, At mealtime come thou hither, and eat of the bread, and dip thy morsel in the vinegar. And she sat beside the reapers: and he reached her parched corn and she did eat and was sufficed, and left. And when she was risen up to glean, Boaz commanded his young men saying, Let her glean even among the sheaves and reproach her not: and let fall also some of the handfuls of purpose for her." I was now a living witness to the fulfilment of that promise, "They that sow in tears shall reap in joy. He that goeth forth and weepeth, bearing precious seed, shall doubtless come again with rejoicing, bringing his sheaves with him." It now seemed as if there was an armful of corn in every promise. I wondered at God's grace to such a sinner; I wondered at His love and I wondered at His wisdom. The glorious Person of Christ was my constant admiration. I could never read a chapter without seeing something which endeared Him to my heart. Right away from the manger in Bethlehem to Calvary's cross I could follow Him, and, amidst all His poverty and persecution, His sufferings and shame, I could still say, "This is my Beloved, and this is my Friend, O daughters of Jerusalem."

CHAPTER 3

THE PRECIOUSNESS OF CHRIST IN THE SCRIPTURES

His condescension seemed amazing and shone forth in such passages as these: "Ye know the grace of our Lord Jesus Christ that, though He was rich yet, for your sakes, He became poor, that ye through His poverty might be rich!" "In the beginning was the Word and the Word was with God, and the Word was God. . . . And the Word was made flesh and dwelt among us (and we beheld His glory, the glory as of the only begotten of the Father) full of grace and truth." His love seemed "wonderful, passing the love of women," and shone forth in every word He spake and in every act He performed but, above all, in His substitutionary sacrifice and death.

The following were some of the passages that I did eat, and they were the joy and rejoicing of my heart; they were like grapes from Eshcol. I sucked the juice out of them and they were sweet to my soul: "The Son of Man came not to be ministered unto but to minister, and to give His life a ransom for many." "Christ died for our sins according to the Scriptures." "Christ also hath loved us and hath given Himself for us an offering and a sacrifice to God." "But now once in the end of the world hath He appeared to put away sin by the sacrifice of Himself." "And as it is appointed unto men once to die, but after this the judgment: so Christ was once offered to bear the sins of many; and unto them that look for Him shall He appear the second time without sin unto salvation." "But this Man, after He had offered one sacrifice for sins for ever, sat down on the right hand of God." "Whom God hath set forth to be a propitiation through faith in His blood, to declare His righteousness for the remission of sins that are past, through the forbearance of God." "Neither is there salvation in any other: for there is none other name under heaven given among men whereby we must be saved."

FIRST CHAPEL CONNECTIONS

I now began to be concerned about joining myself to some religious denomination, and resolved to cast in my lot with the

Methodists, regarding them as the most lively and zealous of any in the neighbourhood. But I soon found that my conduct gave great offence to certain leading people among the Independents. They professed to have the first claim upon me, as I had been brought up a scholar in their Sunday School, and, had I been sufficiently thoughtful and sober-minded, I should probably have hearkened to their entreaties. But I believe that in this, as in all other things, "The lot is cast into the lap; but the whole disposing thereof is of the Lord." I found among the Methodists some of the kindest of friends and the choicest of companions. We read and prayed and sang and talked with each other, and my days passed away with pleasure. I was earnest and attentive at all the means of grace, and talked about a precious Jesus wherever I went.

A FEW FAVOURITE HYMNS

I now took part in almost every prayer meeting, and I had a few favourite hymns that I always wanted to sing; they so expressed my feelings and desires.

One was by Miss Steele:

> "And did the Holy and the Just,
> The Sovereign of the skies,
> Stoop down to wretchedness and dust
> That guilty worms might rise?"

I often felt this hymn to be good and could join in the last verse with all my heart and soul:

> "What glad returns can I impart
> For favours so divine?
> O take my all, this worthless heart,
> And make it wholly Thine."

Another was by dear John Newton:

> "How sweet the name of Jesus sounds
> In a believer's ear!"

Many times at my home have I sung the above with feelings of delight. Another was by Ryland:

> "O Lord, I would delight in Thee,
> And on Thy care depend."

Another was by Cowper:

> "There is a fountain filled with blood,
> Drawn from Immanuel's veins."

Another was by Montgomery:

> "Prayer is the soul's sincere desire
> Uttered or unexpressed."

And others by Watts, such as the following:

> "Come, let us join our cheerful songs."
> "When I can read my title clear."
> "There is a land of pure delight."

These were the days of my youth, and I thought they would surely continue for ever.

My First Serious Affliction

After a lapse of a few months, I was taken seriously ill with rheumatic fever and was confined to bed for many weeks. This was a prison for both my body and my soul and, for a time, I was left and well nigh forsaken by both God and man. I dare say some were afraid, and others were forbidden to see me, so that I had to pass most of my time alone. It was now, for the first time in my life, that I knew real affliction of body. I was made to possess months of vanity, and wearisome nights were appointed to me. I was full of tossings to and fro. In certain instances my days were spent without hope and I thought I should see no more good. It was here that I learned a little of the difference between waiting upon God and waiting for God; the difference between praising God and desiring to praise Him. I was brought where I could do nothing but lie down and wait. But this I must say, to the glory of God's precious name, that during the whole of my affliction I never felt a murmur in my breast either against God or the strokes which He laid upon me. I felt more as Medley describes:

> "When sore afflictions on me lie,
> He is (though I am blind)
> Too wise to be mistaken, yea,
> Too good to be unkind.

"What though I can't His goings see,
Nor all His footsteps find;
Too wise to be mistaken, He
Too good to be unkind."

COMMENCEMENT OF PREACHING

After I was restored to my wonted health, my love to, my longing for and my zeal in the means of grace knew no abatement, no matter what the service was. I can truly say that I never felt the slightest tendency to either weariness or sleep for the space of seven years. And, if I had turned my head during service or opened my eyes during prayer, I should have felt it to be a sin against God. My earnestness was noticed and admired by all who knew me and, after about twelve months from the time of my illness, I was waited upon by the minister in order to obtain my consent to exercise my gifts as an occasional preacher, to which I was solicited by all the church. After much anxiety of mind and prayer to God, I yielded to the entreaties of my friends, and the first time I stood up before them was on a week evening. The chapel was crowded to excess, and my text was: "For He hath said, I will never leave thee nor forsake thee. So that we may boldly say, The Lord is my Helper." I tried to show how the Lord had helped me to believe on Him, to feel His preciousness and to rejoice in His pardoning mercy; how He had helped me in my afflictions and raised me up again to show forth His praise; and I tried to show them that the Lord would never leave those that put their trust in Him.

Shortly after this I became a regular preacher, and the first place I spoke at from home was Burton, near Barnsley. My text was: "Before I was afflicted I went astray, but now have I kept Thy word." I tried to show them that God had gracious ends in afflicting His children, and dwelt particularly upon the case of Manasseh, whose wickedness knew no bounds; showing also that, when one means would not do, the Lord would adopt others, as He did in his case by taking him as a captive to Babylon, and that, when he was in his affliction, he besought the Lord his God and humbled himself greatly before the God of his fathers. After I had done preaching, a few of the friends came to shake hands with me and took their departure. Thus I was left alone, until a person came in with a little tea in a pitcher and some bread and butter on a plate, and abruptly left me either to eat it or to leave it. This was the coolest reception and the humblest entertainment that I ever received. The manager of this chapel was supposed to be worth thousands of pounds. The last account I heard of him was that he had become bankrupt and had given to a worldly man, as security for borrowed money, the deeds of the chapel which, on investigation, were found to be entirely worthless.

JOSEPH HANBY

Some time after this I went to preach at a little place called Bretton West, rather more than two miles from home. I took for my text: "For a day in Thy courts is better than a thousand. I had rather be a doorkeeper in the house of my God than to dwell in the tents of wickedness." Many years after this, when preaching at Clayton West Baptist chapel, a person named Joseph Hanby came to me after service and said, "Do you recollect preaching at Bretton West many years ago?" I said I had tried to preach there many times. He said, "Do you remember preaching from those words, 'I had rather be a doorkeeper,' etc.?" I replied that I had a distinct recollection of the text. He said, "Well, I was there and heard you, and I said to the friends after you were gone, 'Yonder young man will never remain among the Methodists'"; and then he added, "Here you are among the Baptists; I could see you were not a Methodist." This Joseph Hanby lived at Bretton West, but usually went to Flockton, a distance of three miles, to hear a good old Independent minister of the name of Walton. Occasionally he would go to hear Mr. Pym[1] of Elmley, and sometimes he would come to the Baptist chapel, Clayton West. He succeeded my grandfather as shepherd of Bretton Hall, which post he honourably filled until he was unable to walk about. During the greater part of his time at Bretton Hall, Mr. John Kaye was steward. He had both heard the talk and noticed the walk of this humble shepherd; and, when he came to lie on a bed of death, he sent for this poor

---

[1]Robert Pym, Rector of Elmley; see *Gospel Standard*: 1864, p. 27.

servant to pray with him. After he had gone away, he told his friends he felt sure there was something in poor Joseph's prayers that did him more good than anything he could get beside: and I would hope that those prayers of Joseph on his master's behalf were heard and answered and that the rich steward is now in heaven.

SWEET CONFIRMATIONS

It was about this time that I had occasion to take a parcel of boots one week-day to the little village just now referred to. It being a lonely journey, I took in my pocket Doddridge's *Rise and Progress of Religion in the Soul*; and when I got outside Clayton West, I began to read. The portion which took my attention was "The soul's preparation for death and eternity." While reading, I felt both death and eternity to be solemn realities and an earnest desire in my soul to be right, whenever it should please the Lord to call me away. I had a desire to pray. I looked forward and backward, on my right hand and on my left; and, when I could see no one, I knelt down on the grass. But, instead of prayer, all I could do was to bless and praise, having such a sweet and glorious manifestation of God's gracious presence to my soul as I expect hardly ever to have again in this vale of tears. My peace flowed like a river, and my cup ran over with a sacred sense of God's love to my soul. Both the fear and the sting of death were removed, and I felt a desire to be with Him, where I could praise Him better.

I remember feeling, on another occasion, anxiously impressed about the salvation of an individual that I thought was making a profession without a possession. I wrote a letter to him and laid his case before the Lord in prayer, and I had such a sweet season of communion and fellowship with the Lord, and such longing desire to be with Him, that I kept repeating those words in the last chapter of Revelation: "He which testifieth these things saith, Surely I come quickly. Amen. Even so, come, Lord Jesus." What grace and love shine in such manifestations to the soul as these! What a wonder that a poor sinner should be so transported in heavenly feeling and bliss as to lose relish and desire for earthly things! Yet such was the case with me, and I wondered why the

Lord did not answer my request. Many times I looked for His coming. If a little pain or sickness came upon me I thought, "Surely He is coming now!"

I remember one Sunday evening, when I got to bed, feeling a very strange unnatural sensation come over me, as though someone gently pressed the clothes which covered me; and, after a slight rustling, I thought I heard those words distinctly spoken, "Sister spirit, come away"; to which I answered:

> "If this be death, I soon shall be
> From sin and fear for ever free,
> And shall the King of Glory see –
> All is well, all is well;"

and I then felt it would have been a blessed exchange, a swallowing up of mortality (with all its weaknesses and sinfulness) in immortality and eternal life.

I remember relating the above-mentioned circumstance to Mr. Fawcett[2], a dear friend of mine. It so impressed his mind that he got quite a number of selections of hymns in order to find the verse given above and, if I remember aright, he found it at last, similar in form to that recorded here.

CLASS MEETINGS

It is somewhat important that I should state a little of my experience in connection with class meetings. This kind of service I attended regularly on the Sunday morning for years. The class leader was, I believe, a godly man. His name was Joseph Tinsley. He lived in a little cottage at the corner of a wood on the roadside between Denby Dale and Clayton West. His habitation, his appearance and his conversation all reminded me of the patriarchal times. He never took any part in what are called revivals of religion. He did not believe in anything sensational or spasmodic. When told of the great things that were taking place in the churches, he would smilingly say: "Now friends, come, come. Let us see how it wears." He had evidently read well *The Pilgrim's*

---

[2] Enoch Fawcett, deacon at Thurlstone; see *Gospel Standard:* 1879, p. 338.

Progress and, in his remarks to the members of his class, he would sometimes speak of the trials in the path of pilgrims before they reach the Celestial City.

But it is little I can remember that ever was made of use to me at any of those meetings. Most of the members appeared to be altogether ahead of me. When they were telling what great things they had done for the Lord, how happy they were and how determined to hold on to the end, my soul would sometimes sink fathoms deep, and I said within myself, "I ought to be like them, but I am not. O, what shall I say?" At times my feelings were such that I did not know what I *did* say. One thing I have particularly noticed all through life: that is, when God the Spirit has shone into my soul, it has been daylight and I could rejoice, walk in the light, and see where I was going without stumbling; but, when left to myself, down I have gone like a bird that is shot. These sudden changes from light to darkness made me feel that the power of religion was of God, not of man.

———————

CHAPTER 4

THE DOCTRINES OF GRACE

One Sabbath morning, as a few friends were accompanying me from the class meeting, I began to relate some things in connection with my own experience to show that I could do nothing without the Lord's help, when one of the oldest members of the class said: "You must not talk like that, or else you will be a Calvinist." This closed my mouth and set me wondering whatever a Calvinist could be. I began to make enquiry for the writings of Calvin, but I could not obtain any in the village. There was, however, one young man whose father was a member of the Baptist chapel at Clayton West and he, knowing what I wanted, kindly lent me the work of Elisha Coles on the sovereignty of God. I did not then know whether the book was in harmony with Calvinism or not, and, when I read it, I found many things in it that I could not understand. But this much I do remember, that from first to last all the glory in the salvation of the sinner was given to God, and my mind, while I was reading it, was awed with the greatness and goodness, the wisdom and faithfulness of Father, Son and Holy Ghost in saving poor, lost, ruined sinners.

DEEP THINGS OF GOD

Secretly I gloried in these things, and on one occasion I said to a dear minister now in heaven: "Mr. Reynolds, do you believe that God knows everything, from the birth of creation to the last moment of time?" He said, "Yes, I do." I did not want to know more just then. I felt satisfied. His mind was in harmony with mine, and to me he was an authority. I always found him a father and a faithful friend.

The seed was now sown in my heart which was designed by God to bring forth fruit in after life. I began to reason thus: God knows who will be saved, and He knows who will be lost. This knowledge was just as perfect before the birth of time as it will be when the last stroke of the pendulum of time shall be heard to tick, and to this agrees the scripture, "Known unto God are all His works from the beginning of the world."

Shortly after this I purchased a book upon the attributes of God, written by the leading minister in the denomination, in which a comparison is drawn between divine foreknowledge and human knowledge. Thus, human knowledge of transactions in the past does not in any wise interfere with them. They are what they are, but my acquaintance with them does not at all make them what they are; they would have remained exactly what they are if I had never known them. Therefore, my bare knowledge of them can have no influence upon them whatever. In like manner, the divine foreknowledge of all events that can and will ever happen has no influence whatever upon them, any more than my memory has upon transactions which are past. I thought this was deep reasoning, and I was anxious to be a Methodist; therefore, I was pleased to think I could consistently remain among them and advocate the foreknowledge of God. Thus I went on preaching and teaching, east, west, north and south, the doctrines of free will, creature power, human merit, universal redemption, offers and proffers, together with endless "ought-to-be's" and "should-be's" of obligations and duties which neither you nor I, nor any of our fellow creatures, were ever able to perform since the disobedience of our first parents in Paradise.

DIVINE SOVEREIGNTY CLEARLY MADE KNOWN

One Sunday evening, while I was conducting the service at Low Swithin, near Barnsley, I read for my lesson the fourth chapter of Luke. When I came to verses 25, 26 and 27, I felt as if I could proceed no further. The doctrine of election stared me in the face, and I was like a person who had had a slight stroke. I thought, "How is this?" "Many widows were in Israel in the days of Elias, when the heaven was shut three years and six months, when great famine was throughout all the land; but unto none of them was Elias sent, save unto Sarepta, a city of Sidon, unto a woman that was a widow." O how strange is this! If God cares for all alike, why is this one widow singled out from the rest and miraculously fed, her little cruse of oil never failing and her handful of meal never wasting, until God sent rain on the earth? The other widows were probably as poor as she was, and as desirous of life; yet hunger is permitted to make its last meal upon them, and they fall a prey to the ravages of famine and death. Then, again, "Many lepers were in Israel in the time of Eliseus the prophet; and none of them was cleansed, saving Naaman the Syrian." Here, I thought, is God's discrimination. He could easily have cleansed every one of them in a moment, but only one of them is chosen to be cured of his disease. That Sunday evening was the time, and that Methodist pulpit was the place, where the doctrine of election and God's sovereign choice of both men and things were clearly revealed to my soul; and I resolved that if I were spared to get safely home, I would never again attempt to preach the doctrine of man's free will in salvation matters, but that all the glory from first to last must be to the Lord. When I got home, I told my friends what had taken place and what I intended to do. I said: "I am no longer an Arminian, but a Calvinist; no longer on the side of free will, but an advocate for free and sovereign grace."

Attempts to Overturn the Witness for Truth
It was soon noised abroad as to what had taken place. Some thought it was of God; others, that it was the influence of my wife. One rich gentleman, Mr. Hinchliff, the chief supporter of the place where the Methodists met, entreated me to reconsider the steps I had taken and fill up my place as before, and added that, if I would do so, he would give me anything I desired. I replied that it was not a question of giving or receiving, but a matter of principle and faith.

After this the circuit minister was deputed to wait upon me. His name was Mr. Wainman. I do not think he has forgotten, or ever will forget, the interview we had together. Although he was a Goliath in comparison with myself, he seemed tongue-tied and in fetters while he talked to me; while, on the other hand, I felt like a hind let loose. Both words and arguments flowed apace until my instructor was confounded. There were certain appointments on the preachers' plan for me; I was reminded that these ought to be fulfilled. I said I thought it better to withdraw altogether, but my friend urged upon me the importance of discharging my duties as a local preacher. I replied: "If you think it is my duty to carry out those engagements, I will do so, but let me assure you before I do, that wherever I go I shall carry a different story. If I preach again, I shall preach electing love and grace." "O," he said, "If you cannot preach as before, you had better give it up altogether." I said, "That is just what I think." He then left me very abruptly, saying the dinner would be spoiling, evidently caring more about his stomach than he did about my soul.

CHAPTER 5

Attending the Baptist Chapel

I now began to attend the Baptist chapel at Clayton West, and to read such books and magazines as were published by the Baptists, and among these the *Gospel Standard* was the chief.

I ought here to relate a circumstance respecting that periodical. When I was married, my wife brought to her new home a quantity of these magazines; and oftentimes on a Sunday evening she would read in them and seem very much interested and profited. I have seen the tears roll down her cheeks, but she never said anything to me about them. I had often heard the *Gospel Standard* condemned, so I thought the best thing that I could do would be to hide them from my wife lest she should be led astray. So I watched for an opportunity, collected every copy that I could find, and stored them up in an unused attic where I knew she could not get them; and there they remained until they were partially eaten by the vermin. My wife never once asked me if I had taken them away, or where I had put them; but, when I began to read such books, I felt ashamed of my conduct in hiding what I now so much realised the need of. I went and hunted them all up, cleaned them, and began to read; and I have kept on taking and reading them ever since that time to this.

I can truly say that I have often felt the precious truth contained in the *Gospel Standard* to be a word in season to my weary soul. I have found wholesome doctrine, harmonizing with what God has, I trust, taught me by His Spirit. Many times have I had to say, "This is savoury meat that my soul loves"; and when the experience of some tried child of God has been recorded, I have felt like Ruth: "This people shall be my people, and their God my God."

My attendance at chapel was very regular, I was very attentive, and many times the preached word was made a blessing to my soul. My own case was pointed out. Every in and out, hole and corner, was described. I felt sometimes as if the minister was acquainted with my very inside: the fears and doubts, the clouds

333

and darkness, the temptations and trials, the poverty and losses, the slips and falls of word and thought, together with the hungerings and thirstings, the prayers and cries, the wishes and desires, the bubblings of hope and the flutterings of faith, and the poor attempts at love to, and service of, so great and kind a Saviour. Then again, Christ Jesus was sometimes set forth blessedly to my soul in the majesty and glory of His Person and grace, the unchangeableness of His love, the sureness of His purpose and promise; and many encouraging words were spoken by which I was helped to hope that my soul was interested in that covenant which is ordered in all things and sure, and which to this day is all my salvation and all my desire.

TRIALS AND DELIVERANCES

For a while things went on pretty comfortably both with my soul and with the friends; and, although the sky was not without clouds, I found that promise true: "Thine eyes shall see Jerusalem a quiet habitation." I felt that the house of God was my home and that the Lord's people were my companions. With dear old Dr. Watts I could both say and feel:

> "There would I find a settled rest,
>   While others go and come;
> No more a stranger or a guest,
>   But like a child at home."

After a while I was requested by the dear old deacon, Mr. Elijah Bedford, to take a part in the prayer meetings, and the first hymn that I ever ventured to give out was No. 119 (Gadsby's):

> "Great God! from thee there's nought concealed,
>   Thou seest my inward frame;
> To thee I always stand revealed
>   Exactly as I am."

It contained just what I felt as a poor, naked, filthy sinner, and just what I desired to feel of the blood and righteousness of the Son of God; but such were my fears and confusion while on my knees in prayer that I hardly knew what I said, and I was afraid lest someone should pull my coat and request me to give it up. After the meeting, there was some conversation before going home, and the old deacon said: "Sometimes I dream that I am in the chapel, hearing the gospel preached; and, for anything I know to the contrary, I have heard ministers just as well in my sleep as ever I did when I was awake." To this I made no reply whatever, but it distressed me sorely. For, just about that time, I had been repeatedly dreaming; but all my dreams were so filthy and base that I durst not tell anyone of them. "Well," thought I, "this is a man of God – the Lord is with him indeed and of truth; but here I am, destitute of such a favour as that." I went home very sad, but early next morning I was awakened with these words: "My Beloved is mine, and I am His." That was a wonderful help to my soul. O how I did try to thank the Lord for such a timely appearance!

On another occasion some little unpleasantness arose between me and a friend that I dearly loved. I was told that he had said something injurious to my character; I felt determined that I would have this matter out face to face, and that I would tell him something that he would not soon forget. But, just as I was planning how to proceed in this matter, and walking quietly along the road, these words dropped sweetly into my mind:

> "Trials must and will befall,
> But with humble faith to see
> Love inscribed upon them all,
> This is happiness to me."

In a moment, all my enmity and animosity fell to the ground, and I felt that I could have laid myself down on the floor for my brother to wipe his feet upon me. I mention this to show that God is just the same now as He was in Jacob's day; I am sure that Esau's anger was not much more subdued than I felt mine to be.

BELIEVERS' BAPTISM

After a time I began to be exercised in my mind about the ordinance of baptism. Sometimes in reading the Scriptures, sometimes in the preaching, and sometimes in conversation, the subject would be brought before me. At times, when I felt a little of the presence and blessing of the Lord resting upon my branch, I resolved that I would go and present myself before the church as a candidate. Then fears would steal over me, and something would whisper in my heart: "But if, after all, you are not one of the Lord's people, what a sin it will be! You had better wait a little longer." Sometimes I thought it was best not to be in haste, and at other times I felt very much condemned in not attending to it. Once, when I was laid aside by God's afflicting hand, those words awakened me from my sleep, "Ho, every one that thirsteth, come ye to the waters"; and, although these words have reference to gospel blessings, I feel that they were addressed to me in reference to baptism. I fell asleep, and was awakened again by the same words, "Ho, every one that thirsteth, come ye to the waters"; and again, I could see nothing but baptism. On that bed, I then resolved that, if the Lord should raise me up, I would ask the church if I might be baptized.

Well, after a time I was raised up, but my resolutions fell to the ground, and years rolled on before I could see my way into the valley of decision on this despised ordinance of Christ. Even when I felt fully settled in my mind about the course I intended to take, I was not without my fears. There were three things that greatly perplexed me, and how to deal with them I could not tell. The first was, what I should say when before the church. "O," I thought, "will they receive my poor testimony? Shall I be able to say anything that will be commended to the brethren?" The second thing was, "How will my poor body undergo the shock of the cold water? And if anything happens, what will people think?" And the third thing was, "How can I endure the mockery and scorn that the world will heap upon me and upon the Lord's blessed institution?" All these three matters were settled in one moment. I went into a secret place to pray, and while there the following passages came flowing into my heart. With regard to the first difficulty, "Take ye no thought how or what thing ye shall answer or what ye shall say: for the Holy Ghost shall teach you in the same hour what ye ought to say." As to the second, "When thou passest through the waters, I will be with thee." And with regard to the third, "But call to remembrance the former days, in which, after ye were illuminated, ye endured a great fight of afflictions; partly, whilst ye were made a gazingstock both by reproaches and afflictions; and partly, whilst ye became companions of them that were so used."

I was baptized on the first Sunday in August, 1872, by Mr. Eddison[3], along with three other gracious and worthy men of God – namely, George Bedford, Charles Bedford, and Joseph Horbury. I believe the Lord's smile was upon us; for, while we were attending to the ordinance, the sun shone upon the water through the threatening clouds, so that people could not help remarking that the sight was similar to what took place at Jordan, when there came "a voice from heaven, saying, This is My beloved Son, in whom I am well pleased." Such were the sweet feelings I had that I remarked to a friend, "I should like to be baptized every day if I could feel the same blessedness in my soul."

I believe it was a time of rejoicing to the people generally, and we were somewhat like the apostolic church: we met together for prayer both in the chapel and from house to house. Many were the sweet seasons we enjoyed, yet intermingled with many trying dispensations both in the church and at our homes. Some that we loved as dearly as our own selves were removed by death, and others that once ran well made total shipwreck of faith. Sometimes trade was very bad and the price of provisions high, and afflictions in our persons and in our families made us cry to the Lord for help. Often were we afraid that both the church and our businesses would all come to nought; but we were held together and cemented in the bonds of brotherly love, walking in the same path, exercised with the same trials, longing for the same deliverance, and hoping to dwell finally in the same everlasting home – which may God grant, and raise up after us a seed to serve Him and a generation to call Him blessed, in this very place, Clayton West!

------

[3]Jabez Eddison, pastor at Hope Chapel, Rochdale, from 1884 to 1914.

CHAPTER 6

A CALL TO PREACH GIVEN

Let me pass over a few years of worldly prosperity with worldly associates, which brought leanness and death into my soul, proving the truth of Christ's words, "Ye cannot serve God and mammon." But while in the very midst of worldly, vain pursuits, a voice as from heaven spake these words to me, "Robert, thou wilt have to retrace thy steps." I stood still and looked to see if there were anybody near (I felt like the poor publican, a miserable sinner); but, seeing no one, I went on my way reflecting upon my sad state and case. I purposed and resolved to quit and abandon all companies, however pleasing and profitable they were to my carnal mind. I was obliged to mix with them in the discharge of my duties, but I tried to shun their company without giving offence. I was afraid that every member of the church would discover the declension of my love. I verily thought that I should lose all my religion and my immortal soul too.

All my confidence in some who appeared to be great and good men was shaken to the very foundation. I forbear to mention any names, but my friends at Clayton West who are connected with me, in seeking the honour of God by contending for His truth, will at once recall the painful circumstance to which I allude. I thought: "Some worldly, wicked people cannot, will not, deliberately deceive and lie; but some professors will do both." What a stumbling-block this was to me!

But, strange to say, when all the comforts of religion were gone, and nothing but groans and sighs could I pour out before the Lord, at that very juncture the members of the church were deliberating among themselves, and finally drew up a document, signed by every male member and read at a church meeting, to this effect: "That we, the undersigned, having met together for prayer and to consult with each other, are unanimous in our opinion that the Lord has qualified and called our brother, Robert Moxon to the work of the ministry; and we desire to ask him if the Lord has not also laid this matter upon his mind; and, if so, to appoint a day for him to exercise his gift in our midst."

Solemn Exercises

If this had been done years before, I could have better understood it; for there had been a time when God, I trust, wrought powerfully on my mind in divers ways with regard to the work of the ministry. Sometimes I felt very backward, and made every excuse in my power before the Lord when He presented the work before my mind. I used to say something like this: "How is it that I am continually being impressed that I shall have to preach? Thou hast given me no gifts, no memory, no voice, no utterance, no bodily strength, and, what is still worse, no learning, no knowledge, no insight into Thy Word. O do take these thoughts away from me!" Then at other times I used to feel such a willingness come over me that I would say, "O Lord, I do not want to fight against Thee. If I can only be made useful to Thy people, Thy will be done!" But soon again the thoughts of my incapacity would stare me in the face, and then I shrank from it as from death. Now and again I felt a little respite, and thought all would ultimately subside. But not so; the Lord gave me lesson upon lesson. Once, while I was at my work, it was just as if a voice spoke at my left hand saying, "Why stand ye here all the day idle?" I turned to look, and in a moment said, "Because no man hath hired me." And then the voice spoke again, "Go, work in My vineyard."

At another time, when in the chapel before service, I took my Bible to read a portion for the comfort of my soul, and the first place that I opened at was Exodus 3. 10 and following verses. As soon as I began to read, it seemed all meant for me: "Come now therefore, and I will send thee unto Pharaoh," and again, "Certainly I will be with thee." I said to myself, "That is not what I want; I want something for my soul." So I turned to another place, which was Ezekiel 29, and the verse that caught my attention was the last in the chapter: "And I will give thee the opening of the mouth in the midst of them; and they shall know that I am the Lord." "O," I thought, "the same subject again; but, really, I don't want that." So I turned into the New Testament to see if anything different would come; and the place where I opened was Luke 10. 1, 2: "After these things the Lord appointed other seventy also, and sent them two and two before His face into every city and place, whither He Himself would come," etc. At this I felt great surprise; but still I thought I would find some other subject if possible. So I turned a number of leaves over again, and the next time I found myself looking at 2 Tim. 2. 15: "Study to show thyself approved of God, a workman that needeth not to be ashamed, rightly dividing the word of truth." After this I closed my Bible and began to reflect upon what had passed; I felt a solemn persuasion that God's hand was in the matter, and that He thereby was preparing my mind for what was to follow.

On another occasion, I started for a walk from home towards Clayton Hall, and when in the fields and wood I felt a spirit of prayer come over me that God would indeed bless me and be with me. As soon as I got through the wood into that steep field called "The Doles," it appeared as if a voice said, "Cry! Cry!" I thought: "Ah, that is just what I have been doing and what I should still like to do." But in a moment these words came to my mind, and I uttered them aloud, "What shall I cry?" And just as suddenly the reply was given: "Cry 'all flesh is grass, and all the glory of man as the flower of grass. The grass withereth, and the flower thereof falleth away: but the word of the Lord endureth for ever. And this is the word which by the gospel is preached unto you'" (1 Pet. 1. 24, 25). I felt such an opening of this scripture that, as I stood in that field, I thought that if there had been a congregation before me, I could have preached to them. It seemed as if something said: "That is what you will have to do: cry 'all flesh is grass.' All the doings of man in a state of nature are as fading grass, but the Word of God – both in its promises and blessings, above all, the incarnate Word, the Son of God – endureth for ever." O, what security shone forth in the gospel for a poor ruined sinner!

Now, all these things, and others that I could name, had taken place long before the church moved in the matter at all, though their influence upon my soul had in a great measure subsided. So that it was a surprise to me to hear that document read and to see their determination that I should exercise my gifts in their midst. They appointed a Sabbath for me, and said that they should expect me to say a few words to them. I made no promise to them, but rather desired to be excused; but, when I saw that I prevailed nothing, I left them, and for several days I pondered the matter and cried mightily unto God for help and direction. Yet nothing seemed to come to satisfy my mind, so I wrote to a minister asking him if he would kindly oblige us by preaching for us on the Sunday that the church had appointed for me. I received his reply, stating that, if all was well, he would oblige us. I then felt a great relief in my mind, but did not say a word to them about what I had done.

First Sermon at Clayton West

Well, when the Sunday morning came, I was looking for the minister and the friends at the chapel were looking for me. The minister did not come, so I felt at my wit's end. I went into my pew, and could not by any means be prevailed upon to try to speak; so all was confusion and disappointment. The deacon read a sermon and conducted the service, but at the close I was severely censured and repeatedly requested to say a word or two in the afternoon. I could not, however, see my way to do so, and took my seat in the usual place. First one and then another came to me, asking me to try; they said they would be satisfied if I would only try. Just as the time for service drew near, the deacon came in and said he was obliged to go away, and that he would leave the conduct of the service entirely in my hands; if I could not preach, I must try to read. I thought: "Well, if he is going away, I will try to begin the service, and read a sermon as he has done in the forenoon." To this end I got a volume of Mr. Philpot's sermons ready. I gave out a hymn, read a chapter, prayed, then gave out another hymn, and, while they were singing it, none but myself knew what was going on within. My eye was first on the Bible, then on the volume of sermons. I could not tell whatever to do; but at the last moment I could no more dare to touch those sermons than as if they had been a nest of vipers. So I got the Bible, and, with great fear and trembling, stood up before the people and read my first text in their hearing. It was Acts 26. 16:

"But rise, and stand upon thy feet: for I have appeared unto thee for this purpose, to make thee a minister and a witness both of these things which thou hast seen, and of those things in the which I will appear unto thee." I felt in a solemn position, and tried to relate a few things that I trust God had shown unto me. The people were greatly affected, and I was greatly humbled both before them and before the Lord. This was on April 22nd, 1877.

PREACHING AS A SUPPLY

The news spread far and wide, and soon letters came pouring in, asking me to supply the different churches round about; but I felt that I could not comply with any invitations until I had first received the consent of the church at Clayton West. This they soon gave to me, and the first time I went away from home was on May 13th, 1877, to Lincoln. The text that I spoke from was Luke 10. 42: "But one thing is needful: and Mary hath chosen that good part, which shall not be taken away from her." I tried to show how needful the Lord Jesus is in His Person, work, blood, righteousness, intercession, promises, visits and manifestations. But, O how tried I felt! And, as I walked backward and forward in that room of my dearly beloved friend Mr. Blinkhorn, I wished that I had never come. Dear Mrs. Blinkhorn, coming into the room and seeing me so cast down, spoke these words and went back:

"I can do all things, or can bear
All sufferings, if my Lord be there;
Sweet pleasures mingle with the pains
While His left hand my head sustains."

What a comfort they were to me! "A word spoken in due season, how good is it!" "A word fitly spoken is like apples of gold in pictures of silver." I frequently went to supply for them afterwards, and many sweet seasons have I enjoyed in their midst.

CALLS TO A PASTORATE

Shortly after the above-mentioned date, the applications for my poor services came from over thirty different churches, and I tried to the best of my ability to apportion a few crumbs to each and to all. But this caused the friends at home to complain, and I noticed that oftentimes in their prayers they requested God to order it in His good providence for me to remain more at home. Yet every time that I heard these petitions, the words spoken to Paul came to my mind: "I will send thee far hence unto the Gentiles." After a time I told them how singular it was that, when they prayed for me to be more at home, something seemed to convince me that I should have to go more and more away from them. This proved to be the case, for shortly afterwards I received a letter from a distant church, asking me to take the oversight of them, and another church did the same. The first one was Bacup, and the other was Blackburn. But in neither case could I see the hand of the Lord so clearly as I desired; yet at Blackburn a striking circumstance took place which for a time staggered me very much. I had been preaching for them and, after service, they asked me to remain a short time, which I did. The deacons then told me their wish, and that of the church, which was that I should preach to them for three months, with a view of taking the pastorate; but I answered that I could not think of any such thing.

Well, when I got to bed that night, I began to think about the matter very seriously, and wondered if I had been too hasty in refusing to consider their proposal. This kept me awake for a considerable time but, when I felt overcome by sleep and was just losing myself, these words came with such power that I started up as if a burglar had entered the room: "Behold, I have set before thee an open door, and no man can shut it." This happened on Sunday evening, January 4th, 1880.

The following Sabbath I was at Preston, when I dreamed that I was walking up the street panting for breath, like a person with asthma or bronchitis, until I was compelled to rest. While doing so, I saw a Prince, a King's Son, come walking along. Eventually he overtook me. I stepped aside for him to pass by, when he stood and said, "Do you always breathe so heavily?" I replied, "I think I do." He then put his hand into his pocket and gave me a quantity of money, saying, "Take that; you will need it all before you get to your journey's end." I took it without a word. He then turned aside and left me, and, when I had gone a few steps further, I turned to have another look at him, and I saw that he was looking anxiously after me. I then turned back towards him and said: "Don't be surprised if you hear from me again; I feel so thankful for what you have given to me." He smiled, but did not speak, and right before me I saw a very steep hill; but before I could climb over it, I awoke.

Afterwards I thought this Prince is the Lord Jesus Christ, the Prince of Peace. O how neat and plain, how humble and gracious He appeared to be! I thought this heavy breathing represents the groaning and sighing of a poor sinner by reason of the difficulties of the way. I thought the gift of money sets forth the readiness and care of Christ towards His people, the grace that He gives in the time of distress and trial. The hill that I saw appears to signify that the way to heaven is with difficulty.

CALL TO THE PASTORATE AT BURY
Shortly after this I received a letter from the church at Bury, asking me if I could see my way to become their stated minister. This letter the postman gave to me as I was starting on my way to Barnsley market and, when I got through the little village of High Hoyland, I took this letter out of my pocket and read it, and, like Hezekiah, spread the case before the Lord.

I must here state two or three things that had happened previously. I had been supplying at Bury for nearly three years, and on my visit there I had such a sweet time in prayer, such a nearness of access at the throne of grace, such a pleading with the Lord for His people there, that I felt an indescribable union to them for which I could not at all account. Wherever I went to supply, these people were upon my mind. So much were my thoughts taken up with the friends at Bury that when at Bacup conferring with them about settling over them, I said, "I cannot at all see my way to come among you; there is no inward movement from the Lord with regard to this matter. There is a place where for numbers they are less than you; yet I feel that, if they were to give me a call, I would not refuse them whatever the consequences might be." I did not tell them the name of the place, but at that very time I had Bury on my mind.

You may guess what my feelings were when, as related above, the letter came. Why did I spread it before the Lord when it was just the place, the only place, that my heart felt inclined to? The reason was this: I felt my unfitness and my unworthiness. I said: "O Lord, if I accept of this invitation, how can I stand up before them? How can I preach to them? I feel as if I could not hold on for three months at most." But these words came very powerfully to my mind, "Who made man's mouth?" I said, "Thou, Lord." Then it came again: "Cannot I, who made man's mouth, open it and keep it open?" I said, "Lord, Thou canst do everything; there is nothing too hard for Thee to do." As I walked down the road, I felt ashamed that I should doubt the power of God to help me to speak in His great name. After a time I wrote, stating my willingness to come and begin my labours (D.V.) on the first Lord's day in January, 1881.

There are a few more pages of Mr. Moxon's autobiography, but they are not of the same quality. They consist mainly of diary extracts – many only of personal interest and of little spiritual value.

CHAPTER 7

A REMARKABLE DREAM AND ITS FULFILMENT

Mr, Link, deacon of Gower Street Chapel, sent me a letter, asking me to supply their pulpit on the first Lord's day in May, 1891. Having had a dream some time previously that I was preaching in London, I felt very desirous to oblige them if I could. I obtained the services of Mr. Carr for our anniversary, and then promised Mr. Link that I would try to oblige them. I accordingly went, and found a goodly number of the Lord's people. I felt a knitting together to them in the bonds of the gospel. I did not feel very well in body, but on the whole I much enjoyed my short visit among them.

When I was at Gower Street Chapel, I did not think it was the place I had seen in my dream. After a time I received an invitation from Mr. Ashdown to visit Great Alie Street. I felt a desire to go there, to see if that chapel was anything like the one I had seen in my dream. When I was preaching there (October 18th, 1891), I told them my dream and that I thought that was the place I had seen. "And if it is," I said, "I have one particular message to deliver to you, which I distinctly remember in my dream:

'It rises high, and drowns the hills
Has neither shore nor bound;
Now if we search to find our sins,
Our sins can ne'er be found.'"

On the first two Sabbaths in June 1892, I was supplying at Trowbridge, and during the weeks after the Sabbaths, I preached at the following places: Swindon, Calne, Hilperton, Studley, Bampton and Grove. On my way to Bampton, I was met at Faringdon station by my very kind friends, Mr. Pembrey and Mrs. Goold, his dear sister. The distance from Faringdon to Bampton is about six or seven miles. It was a very pleasant drive; but one thing impressed my mind more than all the beauties of nature in God's fair creation. It was this. Mrs. Goold said, "I always think that if God gives a message to His ministers, there is someone to whom that message is sent." She asked, "Do you remember that, when in London supplying for Mr. Ashdown at Great Alie Street, you mentioned having had a dream in which you thought you were in London and that in preaching you had to say the following words:

> 'It rises high, and drowns the hills
> Has neither shore nor bound;
> Now if we search to find our sins,
> Our sins can ne'er be found'?"

I said, "Yes, I remember it very well." She replied, "So do I, and I believe it was for me. I was then about to undergo an operation, which had caused me much anxiety and fear, and many prayers to God for His blessing and help. Those words were made a comfort and deliverance to me before, during and after the operation. Again and again they dropped like honey into my soul. I felt that all sin was put away, all blotted out, all forgiven, all removed, and, with it, all fear. I could neither find nor feel sin, guilt, or fear; and the words kept coming:

> 'It rises high, and drowns the hills
> Has neither shore nor bound;
> Now if we search to find our sins,
> Our sins can ne'er be found.'"

DEATH OF MR. MOXON

Mr. Moxon died on May 23rd, 1906, aged 65. He had been pastor at Bury for twenty-five years. After preaching for the last time on March 18th, he seemed gradually to sink. He was blessed with sweet communion with the Lord and kept very calm and peaceful, saying that the everlasting gospel he had preached would do for him to die with.

On one occasion, he sweetly repeated:

> "Now I have found the ground wherein
> My anchor, hope, shall firm remain,
> The wounds of Jesus for my sin
> Before the world's foundation slain.
>
> "Covered is my unrighteousness,
> From condemnation I *feel* free."

Another time, he said he felt weaned from everything here below, and longed to have a peep at his dear Lord Himself. The day before he died, he testified that the Lord was with him. During his last day on earth, he was only able to speak broken words, but often said, "Jesus, Lord." Just before he died, he pointed upwards and said, "Home, home," and then peacefully fell asleep in Jesus.